Lorca's Legacy

American University Studies

Series II
Romance Languages and Literature

Vol. 138

PETER LANG
New York · San Francisco · Bern
Frankfurt am Main · Paris · London

Lorca's Legacy

Essays on Lorca's Life, Poetry, and Theatre

Edited by
Manuel Durán and
Francesca Colecchia

PETER LANG
New York · San Francisco · Bern
Frankfurt am Main · Paris · London

Library of Congress Cataloging-in-Publication Data

Lorca's legacy : essays on Lorca's life, poetry, and theatre /
edited by Manuel Durán and Francesca Colecchia.
    p. cm. — (American university studies. Series II,
Romance languages and literature ; vol. 138)
    Includes bibliographical references.
    1. García Lorca, Federico, 1898-1936. I. Durán,
Manuel, 1925- . II. Colecchia, Francesca. III. Series.
PQ6613.A763Z7379   1991   868'.6209 — dc20   90-22166
ISBN 0-8204-1253-8   CIP
ISSN 0740-9257

© Peter Lang Publishing, Inc., New York 1991

Printed in the United States of America.

Acknowledgments

Javier Herrero, "The Father Against the Son: Lorca's Christian Vision". Reprinted by permission of the editors from *Essays on Hispanic Themes in Honour of Edward C. Riley*. Edited by Jennifer Lowe and Philip Swanson. (Edinburgh: Department of Hispanic Studies, University of Edinburgh, 1989).

Robert Lima, "Toward the Dionysiac: Pagan Elements and Rites in *Yerma*". Reprinted by permission of the publisher of *Journal of Dramatic Theory and Criticism*. Vol. IV, 2 (Spring 90)

Bettina L. Knapp. "García Lorca's *Yerma:* A Woman's Mystery." Reprinted by permission of Bettina Knapp, *Women in Twentieth-Century Literature*, University Park, PA, Penn State Press, 1987, pp. 11–23.

Appendix: Drawings by Federico García Lorca. Reproduced by permission of the García Lorca estate.

Table of Contents

Preface

Since 1936 the body of Federico Garcia Lorca lies in an unmarked grave near the city of Granada. This fate may remind us of other unmarked graves such as Mozart's or Cervantes'. What is peculiar to the Andalusian poet is of course that he was murdered and that hatred, not poverty or neglect, played an important role in his physical annihilation and the ultimate anonymity of his body. A paradoxical end to a life which, according to all those who knew him well, radiated friendliness and love.

Paradoxes and contradictions are constant in his life and his works. He managed to baffle critics trying to define his ideology by proclaiming that he was simultaneously a ... "Catholic, communist, anarchist, liberal, conservative, and monarchist." In spite of his easygoing manners and friendly directness he was often in the habit of blurring or distorting details of his biography. For example, he lied several times about his year of birth. A poet is also a myth maker. Lorca was working on his own life, slowly turning it into a legend, when he was interrupted by the Spanish Civil War and death.

If we want to grasp the real dimensions of Lorca as a man and artist, we must approach him with the same sense of wonder elicited by a mythical figure from ancient Greece or a medieval legend. At the same time we must approach his poetry, his plays and his prose with a rigorous critical attitude, one that reveals the secrets of his craftmanship and points out the beauty and the ambiguity of his texts.

*   *   *

Writing about Lorca more than fifty years after his death offers several advantages. In the first place we can be sure we are dealing with a writer who is not about to disappear from sight. Lorca is today as well established as a twentieth-century author can hope to be. His works have been translated into dozens of languages and analyzed by hundreds of critics all over the world. His books continue to sell in many editions. His plays are performed and applauded every year. We can be reasonably sure that we know and can study the whole of his considerable output. Yet our knowledge of Lorca's work may be less complete than we had hoped for. For instance, his *Sonetos del amor oscuro* are perhaps not the whole of the sonnets Lorca wrote on a subject that was important to him. In any case the publication of this book has yet to elicit a full response from Lorca's critics. Moreover, Lorca's nephew, Manuel Fernández-Montesinos, announced not too long ago the discovery of an unpublished Lorca manuscript bearing the title of *Místicas* containing 22 texts and 114 pages: most of these texts are incomplete fragments of short essays dealing with Lorca's metaphysical doubts about God's existence, Lorca's dialogue with God if indeed God did exist, Lorca's comments on social injustice and the need for rebellion. The texts are juvenile and naive, yet obviously important for our understanding of Lorca as a man and as a writer. Nonetheless they have neither been read nor analyzed by most of Lorca's critics.

Basically we are close enough to Lorca's life and times so that it is still possible to talk to people who knew him personally, who lived historical experiences similar to his, and who therefore may help us to understand what it was to be a young poet in Spain in the first third of the twentieth century, to hunger for change and yet respect and enjoy most aspects of tradition, to be a liberal without wanting to renounce Spain's glorious past. Yet we are far enough from his life and times that it becomes possible to place Lorca in proper perspective, to see him as an individual and also as a member of a group, as a star in a constellation, as part of a generation of poets and playwrights.

*   *   *

It is fitting that the present book should be a product of American hispanists and other hispanists working in the United States. It can be argued that no other country, with the exception of his native Spain, had such an impact upon Lorca's life and works as the United States. Lorca's New York poems constitute an enduring statement. As Richard Predmore puts it, "it has been nearly fifty years now since Federico García Lorca wrote the poems that constitute *Poeta en Nueva York,* and yet in some ways they read like a book written yesterday. Their themes of materialism, of dehumanization, of violence, of social and racial injustice could have been taken from today's headlines. Because they seem to speak so powerfully to and about the contemporary world, one could imagine them attracting more readers today than they did when first published in 1940."[1]

During his stay in New York Lorca achieved two goals that would seem to be mutually exclusive and even contradictory. The first was to write in a subjective, elusive, obscure style, one which owes much to Surrealism and which effectively erased the label of folksy Andalusian poet that had been affixed to Lorca by the huge success of his *Gypsy Ballads.* With his New York poems Lorca became the foremost representative in Spain of the new "international" style fostered by the avant-garde and the Surrealists. Yet at the same time that he was becoming more subjective and difficult in his style he was approaching a deeper awareness of social problems, a warmer feeling of solidarity with the poor, the oppressed and the downtrodden.

It was often stated during his lifetime that the poets of his generation (often called the Generation of 1927) were cerebral artists devoted to a playful art. For them poetry was merely a game, a pastime, and they were not much given to expressing the deeper feelings of the human heart. This characterization was basically untrue, even maliciously so, and in any case more applicable to the early works of that generation than to their mature works. Ortega y Gasset had unwittingly contributed to the creation of such an inaccurate cliché with the title of one of his books, *The Dehumanization of Art,* in which he discussed the new poetic styles with a mixture of brilliant intuitions and flippant generalizations. Lorca's poetry was never as cold and intellectual as the first works of some of the other poets of his generation, but it too changed in a similar way. His stay in New York probably marked a crucial moment in the evolution of his art.

*   *   *

A great Spanish poet who knew Lorca well, Vicente Aleixandre, states that "with Federico everything was inspiration, and his life, so beautifully in accord with his work, was the triumph of liberty, and between his life and his work there is a spiritual and physical interchange so constant, so passionate and fruitful, that it makes them eternally inseparable and indivisible."[2] We are dealing with a poet who, far from being only cerebral or intellectual, knew how to fuse personal experience, intuition, dreams and feelings into a whole, and knew how to express himself in a style that was flexible enough to respond to the needs of his evolution and his experience. He was a warm personality, a warm artist. Hence the need to remember his warmth even when approaching his work with the detachment and the objectivity that any scholarly enterprise implies. At the very end of his lecture, "Imagination, Inspiration, Evasion," Lorca said: "Poetry does not want initiates but lovers. It puts up brambles and broken glass so that the hands which seek it may wound themselves for love."[3] We believe that the best way to remember the poet's life and commemorate his death is to approach his work in a spirit of "objective sympathy" where the analysis of the many problems posed by Lorca's texts will always try to be as precise and rigorous as possible, yet will never be devoid of love.

Manuel Durán
Yale University

Francesca Colecchia
Duquesne University

---

[1] Predmore, Richard L., *Lorca's New York Poetry. Social Injustice, Dark Love, Lost Faith.* Durham, N.C.: Duke University Press, 1980. P. vii.

[2] Aleixandre, Vicente. "Federico". In: Garcia Lorca, Federico. *Obras completas.* Madrid: Aguilar, 1966. p. 1830.

[3] *Obras completas*, p. 91.

I. Intimations of Glory

JAVIER HERRERO
University of Virginia

The Father Against the Son: Lorca's Christian Vision*

Recent criticism has shown considerable disagreement regarding Lorca's spiritual outlook. Certain facts, however, are beyond doubt. Reared in the bosom of a Catholic family and in an environment rich in Christian folklore, Lorca's sensibility develops among religious symbols and rituals. From his early years he was deeply affected by their beauty: as a child he was fond of gathering his playmates and 'performing' the Mass for them, preaching devout sermons, enthusiastically decorating the altar.[1] This passion remained with him for life: he was perfectly capable of leaving a pleasant gathering to attend a solemn Mass, or of leaving Madrid, with two friends, to spend several days following the Holy Week celebrations in a small Castilian town.[2] He seems to have attended with certain regularity religious functions, at least when he was in an intimate atmosphere, or in especially important liturgical seasons, such as Easter, Christmas, etc.[3]

Derek Harris, in several important studies, has pointed out the powerful imprint left by Catholic images and rituals both in the *Romancero gitano* and in *Poeta en Nueva York*. He shows how metaphors, that had been read traditionally as expression of an Andalusian pagan vitalism, were rooted, in fact, in religious imagery and feeling. Harris, with deliberate British sobriety, avoids philosophical generalisations and focuses his analysis, above all, on the expressive function of these images in the context of the poems in which they are found.[4] Miguel García Posada, in his penetrating and well documented study *Lorca: interpretación de 'Poeta en Nueva York,'*[5] aims to achieve a coherent vision of the different interpretative levels of this difficult and complex book, among them, of course, the religious one. For García Posada, Lorca develops in *Poeta en Nueva York* a biblical myth, clothing in a religious, apocalyptic vision, the class conflicts that divided the society of his time: social evolution, and the final deliverance of the oppressed, entails the successive stages of Paradise, Fall, Apocalypse, and Restoration. Religious imagination, in this interpretation, becomes the rhetorical device through which a social content is expressed with the greatest and deepest vigor.[6]

A social interpretation of Lorca's use of religious imagery is certainly possible. His frequent statements (especially in the many interviews granted in the

* This article was written originally for *Lorca's Legacy*. A subsequent longer, more complete version was published in *Essays on Hispanic Themes in Honour of Edward C. Riley*, ed. by Jennifer Lowe and Philip Swanson. Dept. of Hispanic Studies, Univ. of Edinburgh, Edinburgh, Scotland, 1988. We reprint this longer version by permission of the editors.

final years of his short life) of passionate concern for the tensions and sufferings of contemporary society, witness to a genuine anguish regarding the great socio-political problems that brought Spain, and the world, to the terrible crisis of the 1930s and the second World War. But there is nothing unusual in this; could a humane, generous spirit, who lived through the years that prepared the catastrophe, not be so concerned? And, could not such anguish transcend the social dimension and acquire a religious one? This question may not respond to contemporary intellectual trends, but its interest for our understanding of Lorca is undeniable.

Three critics have asserted in recent years the Christian character of Lorca's poetry. In 1975 Piero Menarini, in his solid work *'Poeta en Nueva York' di Federico García-Lorca. Lettura critica*,[7] suggests that Lorca's thought evolves, under the influence of Fernando de los Ríos, towards a socialist humanism that reaches its final point in a Christian vision: social transformation implies a personal engagement and sacrifice whose model should be found in the Crucifixion.[8] For Lorca, then, according to Menarini, Christianity becomes the highest point, and the basis, of a social humanism. Menarini supports his argument, above all, with a close reading of the 'Oda al Santísimo Sacramento del Altar' and of some poems of *Poet in New York,* but he claims that this Christian humanism reflects a permanent attitude that pervades Lorca's work. More recently André Belamich has argued that it is impossible to assert (as he himself had done previously in his book *Lorca*) that Lorca's spiritual evolution moves from a religious childhood and adolescence to a pagan maturity; for Belamich the crisis that Lorca underwent in 1928 caused a deep spiritual convulsion which resulted in a rebirth of religious feeling.[9] Finally Eutimio Martín brings to an extreme the consideration of Lorca's social commitment, making of him a *precursor* of modern revolutionaries:

> El movimiento de liberación social desencadenado por la *teología de liberación* ha alcanzado tal fuerza, sobre todo en el tercer mundo, que incluso la *Congregación romana por la doctrina de la fe* se ve obligada a declarar oficialmente: *El evangelio es un mensaje de libertad y de liberación*. Es muy posible que no sea otra cosa la obra literaria de Federico García Lorca.[10]

It has been, above all, the recent publication by Christopher Maurer and Eutimio Martín, of a series of early writings of Lorca, as well as the opening of the family archives to the public, that have brought to light a young Lorca obviously dominated by religious preoccupations. We really owe to the works of these scholars the discovery of a new and unsuspected Lorca, and if we take into account that Lorca has said that his early writings 'serán como el andamio donde anidarán mis ideas de niño fundidas en el crisol de la pubertad'[11] it is obvious that their discovery is an important one. Eutimio Martín, in fact, has come to the conclusion that 'Es, pues, a la luz del verbo de Cristo como se opera el nacimiento, como hombre y como poeta, de Federico García Lorca',[12] and that this religious passion, even if it will play a less overwhelming role in his later work (with the exception of the 'Oda al Santisímo Sacramento del Altar') will remain present in it: 'el sustrato religioso de los escritos inéditos juveniles nutrirá toda su obra.'[13]

The central idea at which we arrive through the analysis of this considerable body of new material is that the core of Lorca's religious vision is formed by the experience of life as a conflict between the spirit and the flesh. The flesh seduces man with a religious-demonic intensity: by it Lorca finds himself in a 'grandiosa catedral de bellísimos pecados' and tempted by a 'sagrario de pasiones' that, in a blasphemous way, seems to supplant the Christian temple and sacrament ('San Antonio, Poema raro').[14] But the hero of the early piece where these images appear, an autobiographical Antonio-Lorca, abandons his garden of delights to search for an answer to this basic question: if we die, can carnal pleasure be the aim of life? In his pilgrimage he rejects the dogma of the Catholic Church whose teaching he sees as the perversion of the Gospel. This seems to be, for the young Lorca, the contemporary state of Catholic spirituality, 'Espectros negros — el clero — mantienen encendida una hoguera salvaje — brutal — donde arde el espíritu y que despide sombra pestilentes que ocultan el evangelio'.[15] However, beyond the corruption of these dark ghosts, the sublime light of Christ reaches us, 'el resplandor azulado y tibio de las bienaventuranzas que dejó tras sí aquella paz celeste con cuerpo de hombre que pasó por la tierra.'[16] It is through art that man can approach the gigantic ideal that the church has betrayed: 'La melodía decía un alma grandiosa que nunca consiguió, una ansia de lejanía inacabable, un deseo vehemente de azul hecho carne ...'[17] The ideal can be seen, but it seems to be unreachable: the flesh interposes itself as an unbreakable barrier. Many texts bear witness to the persistence of this tragic conflict. I choose here one from *Místicas* that is contemporary to the ones just quoted: 'Muchas veces mi corazón salta sobre el cuerpo y ama a las estrellas y a las flores, pero enseguida la sensualidad me envuelve en su luz roja. ¡Cuándo terminará mi calvario carnal!' *(OC,* III, 180).[18]

To what extent did these religious preoccupations persist in his later work? Did Lorca, as Eutimio Martín asserts, replace Christian spirituality by a 'moral pagana que, para Lorca, Jesús no vino a destruir — contrariamente a lo que preconizan los Padres de la Iglesia — sino a completar'?[19] I shall try to show, through the analysis of texts that span through Lorca's later years, that this conflict between flesh and spirit and between dogmatic authority and personal religious elan, not only persisted but constituted the basis of his deepest preoccupations as reflected in his work, and that this essential struggle took the poetic form of the sacrificial suffering of the Son against the cruel persecution of God the Father.

****

We have, then, a Christian, but anticatholic Lorca. We also have a pagan one. The pagan Lorca sings with unashamed joy the beauty of the nude body of

New York's adolescents that appear in the 'Oda a Walt Whitman' as young fauns who, pulled out of the East River (separated from nature), are imprisoned in enormous factories:

> Por el East River y el Bronx
> los muchachos cantaban enseñando sus cinturas,
> con la rueda, el aceite, el cuero y el martillo.
>
> . . . .
> Nueva York de cieno,
> Nueva York de alambre y de muerte,
> ¿Qué ángel llevas oculto en la mejilla?
>
> . . . .
> y el sol canta por los ombligos
> de los muchachos que juegan bajo los puentes.
> *(OC,* I, 528–30)

It is clear that the erotic joy of these verses darkens under the threat of a sinister New York. Through the waists, through the navels (through the loins, really) of the boys a sun (undoubtedly a homoerotic sun) sings; but this sun is besieged, threatened, by 'la rueda, el aceite, el cuero y el martillo', in fact by the 'cieno' (corruption) and the 'alambre' (prison) of a civilization of death, a dehumanised and dehumanising society that destroys a glorious nature that Lorca had seen as the promise of a possible paradise. In the tragic confrontation described by these verses we have, on the one hand the sun-eros that rises, dazzling us, from the youthful flesh, on the other the mud, the wire, the stains of oil, the leather belts and the hammers, that imprison, soil and degrade it.

If we search back towards the cosmology that pervades Lorca's early lyric we find that this erotic sun is part of a world in which tragedy is already present; a discordant world precisely because it is in the nature of this sun to introduce, through its turns and returns, time and death in the cosmos. Already in some magnificent verses of the *Libro de poemas* Lorca introduces the theme of the essential contradiction between life's inner struggle for permanent joy and the unstoppable march of the cosmic circle towards death:

> EL DIAMANTE
> (Granada: November 1920)
>
> El diamante de una estrella
> ha rayado el hondo cielo,
> pájaro de luz que quiere
> escapar del universo
> y huye del enorme nido
> donde estaba prisionero
> sin saber que lleva atada
> una cadena en el cuello.

. . . .
Se agitan en mi cerebro
dos palomas campesinas
y en el horizonte, ¡lejos!,
se hunde el arcaduz del día.
¡Terrible noria del tiempo!
(OC, I, 47–48)

I have selected the first and the last stanzas of this poem in which Lorca points to the contrast between the spirit's aspiration towards a transcendence that soars beyond the boundaries of the cosmos and the joyful (?) acceptance of earthly limits. In verses 1–8 the religious desire to transcend the cosmic sky-roof (or Heaven-floor; the Heaven that receives us beyond time, that is to say, the Heaven of the Catholic tradition in which Lorca was educated) is expressed through the image of a bird of light that tries to escape from the huge cosmic nest, but is retained in place by a chain fastened to its neck. This metaphor rests upon a previous one: a shooting-star is seen as a diamond that tries, and fails, to cut through the sphere of crystal that encloses the cosmos. Both images, then, signify the soul's desire to transcend the spatial dimension of the cosmos, and deny it. Verses 9–13 express a contradictory spiritual mood. The two rustic doves, as we shall see later, signify the sun and the moon; their agitation in Lorca's brain expressing his experience, and acceptance of temporal limitations. In this sense the cosmos opposes the religious aspiration described in the first stanza: Lorca replaces the spiritual desire for infinitude with a joyful, pagan, assertion of the earth. But such affirmation is immediately denied by a second metaphor superimposed upon the previous one: day and night, the flight of the two doves of sun and moon, is seen as the rising and sinking of a water-wheel, and is qualified as 'terrible'; Lorca could never bring himself to accept mortality.

****

I have made two assertions that should be supported. One is that the star that, like a diamond, cuts along the crystalline sphere of the cosmic prison, signifies the aspiration of the soul to infinity. The other that the doves that agitate in Lorca's brain signify the movements of the sun and the moon, creators of the day and night, and consequently of time. The first assertion does not need a very elaborated proof. *Azul* stands, first and foremost, for the ideal world that, through the metaphor of music, embodies the soul's aspirations towards infinity and transcendence. We saw above that Jesus left behind him, through his gospels, 'el resplandor azulado y tibio de las bienaventuranzas', his 'paz celeste'. This blue, so closely connected with the God-man, is the heavenly blue, and from it the stars gaze at us with welcoming, appealing beams: 'Los hombres que con el pecho lleno de amor a otro amor ideal se pasean por los campos mirando a las enigmáticas estrellas imposibles, esos son los *extrahumanos*,' *(OC, III, 181)*. These *extrahumanos,* the artists, the saints, the great revolutionaries, are the true *hijos de Dios:* 'Pero bienaventurados vosotros porque seréis llamados por una sociedad ideal hijos de Dios ... si queréis soñar imposibles ... mirad a las estrellas *(OC,* III, 183). Jesus' soul itself is a gigantic star to whom Lorca looks up for ideal support: '¡Jesús nazareno! Estos nuevos fariseos te han robado tu grandeza ... haz que la estrella gigante de tu alma caiga sobre los templos irrisorios y los sacerdotes sarcásticos' *(OC,* III, 186).

But the religious meaning is only the supreme form of ideal love. The pure love of the artist for the muse, foreshadowed by the first, romantic, love of the child-adolescent for his beloved, is also tinted by the same celestial blue. Ian Gibson has shown that the *estrella azul* that often appears in the *Libros de poemas* embodies the dream-like, platonic, love incarnated in children's songs and games, for a pure 'damsel' that comes to him from a radiant, magic beyond.[20] As such it signifies their innocent dreams of childhood: the child is the knight that soars towards an angelical body:

> Fui también caballero
> una tarde fresquita de mayo.
> Ella era entonces para mí el enigma,
> estrella azul sobre mi pecho intacto.
> Cabalgué lentamente hacia los cielos. ...
> *(OC,* I, 27)

The 'estrella azul', then, is an enigmatic 'she' that is pinned, like a decoration, on his 'pecho intacto'; the child sees himself as a knight that, moved by this star (we shall see presently that the star on his chest is a reflection of a loving blue star in the sky), rides slowly towards that sky that, obviously, is the same sky-heavens that had already appeared in the first poem and whose religious character we have just established. We have, then, here a different poetic interpretation of the same signified: the religious aspiration that incites the soul to soar, that moves it through love. Such movement, here as in the previous poem, is finally frustrated by the cosmic limitation of the sky-roof:

> Yo solo...
> Hacia el techo imposible de los cielos ...
> *(OC,* I, 28)

This appeal of the 'lucero azul' is essentially anti-erotic. We have seen already that the young Lorca exclaimed: 'Muchas veces mi corazón salta sobre mi cuerpo y ama a las estrellas y a las flores, pero enseguida la sensualidad me envuelve en su luz roja.' We have here established the terms of a conflict that, in my opinion, Lorca carried with him until his premature death. A conflict that for him is the essence itself of the religious experience: not only does the spirit oppose the flesh, it freezes it. In an unpublished drama that Eutimio Martín dates as early as June 1917 to June 1918, Lorca expresses the sense of vocation of Jesus as a conflict between the appeal of the stars and the call of all flesh: '... al mirar hacia el cielo, todas las estrelles que se ven y las que no se ven cayeron sobre mí y me taladraron con sus puñales de luz la carne y el alma y me incendiaron este corazón que era de fuego, dejándome la carne fría y dura como la nieve de las cumbres.'[21] Man, then, can burn with two fires, the ideal and the carnal, but the ideal light is jealously exclusive: it freezes the flames of eros. In poetic terms Lorca expresses this conflict in the poem 'Hay almas que tienen... ' of the *Libro de poemas*. In it Lorca establishes a clear difference between souls that maintain a remnant of the innocence of childhood and those in which the sins of the flesh (the erotic awakening of adolescence) do away with the chaste and fragile spiritual aspirations of the child:

> Hay almas que tienen
> azules luceros,
> mañanas marchitas
> entre hojas del tiempo,
> y castos rincones
> que guardan un viejo
> rumor de nostalgias
> y sueños.
>
> Otras almas tienen
> dolientes espectros
> de pasiones. Frutas
> con gusanos. ...
>
> *(OC,* I, 84–85)

'Estrellas azules' are identified (vv 3–4) with flowers ('mañanas marchitas' = childhood) that although they have withered, remain in the tree of time. The stars in the sky are metaphorically identified with the flowers of a tree; an organic image, then, superimposed on the more familiar cosmic one. A third image appears immediately: the 'estrellas azules' and 'mañanas marchitas' are now likened to 'castos rincones' in the *building* that is man. The image of organic growth is replaced by the mechanic one of man as *built,* and in the grown man (the final building) we find sometimes 'castos rincones' where old souvenirs and dreams of childhood (worn out dresses, toys = 'rumor de nostalgias') remain almost forgotten. Verses 9–12 state that in other souls the chaste souvenirs of the child's illusions and games have been replaced by the 'dolientes espectros de pasiones,' by the corruption of sin 'frutas con gusanos'. Such fruit, of course, points to Eve's apple = original sin (probably the sins of the flesh);[22] in this case, then, the chaste corners are replaced by haunted ones. At the light of these images of organic (tree) or mechanic (building) growth, it seems superfluous to argue that the contrast between childhood ('estrella azul') and youth ('espectros de pasiones') is marked often by a spiritual fall that includes an erotic awakening ('flor' against 'frutas con gusanos').

The meaning of 'estrella azul' is, then, well established. Before leaving this analysis, however, it seems appropriate to give a brief thought to the nature of the crystalline sphere that encloses it. In the poem 'El diamante' we saw that the sudden flare of a shooting star was poetically interpreted as the cut of a diamond against the hard surface of the cosmic sphere and as the flight of a bird that cannot escape from the huge cosmic nest. What is the essence of that hardness? Lorca's answer is swift and brutal: the sky is closed and hard because it is the skull of God. The God of his childhood has died and consequently the cosmos has lost its dimension of infinitude, has become confined, denying the soul's aspiration to soar towards the unlimited space of dream. But this image of the death of God (the 'cielo' as 'calavera') is not final; *if God exists,* then he is a tyrant that answers our prayers with curses. In his poem 'Madrigal', also of 1920 (October) Lorca writes:

> En la agujereada
> calavera azul
> hicieron estalactitas
> mis te quiero.
> *(OC,* I, 78–79)

Surprising, original verses, but clear. The title 'Madrigal' is sardonic: we are dealing with a desolate poem, a poem of rejected love. The sky-heavens is now a prison because the God of our childhood is dead; the Father who opened his arms to us with unlimited love has been replaced by a brutal stranger. The cosmic sphere has been replaced by a blue skull; Lorca's prayers (his 'I love you') fall like drops of water on the calcic cave and, far from awakening a loving echo, they grow stalactites that, like swords, threaten him with the implacable hostility of a tyrannical father. Such is, then, the tragic destiny of a soul that tries to fly beyond the boundaries of the cosmic prison.

This harshness of the Father has been explicitly asserted by Lorca in a fragment that was published by Gibson in 1985[23] and more extensively by Eutimio Martín in 1986.[24] It consists of a dialogue between *Jehová* and an *Angel,* and in it 'Jehová aparece solemne y malhumorado; le sigue un angelote viejo, con la cara despintada y las alas pegadas con sindetikón.' *Jehová* appears all along as a doting old man who is terrified of the revolution that his son could bring forth at any moment:

JEHOVA:	¿Cargaste de cadenas al Cristo?
ANGEL:	Sí.
JEHOVA:	Ten mucho cuidado con él. Un loco así nos puede dar un disgusto el día menos pensado.

In fact, Christ has already managed to recruit some dangerous followers; Saint Teresa seems to be also involved in the conspiracy:

JEHOVA:	Teresa de Jesús, ¿No fue ésta la loca que llegó con el pelo suelto preguntándonos por Cristo?
ANGEL:	Esa misma. Y continúa más loca.
JEHOVA:	Dadle duchas frías.

As we can see, Lorca's despair of the Father's cruelty brings him, not only to blasphemy, but to contemptuous mockery.

****

We now have the meaning of 'estrella azul' and 'hondo cielo', or 'pájaro de luz' and its 'enorme nido'. The signified of the two doves that stir up in Lorca's brain can be established with similar ease. At first sight the assertion that two doves mean 'the sun and the moon' might appear (I am conscious of it) as shocking. I do not have time here to digress regarding the structure of the modern image. Be it enough to quote the well-known remark of Apollinaire, who referring to the new painting (cubism) wrote: 'a real likeness has no importance any longer, since the artist sacrifices everything to the cause of truth';[25] that is to say, the modern image is a creation of the artist that takes some elements from the referent and incorporates them into a new form that serves his expressive needs. The sun and the moon are two bodies that move through space and, in this sense, they can be imagined as flying birds; or, since they are functions of cosmic life, they could be recreated into two breasts of a female torso:

ARLEQUIN

Teta roja del sol.
Teta azul de la luna.

Torso mitad coral,
mitad plata y penumbra
(OC, I, 278)

Obviously, if the sun and the moon can be two tits, there is no reason why they could not be two doves:

CANCION

Por las ramas del laurel
van dos palomas oscuras.
La una era el sol,
la otra la luna.
Vecinitas, les dije,
¿dónde está mi sepultura?
En mi cola, dijo el sol.

En mi garganta, dijo la luna.
(OC, I, 627; I, 598)

Of these two doves only one is essentially luminous: the sun; the moon is simply a mirror (often made of silver) that reflects the sun's light. Lorca writes in his 'Ode to Salvador Dalí':

La Noche, negra estatua de la prudencia, tiene
el espejo redondo de la luna en su mano.
(OC, I, 752)

The continued rounds of the cosmic doves weave the net of time that brings us death. This is the reason for the poet's surprising question: 'vecinitas ... ¿dónde está mi sepultura?' To which the doves answer no less surprisingly: 'En mi cola, dijo el sol. /En mi garganta, dijo la luna.' Let it be enough to say that the association of 'sol' with 'cola' implies an erotic meaning: the 'sol' in Lorca's mythology is closely associated with 'coral', 'naranja', 'sangre', all images of 'desire'. The association of 'luna' with 'garganta' implies song, that is to say art, and art is born from the agony of twilight, of the setting of the sun and the rising of the moon: from the suffering and the remembrance (the reflected light) of lost love.

This is, then, the 'terrible noria del tempo.' Terrible, because from the burning fire of desire, and through the twilight and darkness of disillusion and pain, we move forward, we sail towards death. These wonderful verses of *Así que pasen cinco años* develop with glorious clarity his image of time as a voyage towards death:

> Arlequín
> El sueño va sobre el tiempo
> flotando como un velero.
>
> . . . .
>
> ¡Ay, cómo canta el alba, cómo canta!
> ¡Qué témpanos de hielo azul levanta!
>
> El tiempo va sobre el sueño
> hundido hasta los cabellos.
> Ayer y mañana comen
> oscuras flores de duelo.
>
> . . . .
>
> Sobre la misma columna,
> abrazados sueño y tiempo,
> cruza el gemido del niño,
> la lengua rota del viejo.
> *(OC,* II, 424–25)
>
> . . . .

'Ayer y mañana comen/oscuras flores de duelo.' In dawn and in twilight, light and shadow mixed, dream and disappointment collide and the glory of the new day lights up the blue lumps of ice that will freeze the dreams of the morning (of childhood); that is why, of course, 'cruza el gemido del niño/la lengua rota del viejo' and why dream and time are embraced 'sobre la misma columna.'

****

Because night is the deepest cosmic reality life is seen as sailing over the abyss of night. This obsession with temporality and death is not, in Lorca, simply a literary theme; those who knew him have left considerable evidence of this continuous preoccupation, that at times he confided in intimate conversations, at times through jests or pranks with which he amused his friends and exorcised his own demons. Carlos Morla Lynch, one of the friends who better knew Lorca and who has left a most comprehensive record of his life and concerns, has conveyed to us innumerable testimonies of the depth and almost Unamunian intensity of Lorca's anguish. Among these many references I choose one that, through the awful prose of Lynch, conveys some of the intensity of Lorca's confidence. Lynch had called Lorca 'mimado de las hadas' and Lorca answers:

> 'Mimado por las hadas; quizás, pero aquí en la tierra. Vivo en la angustia del 'más allá' incierto; quisiera creer en la immortalidad de nuestro espíritu consciente a través de las etapas sucesivas de la eternidad … y no lo logro. La duda impera fatal e indomable.'[26]

The pomposity of these sentences belongs undoubtedly to Morla Lynch, but the anguish is real and the spirit is all Lorca. Much more intelligently, and with his sharp and shameless irony, Salvador Dalí mocks Lorca's obsession with death remembering some of Lorca's jests to which I referred above:

> Cinco veces al día, cuando menos, Lorca hacía alusión a su muerte. Por la noche no podía dormirse si, en grupo, no íbamos todos a 'acostarle.' Una vez en la cama, encontraba el medio de prolongar indefinidamente las conversaciones poéticas más trascendentales que han tenido lugar en lo que va de siglo. Casi siempre terminaba por hablar de la muerte y, sobre todo, de su propia muerte.
> Lorca imitaba y poetizaba todo lo que hablaba, en especial su defunción. La ponía en escena recurriendo a la mímica: 'Mirad — decía — cómo seré en el momento de la muerte.' Después de lo cual bailaba una especie de ballet horizontal que representaba los movimientos augustiosos y convulsivos de su cuerpo durante el entierro, cuando el ataúd descendiera por una de las bruscas pendientes de su Granada natal. Después nos enseñaba cómo sería su

rostro unos días después de su muerte. Y sus rasgos, que de costumbre no eran hermosos, se aureolaban de pronto de una belleza desconocida e incluso de una excesiva alegría. Entonces, seguro del efecto que acababa de producir en nosotros, sonreía satisfecho del éxito que le procuraba la absoluta posesión lírica de sus espectadores.[27]

To throw myself directly into the eye of the storm I shall start by asserting that Lorca's anguish has a religious origin. Lorca seems to have been, to judge by the data we possess, as much anticlerical and anticatholic, as antiprotestant: for him religious institutions represented the spirit of the Old Testament, the religion of authority, of oppressive social structures and, especially in protestant capitalism (and by it), of spiritual hardness and cruelty. And, very important for Lorca, in both Catholicism and Protestantism, social repression entails an equally harsh sexual one. The final authority in whom all these repressions are embodied and from whom they originate is the God-Father of the Old Testament; the God who asked Abraham to sacrifice His own Son to Him, the one who sent His own Son, Jesus, to death on the cross, to expiate faults of which He was innocent. We have already found this cruel Father in poems quoted above: He was the cosmic skull who answered Lorca's prayers with the hard swords of stalactites. I would degrade Lorca's original religious vision if I asserted that this conception of God the Father as a cruel tyrant had its final root in his homoerotism; but it is obvious (and an attentive reading of the *Libro de poemas* and of *Místicas* leaves little doubt about it) that the violent rejection by contemporary Catholicism of homosexuality as the unspeakable sin, the lived experience of emotional repulsion that he was bound to feel, as well as the tragic social exclusion that the curse that had fallen on him, and of which he felt innocent, entailed, all these shattering convulsions had to leave a profound imprint in his art, and they did. By them Lorca felt a profound sense of identity with the forsaken and the persecuted, with the Andalusian gypsies, the negroes of New York, with all the children of the world that are victims of economic struggle and class oppression, with the little animals, with insects, symbols of everything that is small and defenseless; and finally, of course, with the Son of God, the Crucified, the innocent victim who died for them all.[28]

I believe, with André Belamich, that we must take seriously Lorca's 'Oda al Santísimo Sacramento del Altar', one of the greatest religious poems of the twentieth century. The 'Ode' is divided into four parts. The first one, 'Exposición', serves as introduction, and refers to the liturgical ceremony of presenting the Host in the Monstrance for public adoration. The three following parts are dedicated each to one of the enemies of the soul in Christian theology, and from there their titles: 'Mundo', 'Demonio', 'Carne'. The poem, as a whole, expresses anger against the God-Father that sends his Child to be persecuted and killed by those dreadful enemies, and praises the glory of the God-Child that, through His sacrifice, saves man from them. From the first lines the poem presents the conflict between the Father and the Son:

Exposición

Pange lingua gloriosi corporis mysterium.

Cantaban las mujeres por el muro clavado
cuando te vi, Dios fuerte, vivo en el Sacramento,
palpitante y desnudo, como un niño que corre
perseguido por siete novillos capitales.

Vivo estabas, Dios mío, dentro del ostensorio.
Punzado por tu Padre con aguja de lumbre.
Latiendo como el pobre corazón de la rana
que los médicos ponen en el frasco de vidrio.

Piedra de soledad donde la hierba gime
y donde el agua oscura pierde sus tres acentos,
elevan tu columna de nardo bajo nieve
sobre el mundo de ruedas y falos que circula.
(*OC*, I, 763)

The epigraph of the ode contains the first two verses of the hymn with which the Catholic Church celebrates the divine presence in the Eucharist: 'Sing, oh tongue, the mystery of the glorious body!' It is probable that Eutimio Martín is right when he interprets the 'mujeres por el muro clavado' as the encloistered nuns that sing the sacrament presented in the monstrance (the church does not need to be a convent's private chapel, since many convents possess churches open to the faithful).[29] Lorca describes a monstrance that, as often happens in altars of Catholic churches, consists of a cross in whose centre the ostensory (*ostensorio* or *custodia*) contains, and displays, the Host; the cross is supported by a base (a stone) that rests upon a sphere representing the world. The most frequent icon of this type is the well-known cross of the Child-Jesus of Prague, who holds the sphere in his left hand while blessing the faithful with the right. But the Church is also an arena where a strange bullfight is taking place: seven bullocks persecute a strong Divinity that, for the love of man, has incarnated and become a small child. In this sense the 'muro' would belong, too, to the bull-ring and the image of the arena would be superimposed on the one of the convent-church: humanity both looks from his prison to God the Son and contemplates, as public, his sacrifice.

The world (the cosmic sphere) is seen as sunk under the power of sin, of the seven bullocks that persecute the God-Child; and the root of these sins is found in the two images of the wheels (that here, as in the 'Oda a Walt Whitman,' signify the factory, the modern industrial world, born from greed and creator of oppression) and the phallus, that in his poem is often identified with the sceptre, signifying in this way the double lust of power and sex. I have called this bull-fight strange; it is strange and brutal because we do not see here a bull-fighter facing the beast, armed with his sword and cape, but a defenceless child that has been sent, alone and unarmed, to be torn to pieces by seven deadly sin-bullocks. If the verses 1–4 signify Jesus' sacrifice through the image of a bull-fight, verses 5–8 do it through the metaphor of a scientific experiment. As the biologist, with scientific coldness, places a frog in a glass tube and pierces its heart with a needle to study its reactions (which, we presume, he will use for medical purposes), so the Father pierces with a needle of light (probably any one of the golden arrows of the monstrance) his Son, imprisoned in the walls of the ostensory, that here play the same role (and with the same meaning) as that of the nailed walls of the bull-ring.[30]

The monstrance rests on a base of stone that itself rests on the sphere of the world. I insist that Lorca, in these verses, simply uses, giving to them a spiritual dimension, the iconographic elements generally found in many a traditional Spanish church. The stone, then, serves as the support of the cross, in whose centre is placed the ostensory that displays the Host for public worship. But metaphorically the basis on which Christ's sacrifice rests is his agonic decision to accept the Crucifixion. It is Christ's loneliness, which prefigures his death, that is signified by this stone. Christ's death, then, vanquishes our death ('donde las hierbas gimen') and our sin ('agua oscura') is defeated by His agony on the cross (his three voices corresponding to the three nails that pierced his body to the cross).

Although the general interpretation is now clear, it will be helpful, leaving these verses, to examine briefly some images that we have so far left aside. The cross imagined by Lorca seems to consist of two arms of silver in whose center several arrows of gold surround the ostensory. The vertical arm of the cross, that rests directly on the stone (and which in the referent would correspond to a silvery column) is transformed by Lorca into a double poetic reality: a nard enclosed into a column of ice (v. 11). The key for the interpretation of this image should be found, I believe in verse 76: '¡Sacramento immutable de amor y disciplina!' The nard here, which as so often in Lorca, signifies reckless strength, a vitality that, if left to itself, becomes the brutal energy of the wheel and the phallus and ends finally in anguish, contained by the silvery limits of God's discipline, is transformed into graceful, fertile life.[31]

****

An analysis of the extremely rich *Poeta en Nueva York* would transcend the limits of this paper. The religious anguish that pervades it has been carefully investigated by some of the greater Lorquistas who have made of it an object of inquiry (Marcilly, Harris, Menarini and García Posada have all studied this aspect of the poem). It is clear from their works that the Father, in *Poeta en Nueva York*, has become incarnated in the protestant, Calvinist spirit of modern capitalism, and the Son in the oppressed minorities, in the child whose heart, like the one of the frog in the 'Oda al Santísimo Sacramento del Altar', is pierced by the golden thread that has cut through the chest of all the oppressed in history, from the slaves of Pharaoh to the ones of the mechanic, industrial world:

> De la esfinge a la caja de caudales hay un hilo tenso
> que atraviesa el corazón de todos los niños pobres.
> El ímpetu primitivo baila con el ímpetu mecánico,
> ignorantes en su frenesí de la luz original.
> ('Danza de la muerte', vv 36–39)

Lorca leaves no doubt about where this *frenesí* takes place:

> Cuando … el director del banco observaba el manómetro
> que mide el cruel silencio de la moneda,
> el mascarón llega a Wall Street
> . . . .
> El mascarón bailará entre columnas de sangre y de números
> entre huracanes de oro y gemidos de obreros parados
> que aullarán, noche oscura por tu tiempo sin luces.
> ('Danza de la muerte', vv 3133, 4547)

As García Posada has pointed out it is with an echo of Isaiah 34:13 ['and thorns shall come up in its palaces, nettles and brambles in the fortresses thereof'] that Lorca announces the day of reckoning for New York-Babylon;

> Aguardad bajo la sombra vegetal de vuestro rey
> a que cicutas y cardos y ortigas turben postreras azoteas.
> Entonces, negros, entonces, entonces,
> podréis besar con frenesí las ruedas de las bicicletas
> poner parejas de microscopios en las cuevas de las ardillas
> y danzar al fin, sin duda, mientras flores erizadas
> asesinan a nuestro Moisés casi en los juncos del cielo.
> ('El rey de Harlem', vv 105–111)

The revolution of the oppressed is directed against the tables of the Old Testament. The poem 'Nacimiento de Cristo' makes clear how this great apocalypsis will take place: through the Crucifixion. Lorca has seen, during the Christmas season of 1929, a *nacimiento* among the sky-scrapers of New York, and the vision of the frailty of the Child-God among the giants of materialism has moved him to write a poem in which he foresees in the newborn the future victim that will expel from Manhattan the prophets of protestantism:

> El Cristito de barro se ha partido los dedos

en los filos eternos de la madera rota. (vv 3–4)

Like the golden thread that cuts through the hearts of the oppressed for centuries, so the cross has nailed its victim all through history. But it announces the victory over the Father:

Dos hilillos de sangre quiebran el cielo duro. (v. 6)

San José and the child foresee the victory of the cross:

El niño llora y mira con un tres en la frente
San José ve en el heno tres espinas de bronce. (vv 13–14)

Such victory, finally, will entail the expulsion of the priests of the Old Testament from the new city:

Sacerdotes idiotas y querubes de pluma
van detrás de Lutero por las altas esquinas. (vv 19–20)

****

If we accept my reading, we find in Lorca a flow of images, more or less subterranean, that seem to possess a rather astonishing coherence. Lorca appears as an extremely original heterodox, a poet of religious anguish more than of pagan joy; an anguish that becomes deeply enmeshed with social concerns and apocalyptic frenzy in *Poet in New York*. In this sense Lorca is simply a child of his time: how could a generous and valiant spirit attend without anger to the rise of Fascism and the specter of war? His own death, of course, witnesses to the clarity of his vision. But can we, then, consider our case closed?

It would be useless to deny, or ignore, the many occasions in which Lorca asserts the absolute finality of death. The cry of the 'Llanto por Ignacio Sánchez Mejías' seems to state it with painful despair:

Estamos con un cuerpo presente que se esfuma,
con una forma clara que tuvo ruiseñores
y la vemos llenarse de agujeros sin fondo.
. . . .

Porque te has muerto para siempre,
como todos los muertos de la Tierra,
como todos los muertos que se olvidan
en un montón de perros apagados. *(OC,* I, 557–58)

Lorca has repeated this cry too many times for us to ignore it. But this bitter pessimist is the same man that a few weeks before his tragic death would say to the *caricaturista* Bagaría, in an interview where doubts and hopes mixed in a moving confession:

> Yo no sé, Bagaría, en qué consiste la felicidad. Si voy a creer el texto que estudié, en el Instituto, del inefable catedrático Ortí y Lara, la felicidad no puede hallarse más que en el cielo; pero si el hombre ha inventado la eternidad, creo que hay en el mundo hechos y cosas que son dignos de ella y, por su belleza y trascendencia, uno de los absolutos para un orden permanente. ¿Por qué me preguntas estas cosas? Tú lo que quieres es que nos encontremos en el otro mundo y sigamos nuestra conversación bajo el techo de un prodigioso café de música con alas, risa y eterna cerveza inefable. Bagaría, no temas; ten la seguridad de que nos encontraremos.
> *(OC,* III, 681–82)

There are many Lorcas. We now know that the image of a triumphal Lorca, full of laughter and wit is, although authentic, partial and, to a great extent, mystifying. With the joyful Lorca, mime and buffoon, the soul of elegant parties, there is a deeply sad, a melancholic Lorca. The Lorca dandy and somewhat snob, frequent patron of the bar of the Palace Hotel and of the aristocratic drawing rooms of Madrid society is also the Lorca of the *Barraca,* the students' theater group that roamed the Spanish countryside carrying the Spanish classics to the peasants and laborers. It is a well-established fact that under his indolent appearance and pose lay an untiring reader and worker. I can see no difficulty in finding in the irreverent and skeptical Lorca a great religious poet that may have alternatively shared his overflowing spiritual vitality. I think that Lorca is, with Unamumo, the most important religious poet of modern Spain. But I fully realize that our research, in this respect, is just beginning. The aim of these pages was not to close an argument, but to contribute to a discussion that has only started.

NOTES

1. Francisco García Lorca, Prologue to *Lorca: Three Tragedies* (New York: New Directions, 1955) and *Federico y su mundo* (Madrid: Alianza, 1980), 65–89.

2. Carlos Morla Lynch, *En España con Federico García Lorca* (Madrid: Aguilar, 1957), 218–330.

3. We have numerous testimonies regarding Lorca's religious practice and his enthusiasm for liturgical ceremonies. See Ana María Dalí, *Salvador Dalí visto por su hermana* (Barcelona: Juventud, 1949), Alfredo de la Guardia,*García Lorca, persona y creación* (Buenos Aires: Shapire, 1941) and in Carlos Morla Lynch, *En España con Federico García Lorca* we find frequent references to his attendance at Mass, processions, Easter and Christmas celebrations, etc.

4. Derek R. Harris, 'The Religious Theme in Lorca's *Poeta en Nueva York, Bulletin of Hispanic Studies,* LIV (1977), 315–26; *García Lorca: 'Poeta en Nueva York'* (London: Grant and Cutler/Tamesis, 1978); and 'The Theme of the Crucifixion in Lorca's *Romancero gitano', Bulletin of Hispanic Studies,* LIII (1981), 329-37.

5. Miguel García Posada, *Lorca: interpretación de 'Poeta en Nueva York'* (Madrid: Akal/Universitaria, 1981).

6. García Posada, 178–94.

7. Piero Menarini, *'Poeta en Nueva York' di Federico García Lorca. Lettura critica* (Firenze: La nuova Italia, 1975).

8. Menarini, 198–213. Although the great French critic Charles Marcilly does not aim to give to us a general opinion regarding Lorca's faith, his insightful studies, so important for our understanding of Lorca's religious imagery, seem to me to come very close to Menarini's position. See "Notes pour l'étude de la pensée religieuse de Federico García Lorca. Essai d'interprétation de la 'Burla de don Pedro a caballo.'" *Les langues Néolatines, 141 (1957)."* pp. 9–42; "Notes pour l'étude de la pensée religieuse de Federico García Lorca," BHS, 44, (1962), 507–525. (See also Note 23 below). It could be objected that this religious anguish seems absent from his theater, but although such assertion is doubtful at its best, and incorrect regarding *El público (The Public)* and *Así que pasen cinco años* we must remember that he was writing a biblical trilogy at the time of his assassination. See Christian de Paepe, "García Lorca: posiciones, oposiciones, proposiciones y contraposiciones (Apostillas a la documentación lorquiana)," CHA, 90, (1972), 295–299.

9. André Belamich, 'Cristianesimo e paganesimo nella vita e nella opera di Lorca', In *García Lorca Materiali,* ed. Ubaldo Bardi and Ferruccio Masini (Napoli: Libreria Tullo Pironti, 1979), 98–113.

10. Eutimio Martín, 'Federico García Lorca, ¿un precursor de la "Teologia de la liberación"? (Su primera obra dramática inédita)', in *Lecciones sobre Federico García Lorca,* ed. Andrés Soria Olmedo (Granada: Maracena, 1986), 33.

11. Christopher Maurer, 'Sobre la prosa temprana de García Lorca', *Cuadernos Hispanoamericanos,* 433–434 (1986), 13–22, at 14.

12. Eutimio Martín, *Federico García Lorca, heterodoxo y mártir. Análisis y proyección dela obra junvenil inédita* (Madrid: Siglo XXI, 1986), 192.

13. Martín, *Federico García Lorca, heterodoxo ...*, 321.

14. Martín, *Federico García Lorca, heterodoxo ...*, 161–74.

15. Martín, *Federico García Lorca, heterodoxo ...*, 169, note 18.

16. Martín, *Federico García Lorca, heterodoxo ...*, 167.

17. Martín, *Federico García Lorca, heterodoxo ...*, 169.

18. Federico García Lorca, *Obras completas*, 3 vols., ed. Arturo del Hoyo, 22nd edn. (Madrid, Aguilaz, 1986). All references are to this edition.

19. Martín, *Federico García Lorca, heterodoxo ...*, 247.

20. Ian Gibson, 'Lorca's "Balada triste": Children's Songs and the Theme of Sexual Disharmony in the *Libro de poemas*', *Bulletin of Hispanic Studies*, XLVI (1969), 21–38.

21. Martín, *Federico García Lorca, heterodoxo ...*, 215.

22. Lorca develops the icon of the rotten fruit extensively, and in a purely religious context in the poem 'Prólogo', also of the *Libro de poemas*. In it Lorca likens his heart to a rotten quince and asks God to cleanse it by sinking his sceptre into it: 'Mi corazón está aquí, /Dios mío, /hunde tu cetro en él Señor, /Es un membrillo/demasiado otoñal/y está podrido.' Since this rottenness is due to 'an exam about lust' taken by the author with Satan as a classmate, there can be no doubt about the sexual character of this corruption.

23. Ian Gibson, *Federico García Lorca: De Fuente Vaqueros a Nueva York (1898–1929)* (Barcelona, Buenos Aires, Mexico: Grijalbo, 1985), 200–01.

24. Martín, *Federico García Lorca, heterodoxo ...*, 231–34.

25. Guillame Apollinaire, 'Les peintres cubistes,' In: *Theories of Modern Art. A Source Book by Artists and Critics,* ed. H. B. Chipp; (Berkeley: University of California Press, 1968), p. 222.

26. Morla Lynch, 39–40.

27. Salvador Dalí, *Diario de un genio* (Barcelona: Tusquets, 1983), p. 81.

28. Recent studies have dealt frankly with Lorca's homosexuality and with the traumatic effect that his perception of his sexual inclination had in his spiritual and aesthetic development. See Gibson, *Federico García Lorca. De Fuente Vaqueros...*, especially his Introduction; Martín, *Federico Garcia Lorca, heterodoxo ...*, 216-22; and Angel Sahuquillo, *Federico García Lorca y la cultura de la homosexualidad* (Stockholm: Akademitryck, 1986) where the subject is treated exhaustively.

29. The 'muro' as the constraint that limits human and natural freedom is a frequent image in Lorca. In the 'Oda a Walt Whitman' the modern, mechanical civilisation that imprisons the free man of nature raising modern cities in the prairies is described: 'una danza de muros agita las praderas/y América se llena de máquinas y llanto.' A 'muro' is also the frozen look by which the self surrounds its intimacy, denying communication and love: 'Mi dolor sangraba por las tardes/cuando tus ojos eran dos muros' (*OC*, I, 495); the blonde Americans of New York 'aman los muros porque detienen la mirada' while meanwhile in the humane and natural negro world there is 'un constante cambio de sonrisas' (*OC*,

III, 350). In this sense the nuns would be a metonymy for an imprisoned humanity looking to Christ in their quest for freedom.

30. The Father wounding the Son with an arrow of light reminds us of the God of 'Madrigal' that answers the poet's prayers with stalactities. There is an important textual problem to be considered here. Lorca had written verse 7 first as: 'como el médico aflige por amor a lo vivo', which would imply that the Father sends the Son to the cross for His love for humanity. This, of course, would contradict not only my interpretation but everything that Lorca himself had said so far and would say later. Martín *(Federico García Lorca, heterodoxo ..., 319)* argues that, at least when writing parts I and II, Lorca seems to have returned to Catholic orthodoxy. It may be so; but what is certain is that he decided against the verse, and I can only think that he must have realized that the benevolent feeling he attributed to the doctors could not be properly applied to the Father as he had conceived Him.

31. The best expression of the conciliation of restlessness (nard) and confinement (wall), in a fusion of love that leaves joy with peace and discipline without imprisonment, is found in these verses that praise the balancing power of the Holy Sacrament:

Sólo tu Sacramento de luz en equilibrio
aquietaba la angustia del amor desligado.
(*OC*, I, 766)

HOWARD T. YOUNG
Pomona College

Lorca and the Afflicted Monk

The nineteen-year-old author of *Impresiones y paisajes* (1918),[1] a remarkable literary debut despite its heavy reliance on the texts of others, was a young man bristling with frustration and indecision. His family had just forbidden him to study music in Paris; the puissance of sex threatened to overwhelm him, as the typical adolescent feelings of guilt mingled with doubts about his ultimate sexual preference. It is no surprise, therefore, that his collection of prose pieces, underwritten for publication by his father and imbued already with a sense of color and a clear talent for metaphor, should foreshadow the sense of revolt and iconoclasm associated with Lorca's life and work.

In the summers of 1916 and 1917, Professor Martín Domínguez Berrueta of the University of Granada organized and led student excursions in Andalusia and Castile to study *in situ* examples of architecture, painting, and sculpture. A highly personal record of these tours, *Impresiones y paisajes* takes occasion to denounce the hypocritical sexuality of monastery life, make scathing remarks about the artistic quality of religious objects in side chapels, and leave a record of Castile that while conscious of the austere beauty of its landscape does not hesitate to depict it as a lonesome, arid, depressing and fly-infested place.

A musical encounter between the young Lorca and the Benedictine community in the Monastery of Silos offers an especially rich opportunity to read the revolt and appreciate its layers of implications, including a portent of its final outcome. By filling in gaps and looking at indeterminancies in the narration,[2] the problematic nature of Lorca's iconoclasm and his complicated relation to authority and age acquire deeper hues.

The incident occurs in the section called "Monasterio de Silos," and at a propitious moment in the narration when the point of view, handled until then by a third person of thinly disguised subjectivity who resorted on occasion to *nosotros*, leaves its disguise for the more openly involved *yo,* in effect, abandoning description for narration. An evening alone in a cell in Silos provided an incisive experience that may have prepared the narrator for this more open expression that was to follow. A mournful night chorus of howling dogs provoked a reaction that presages the kind of discourse that will be used to describe the presence of the *duende* in the ritual of the *cante jondo*. In the opinion of Michèle Ramond, this episode of fearful night sounds gives a first indication of Lorca's creative bent toward the dark, the mysterious, and the dionysian. She argues that the night is a *rite de passage* that endows his *yo* with "un destin créateur et médiateur."[3]

In the morning light, however, the dogs' cries seem innocent enough. Lorca attends mass and, although distracted by certain coarse attributes of the monks ("manos ... llenas de cerdas")[4] listens delightedly to the Gregorian chant that is part of the service.

The musician in Lorca has been particularly aroused by an Agnus Dei of rare and ancient nature. After the service, Lorca strikes up a conversation with the organist and discovers that, having entered the monastery as a child, the monk's musical exposure has consisted of nothing but plainsong. He has never listened to a cello, the astonished narrator informs us, been stirred by the sound of trumpets, nor even heard of Beethoven. This is too much for the nineteen-year-old Lorca, who offers to play a sample of this other kind of music on the monastery organ.

Lorca at the piano: the scene is a set piece, in every sense of the phrase, de rigueur in the Lorca legend. The magical hands[5], although *torpe* for every other task,[6] charmed audiences in impromptu recitals at parties on three continents. Despite the denial of formal studies in Paris, Lorca and the piano remained inseparable. It was one of his major means for communication beyond his poetry, and it is also part of the language of music in his verse. The fascist hands that searched the Huerta de San Vicente in August 1936 made a point of rummaging through the insides of the grand piano, as if they were symbolically attacking the poet himself.[7]

In 1916, one year before the excursion to Silos, Professor Berruguete took his group to visit Antonio Machado in Baeza. Inevitably, Lorca played the piano. The *mozalbete* who sat down at the keyboard became transfigured: "Entonces se opera el milagro: la figura sentada crece, se hace adulta, sobrepasa las naturales proporciones y parece llenar la sala por completo."[8]

Now at the Monasterio de Silos, the legend still largely unformed, Lorca proposes to exercise his magic in an enclosed and sacred environment. Of special interest in the Lorca canon is the fact that, as a narrator, he will describe himself for the first time in this performing situation:

Después yo me senté en el órgano. Allí estaban los teclados místicos con pátina amarillenta, filas de pajes de ensueño que despiertan a los sonidos (52).

The youthful author does not hesitate to resort to well-worn romantic conventions. The image of the idle instrument awaiting an inspired hand lay readily accessible in Bécquer's *Rimas,* and Lorca avails himself of it. To see the keys, however, as *pajes de ensueño* adds a touch of playfulness that will grow stronger in later work. It is a trope that points forward to the potent *teclas* of Salinas' "Underwood Girls" as the fingers poised over the typewriter keys are about to unlease a magic world. At the moment, however, the narrator's sense of himself as a avatar of romanticism could hardly be stronger.

Before the period of the *duende* and the *cante jondo*. Lorca's tastes in music were decidedly classical,[9] and Beethoven was his favorite composer. In dedicating *Impresiones y paisajes* to his former music teacher Antonio Segura Mesa, Lorca alluded to the "conjuro de una sonata beethoviana (4)" evoked by the maestro's playing. In one of his earliest prose pieces associated with the series "Místicas," Lorca broods over the confusion of his feelings, but knows that he longs for "lo imposible" "cuando hay luz de tarde y la música de Beethoven lo dice sangrando" (180). It was this quintessential romantic the monk had never heard of, and it was Beethoven's music that came unbidden to Lorca's mind as he poised himself over the organ keyboard:

> Entonces vino a mi memoria esta obra de dolor extrahumano, esa lamentación de amor patético, que se llama el *allegretto* de la *Séptima sinfonía*. Di el primer acorde y entré en el hipo angustioso de su ritmo constante y de pesadilla (52).

If Lorca had been consciously seeking a Beethoven equivalent of the simplicity and austerity of a Gregorian chant, he could hardly have chosen better than the opening bars of the Seventh's allegretto. Its long, sustained single thematic note, expressed by rhythm ("ritmo constante y de pesadilla") agrees with the monodic temperament of the plainsong.[10] The barest information of a musicological nature reinforces the felicitousness of the selection. From the first, the rhythmic element of the Seventh Symphony led Wagner to term it the apotheosis of the dance. The symphony has often been choreographed, and Isidora Duncan at the height of her fame had danced to it.[11] In describing the high mass that had just ended, Lorca also thought in terms of choreography: "Las danzas sagradas de los oficiantes repercuten en el coro" (50). Program notes continue to link the allegretto to a religious setting by use of such word images as "mystic tread" and "a priest's march to a temple amid sacred dancing."[12]

The priests in the heart of Castile, however, turned out to be unwilling dancers. Lorca is not more than three measures into this confrontation between plainsong and Beethoven when the door of the organ loft bursts open.

The *fraile* who unceremoniously enters has appeared previously in the text. To the group of students from Granada he volunteered to explain some of the sculpture in the cloister. Cast in the role of explicator, he is a figure of some authority, and Lorca resorts to superlatives to describe his magnetism:

> En una pared del claustro duerme un caballero de nobleza castellana, que fue el héroe de una hermosísima gesta de amor. Un monje inteligentísimo y sabio nos la cuenta ... Fuerte y serena surge la leyenda de los labios apsaionados del religioso, brillan sus ojos melancólicos en el ensueño de una evocación artística (46).

The fraile who bursts through the organ loft door at the first strains of Beethoven's allegretto now stands divested of the authority and charm that were his in the telling of the *gesta de amor*. The melancholy eyes are covered, and he presents a suddenly vulnerable figure: "Tenía una palidez acentuada. Se acercó a mí y tapándose los ojos con las manos con acento de profundo dolor me dijo: '¡Siga usted, siga usted!' " (52).

This is the cusp of the encounter between plainsong and Beethoven. The iconoclastic young bard, seated at his instrument, has aroused the one individual intelligent and sensitive enough to comprehend fully the message of the individual revolt that underlies Beethoven. As he stands before Lorca with open ears but covered eyes, he conveys an ambiguous attitude: "Let the music continue but my emotions be hidden."

Lorca continues to play, but at a point where the music becomes especially impassioned and full of "amor doloroso" (52), his fingers stumble on the keys and the organ grows silent. His musical memory collapses: "No me acordaba de más" (52).

Lorca's phenomenal memory was a subject of constant family commentary,[13] and, therefore, his memory lapse is doubly significant: that it happened at all, and in this particular place and time. The breakdown is rationalized by Lorca as a "misericordia de Dios" (52), suggesting the compassion of divine intervention in order to silence the profane chords of Beethoven and protect the distressed monk. Undoubtedly present also was the onslaught of nervousness attributable to the realization that, after days of pent-up resentment against the monastery system, he had an opportunity to respond in a performance situation that had, heretofore, been unusually successful. It could be argued that he was musically over his head, but as a pianist, he was not above improvisation. As some of his more discerning listeners were quick to notice, verve and feeling covered a multitude of sins. The point is that he always played, as Pérez Ferrero remembers him in front of Antonio Machado, with heart and soul. The question is what happened now to the heart and soul of this normally brash young man to cause what appears to be a failure of nerve?

The figure of the distraught monk suggests ways in which a fuller understanding of the moment may be achieved. After Lorca's memory fails him, he turns to look at his intruder. What he sees is worth recording:

> El monje apasionado tenía los ojos puestros en un sitio muy
> lejos. Ojos que tenían toda la amargura de [un espíritu que acababa
> de despertar de] un ensueño ficticio, para mirar hacia un ideal de
> hombre perdido quizá para siempre (52).[14]

Beethoven's music has poignantly reminded the monk of another artistic world to which he once belonged. The bitterness that Lorca senses is that of a man momentarily jolted from a peaceful routine, *ficticio* though it may be, and confronted with an ideal long thought lost: the musician (or artist) he never became. The parallel with Lorca's situation cannot escape attention. The narrator, at the time of writing, has just recently suffered frustration occasioned by the parental denial of permission to study the piano in Paris. It is not too far-fetched to suppose that Lorca has identified himself with the intelligent Benedictine, and that the *amargura* perceived in the monk has not a little of self-projection.

Too many gaps exist in the presentation of the narrative to allow the reader to know whether the monk really does consider the cloister "un ensueño ficticio."

Of Lorca's opinion on that matter, however, there can be no doubt. *Impresiones y paisajes* never misses an opportunity to denounce the oppression and hypocrisy that the young author believed to exist in monastery life as he saw it in Cartuja de Miraflores and Silos.

Marie Laffranque, stressing the significance of this scene in the organ loft at Silos, sees it as a watershed in the poet's life. Lorca, she believes, linked the *ideal de hombre* with the freedom of Beethoven, and vowed at that moment "...d'être pleinement lui-même, et de trouver ainsi sa place, son rôle dans le monde."[15]

The degrees of indeterminacy in the text (fluctuating point of view and gaps in the character presentation) do not, however, suggest that the reading should end with such a categorical statement. The phrase *ensueño ficticio,* for example, does not have to be a metaphor for monastic life. It could be concerned with music's well-known ability to breed daydreams, and thus remind the monk of a lost ideal. When Lorca's memory fails and the music stops, the monk awakens from this beguiling fiction. That is certainly the interpretation supplied by the monk, who later in the day appears before the young guest and delivers a strong homily. Music, he opines, "... es la lujuria misma. Yo le doy a usted un consejo: abandónela, si no quiere pasar una vida de tormentos" (55), which is the same advice that Lorca's parents insisted he take.

The impact made by the monk's figure is due, in part, to the fact that of all the inmates of the Cartuja de Miraflores and the Monasterio de Silos, he is the only one viewed affirmatively by Lorca. The rest, to use Klibbe's metaphor for a university excursion, do not receive passing grades from the young narrator.[16] The monk moves in and out of the story in a fascinating way that makes it difficult for the reader to apprehend with any depth his figure, but the overall effect is one of a cultivated and wise individual who counted among his steady visitors Zuloaga and Unamuno (55).[17] We know enough about Lorca's background and his tastes to recognize that he could have easily identified with the monk.

To pinpoint even further the complex nature of this attraction, let us return to the eyes. The end of the music finds them uncovered, fixed on a far off site. But Lorca is not finished describing them:

> Ojos los suyos de españoles centelleares, cobijados por las cejas
> que ya le empezaban a nevar. Ojos los suyos de inteligencia, de
> pasión, de lucha constantes (52).

The description predicates the involvement of the narrator. Lorca intuits passion, intelligence, and struggle, attributes, as Marie Laffranque says, that will characterize the development of his own brilliant career. Eyes may be windows, but they have their share of mirror duties, reflecting images as well as serving as openings onto the world. The curious phrase *españoles centelleares,* used to describe the monk's eyes, must own up to its dash of platitude, but it also emulates Lorca's own eyes and the sparkling defiance that will be associated with his life. In a book that rejects much that literary or general cultural tastes proclaimed as *castizo* — Castile, monasteries, the head of San Bruno by Manuel de Pereira at the Cartuja de Miraflores — no other explanation for the presence of such a near *tópico* satisfies as well. The "Spanish sparklings" look ahead to the magnetism of Lorca's mature personality, the famous "comunicativa vitalidad."[18]

Finally, it would be a mistake to ignore the age of the unnamed monk. The snow of the eyebrows is of a different nature than the Spanish flashes in the eyes, and the monk realizes that he will die in the monastery (55). As a child, Lorca was profoundly moved by the death of a venerable family friend known as el Compadre Pastor (172–173); he had learned at an early age to recognize the ultimate silence lurking in the faces of the old.

Age also implies authority. Lorca came from a large *Latino* clan, sternly led by don Federico, his own father. Lorca sought friendships outside the huge circle of *primos*, and, according to don Federico, would always do "lo que le [diera] la gana."[19] But he admired without reservation such father figures as Federico de Onís, Angel del Río, and Fernando de los Ríos, who, at a crucial moment, steered the young poet in the momentous direction of New York. Just one year before the scene as Silos, Fernando de los Ríos had listened "astonished" as Lorca sat playing Beethoven at a piano in Granada.[20] Lorca's hands, one may safely assume, did not falter then.

On the basis of the reading just undertaken, Lorca's failure of nerve acquires considerable complexity. By filling some gaps in the narrative with material from outside the immediate text, but, nevertheless, part of the larger Lorca text, one can go far towards explaining the reasons for the protracted effect this passage has had on readers. The monk is a vulnerable artist, a confined intellectual, with whom Lorca at once identifies, but whom he also intends to surpass by not falling into the trap of silence and conformity imposed by the cloisters. The dual reaction of recognition and denial helps account for the momentary confusion of the nineteen-year-old narrator and adds to the poignancy of the situation.

Lorca, thus unsettled, is a failure in his role as romantic avatar. He has bewitched no one; the spell of the *Romancero gitano* has yet to be cast. The initiate whose pure Agnus Dei delighted Lorca is simple to the point of being *bobo*, laughing uncomprehendingly at the confusion of the older monk (52). As for Father Pinedo himself, if that is his name, he welcomes the silence and confinement of Silos. "Quiero morir aquí" (55), he tells Lorca, after having assured him that "Ahora mi única música es el canto gregoriano" (55).

Thus ends the confrontation between plainsong and Beethoven.

There is one other startling gap in the narration. When the organ grows silent from Lorca's forgetful hands, the disturbed monk disappears. Lorca and the organist make their way downstairs.

> Al salir de la iglesa sentimos una gran palpitación en el ambiente:
> era un libro enorme que se había cerrado sobre el facistol (52).

After the emotionally charged confrontation that has just taken place — the free romantic spirit of the narrator halted in confusion, the organist laughing mindlessly, the anguish of the intelligent monk — the reader is shocked by this loud clap in the stillness of the church. What can be made of it? Has the music-loving *fraile* vented his frustration and his bitterness by slamming shut a large hymnal? Has some other bystander turned his disapproval into a sonorous gesture?

There are, of course, no clear answers. But the closing of the book is the final commentary on the encounter between the simplicity and order of plainsong and the gigantic freedom of Beethoven. When the monk appears once again in the narration, he is homiletic and avuncular. The institution has remained intact; the tragic tones of the allegretto are not even a memory. However, years ahead, outside of the text under consideration, there will be the clap of another book closing with a sharp, dry sound in a ravine in Víznar.

NOTES

1. Published in the spring of 1918 (Granada Imp. P. V. Traveset), *Impresiones y paisajes* made little impact on the literary scene of its day. In a copy he presented to Campbell Hackforth-Jones, Lorca called it "Este libro de mi niñez." See Andrew A. Anderson, "Una amistad inglesa de García Lorca," *Insula*, 40, núm. 462 (mayo 1985), 3. Portions of the book appeared as early as 1960 in the Aguilar *Obras*, but censorship delayed the full text until 1973 (18th ed. of the *Obras*). Lawrence H. Klibbe, *Lorca's "Impresiones y paisajes": The Young Artist* (Potomac, MD: Studia Humanitatis, 1983) is the only book-length study. The strong sense of revolt that informs *Impresiones* is considered by Howard T. Young "Breaking the Rules in *Impresiones y paisajes*" in *"Cuando yo me muera ..." Essays in Memory of Federico García Lorca*, ed. C. Brian Morris (Lanham, MD: University Press of America, 1988), pp. 11–23.

2. W. Iser, *The Act of Reading: A Theory of Aesthetic Response* (Baltimore, MD: The Johns Hopkins University Press, 1978), pp. 176–183. Lucien Dállenbach claims that when reading is confronted with a hiatus (blank, gap, vacancy, ellipsis, rupture, *Leerstelle*), the reader is forced to lay bridges and to make interpretations not supplied by the text. See *Mirrors and After: Five Essays on Literary Theory and Criticism* (New York: City University of New York, 1986), p. 25.

3. M. Ramond, "Le moi au couvent. L'épisode des chiens dans *Impresiones y paisajes*" in *L'Autobiographie dans le Monde Hispanique* (Provence: Université de Provence, 1980), p. 60.

4. F. García Lorca, *Obras completas* (22nd ed. 3 vols.), III, 49. Subsequent page references will be to this edition.

5. P. Neruda, *Confieso que he vivido: Memorias* (Barcelona: Seix Barral, 1974), p. 171.

6. Francisco García Lorca, *Federico y su mundo*, 2nd ed. (Madrid: Alianza, 1981), p. 56.

7. I. Gibson, *The Assassination of Federico García Lorca* (New York: Penguin, 1983), p. 121.

8. M. Pérez Ferrero, *Vida de Antonio Machado y Manuel* (Buenos Aires: Espasa-Calpe, 1952), pp. 120–121.

9. The pervasive use of music in his work is more and more appreciated. An entire scene of *Bodas de sangre* (1932) is directly modeled on the technique of "imitative entry" used by Bach in his cantatas. C. Maurer, "García Lorca y las formas de la música" in *Lecciones sobre Federico García Lorca*, ed. Andrés Soria Olmedo (Granada: Ediciones del Cincuentenario, 1986), pp. 235-250.

10. I am indebted to my colleague Peter Jaffe for this analysis.

11. O. Downes, "Ludwig van Beethoven: Symphony No. 7" in *The Music Lover's Handbook*, ed. Elie Siegmeister (New York: Morrow, 1943), p. 162.

12. R. Freed, "Program notes to Beethoven's Symphony No. 7 in A." The Philadelphia Orchestra. Riccardo Muti conducting. Angel Record S-37538 (1979).

13. Francisco García Lorca, op. cit., p. 58.

14. The words within brackets were omitted in the early Aguilar editions. The Franco censorship would not condone the comparison of monastery life to an "ensueño ficticio."

15. *Les idées esthétiques de Federico García Lorca* (Paris: Centre de Recherches Hispaniques, 1967), p. 69.

16. L. H. Klibbe, *Lorca's "Impresiones y paisajes": The Young Artist* (Potomac, MD: Studia Humanitatis, 1983), p. 58.

17. The monk has been identified in all likelihood by I. Gibson as fray Ramiro de Pinedo, who after having studied in Paris and made a considerable fortune through the concoction of a tonic, retired to monastery life. *Federico García Lorca. 1. De Fuente Vaqueros a Nueva York* (Barcelona: Grijalbo, 1985), p. 168. Fray Pinedo's actions impressed Lorca enough to reappear in "Las reglas de la música," an article that appeared in *El Diario de Burgos* 18 August 1917: "Yo conozco a personas que se retiraron de oír música, abrumadas por las ideas que sentían" (372).

18. Francisco García Lorca, op. cit., p. 92.

19. Ibid., p. 95.

20. Gibson, *Assassination*, p. 176.

REI BERROA WITH SARAH E. MORGAN
George Mason University

Poetry and Painting: García Lorca's Dual Manifestation of Symbol and Metaphor

> *Senseless speech ...*
> *Does inspiration have eyes, or does it sleepwalk?*[1]
> From *The Diaries of Paul Klee, 183*

1. The Story of an Old Relationship

Poetry and painting, like naming, imagining, or analyzing, are mirror-like reflections of man. They engage the human being in an inquest into both the solitude of the word or the sign trying to give meaning to language, and the isolation of color and line as they attempt to capture reality. The arts of poetry and painting are related modes of conceiving and expressing the real.

The correlation between poetry and painting, the "sister arts", has concerned philosophers, historians, and art critics[2] at least since the sixth century B.C. when the Greek poet Simonides of Ceos, according to Plutarch, stated that while painting is a "mute poetry," poetry is a "speaking picture."[3] This analogy, by which one art is credited with the attributes of another, created the space for rhetorical comparisons between other art forms and produced epigraphs and figures of speech such as "symphonic poem," "harmonic painting," and "rhythmic sculpture."

More than a mere tool for art criticism, the analogy and the actual relationship has always been seen as an implement for creation and a concern for the artists themselves. Such was the case with Horace's mimetic ideas about poetry, Blake's visions of the human shape of the universe, and with the concern of many modern painters, including Picasso, Miró, and Dalí, for sculpture, music and poetry. Victor Hugo, himself a poet and painter,[4] had this comradeship of the arts in mind when he wrote to the French sculptor Froment-Meurice:[5]

> Nous sommes frères; la fleur
> Par deux arts peut être faite.
> Le poète est ciseleur,
> Le ciseleur est poète.

This is the spell that leads us to an understanding of why a poet with the metaphoric perception of García Lorca revealed his poetic needs and obsessions not only through writing but also through painting.

In an article that appeared in *Linguistic Inquiry* in 1970 and was later published in his book *Questions de Poétique,* Roman Jakobson studies the "visual" verbal art of three painters: William Blake, Henri Rousseau, and Paul Klee.[6]

Jakobson's study is an inquiry into the function of words for these painters whose means of aesthetic manifestation — obviously excluding Blake — are primarily line, color, and form. The study that follows, countertracks Jakobson's analysis. It is an inquiry into the poetic function of line and form in García Lorca, an artist who, although frequently seized by the sounds of popular music and the lines of visual form, used the written word as his primary source for expressing the totality of the real: the outer world and the world within.

2. The Total Eye of Federico García Lorca

Federico García Lorca is a *créature extraordinaire*.[7] His poetry, rooted in the inexhaustible flow of the popular talent, continues as fresh today as it was the first day it reached the public. Equally fresh are his theater works, his drawings and sketches, the music he collected and harmonized and, above all, his image: that of a spritely man who comes and goes through the by-ways of art with the surety of the trapeze artist. Of himself he once wrote to Sebastiá Gasch, art critic and director of the art magazine *L'Amic de les Arts*:[8]

> I find myself with an almost physical sensation that carries me to
> levels where it's difficult to find one's footing and where one al-
> most flies over the abyss.

Anyone who makes the acquaintance of even one of Lorca's many facets recognizes at first glance the dramatic force that the total eye of Federico, an eye which weighed equally the tangible and the fantastic, injected into everything which came through the sieve of his imagination. He argued always that the poet should sharpen his five senses so he would not get confused in the turmoil of reality. Especially important to grasp what is beyond the real, he said, is the sense of sight.

> Metaphor is always guided by the sense of sight (a sublimate sight
> at times), but it is the sight that puts limits on metaphor and gives
> reality to it. Even the most evanescent English poets, like Keats,
> feel the need to draw and limit their metaphors and figurations.
> And Keats *is saved* by his admirable plasticity from the dangerous
> poetic world of visions. Later on he would have to exclaim
> naturally: "Only poetry can narrate his [sic] dreams." The sight
> does not let the shadow blur the shape of the image drawn before
> her eyes. (*O.C.*, p. 68.)

The paintings of García Lorca are a study in themselves of the visual perspective from which both painters and poets create. The works of Lorca the painter illuminate some of the most forceful metaphors and symbols of Lorca the poet, and because of this creative interrelation, the closer we examine his paintings, the more we know of his poetry.[9] The paintings should be studied through the total eye which gave birth to them, an eye of all senses and reason combined into one creative and critical apparatus: a pupil which opens to interpret and explain the agonizing reality with which the human identifies.

3. García Lorca's Allusions to Painting

There is movement, a flowing back and forth of symbol and metaphor between Lorca's sketches and his poetic works. This flow or relationship is illuminated again and again in the poetic texts themselves and in his letters. Two of Lorca's most enlightening letters on this correlation were written to Gasch, the first in August of 1927, the second, September 8, 1928.[10]

> Now I'm starting to write and illustrate poems like this one that I'm sending dedicated. When a subject is too lengthy or contains a poetically stale emotion, I resolve it with drawing pencils.
>
> I'm working with great devotion on several things of very different genres. I'm composing all sorts of poems. I'll be sending some to you. If you like the drawings tell me which one or ones you'd like to publish and *I'll send you their corresponding poems.* (Italics mine.)

After this declaration to the director of *L'Amic de les Arts* García Lorca did not speak again of his drawings until 1936[11] when he wrote to Juan Guerrero Ruiz:

> I am sending you my poems corrected. ... I [also] send you three drawings. Publish them their exact size and well arranged. The definitive titles are on the back in red pencil.
>   Publish the three of them if possible ...
>   You must take care of the drawings so that, when reproduced, the lines don't lose the only thing they have: their *emotion.* They have to appear *exact.* Insist on that to the engravers. *(O.C.,* p. 1672)

Before this last letter, Lorca's references to his drawings had been rapid, without pause for reflection or clarification that would give another dimension to the sketches which, on many occasions, illustrated postcards and letters to his friends Jorge Guillén, Guillermo de Torre, and Ana María Dalí.

In February of 1927, he wrote to Guillén:[12]

> ... Perhaps someday I will be able to express the extraordinary *real* drawings that I dream. Now I have a long way to go.

Lorca also wrote to Guillermo de Torre, referring to "some bull sketches" that he was doing and which now are lost (*O.C.*, p. 1631). The greatest number of references to his drawings, however, appeared in his letters to Gasch, probably because of the interest Federico had in Gasch publishing his drawings in *L'Amic*.[13] From these letters, I selected the following, which reflects a spontaneous vision, but penetrating and defined, of his plastic works.[14]

> But without *torture* or *dream* (I detest the art of dreams), or complications. These drawings are pure poetry or pure plasticity at the same time. I feel clean, comforted, happy, *a child* when I do them. And I am horrified by the *words* that I have to use to name them. I'm horrified by the painting that they call *direct,* which is nothing but an anguished struggle with forms in which the painter is *always* vanquished and the work is *dead.* In these abstractions I see *created* reality joining itself to the reality that surrounds us like the real clock is attached to the concept the way a barnacle is to a rock. You're right, my dear Gasch, one must connect abstractions. What's more, I would call these drawings you'll be receiving ..., *Very Human Drawings.* Because all of them pierce the heart with their little arrows.

For García Lorca, then, the act of painting involved no "burst" of inspiration, no creative "fever." "I think no great artist works in a state of fever," he stated (*O.C.*, p. 75). In characterizing poetic inspiration as a "dove wounded by a mysterious hunter" (*O.C.*, p. 150), he underlines that the poet goes out, searching with all his senses to "hunt" the right metaphor.[15] Through this "hunting," he discovers not only the relationship between the senses of words, that's to say their metaphoric figuration, but also their symbolism, what they *represent* or stand for. García Lorca consciously invested time in "hunting" the right metaphor for his poetry through exercises in painting.

In the section that follows, we will explore the flow of metaphor between García Lorca's poetry and his painting. Although we will not distinguish between symbol and metaphor due to the imprecise line which divides them,[16] we will connect metaphor to his poetry (after all, it is a figure of meaning), while the search for symbol will be mainly limited to his drawings and, at times, to his plays because of the visual aspect of theater. We will study how some key symbols in his paintings and sketches reflect the metaphors of his poetry, and highlight the parallels which exist in the two art forms. This will allow us, in Bakhtin's terms, a "chronotopical" stance,[17] which enables us to establish a dialogue between the simultaneity of painting with its synchronic representation (in the space of the painting, everything seems to happen at the same time), and the sequential or diachronical accommodation of a poetic instance (one word comes *after* or *next to* but not *within* the other).

4. Some Key Symbols

Relating the poetry of García Lorca to his paintings is a complex process for several reasons. The strongest metaphors of his poetry are not reflected as the most obvious symbols in his visual works, but as less vivid, more subtle keys to the drawings' meaning. Conversely, the most important visual symbols do not appear as cornerstones in the construction of the poetry. This "hidden" correlation should be kept in mind as the eye searches for the poetic in the drawings.

Although the works of poetry far outnumber the preserved drawings, the visual works present a wealth of symbolism, meaning compressed into an incredible economy of line. Christoph Eich, in a discussion on the economy and intensity of García Lorca, compares him to Racine, another dramatic poet, to show how intensity is obtained directly and ineffably by reducing or economizing the elements that will lead to the desired emotion. Eich quotes from *Phèdre* to show how Racine evokes the shaded freshness of the forest in few terms: "Dieux!, que ne suis-je assise à l'ombre des forêts."[18]

Manos cortadas (Ap. 1) provides a prime example of Lorca's dramatic economy. With a few simple strokes, the effect moves from the sensorial, or the pupil (the extended fingers, the hands alone, the dripping blood) to the spiritual, that which one sees with the total eye (the amputation of the hands from the body becomes a symbol of ultimate destruction).

García Lorca employed an economy of symbol as well as line in his drawings. The same figures appear again and again in different settings, the main ones being hands, eyes, fish and trees. As we have already introduced the symbol of hands in *Manos cortadas,* this is where we will begin the discussion of these symbols individually.

4.1 The Hands

The hands, a symbol of secondary rank in the poetry of García Lorca, acquire outstanding strength as symbol in his drawings. Generally accepted as symbols of work and fertility,[19] the hands appear amputated in *Manos cortadas,* thus symbolizing the castration of man in three senses: the political (the elimination of man's means of labor), the social (interruption of husbandry), and the individual castration (cessation of fertility).[20] The dramatic force of this drawing is paralleled in *Romancero gitano (O.C.,* p. 459), in the poem dedicated to the martyrdom of Santa Eulalia ("Olalla"). In the poem, the saint's breasts (a metaphor for fertility) are amputated, and her hands appear in the same symbolic posture of the drawing:

> On the ground and unruly
> her amputated hands writhe

> still crossing in a tenuous
> decapitated prayer.

Muerte (Ap. 2), recalls the entrance of the masquerade on Wall Street in *Poet in New York (O.C.,* pp. 484–487). "Death" has one foot in the flagstone pavement and the other off the pavement.[21] There are several hands which float or dangle from the head and ribs, hands without movement, but connected by filaments to the rest of the monster that possesses human legs, a trunk full of roots and stamens, a ribcage, and two heads, the head of Death and the head of Death's victim, that are united at the ribcage by a filament serving as an umbilical cord.[22] The bigger head, Death's victim, has closed eyes; by the lips, one can read her anguish. Death's head has two bones instead of eyes, and a series of points in place of the mouth extending to a hand, which can be interpreted as Death's cry.[23] In 1918, García Lorca wrote some verses which correspond in gesture to *Muerte,* quoted here from *Libro de poemas (O.C.,* p. 189):

> Any living thing that passes
> the doors of death
> goes with the head bowed
> and a white sleep-walking air.
> With speech of thoughts.
> Without sounds ...
> Sadly,
> covered with the silent
> veil of death.

The Angel (Ap., 3), is a demonic drawing, with the hands serving to represent a monstrosity. The right hand posed over the side of the heart has six fingers.[24] The "angel" also sports hook-like horns in its curly hair and wings of horrible disproportion. (Recall the verses of *Romancero gitano:* "Angel with impressive wings /like daggers from Albacete," *O.C.,* p. 429.) The angel has a glint in its eyes and a devilish smile on its lips which contrast sharply with the popular, pleasant imagery of angels. García Lorca's is a caricaturesque, deconstructive vision, built in a demiurgic manner, the way in which the artist often perceives reality. Here he presents the angel not as an allegory of goodness, but as a mixture of pride (pheasant's plumes), evil (hooks), and monstrosity (hand with six fingers.) Nevertheless, García Lorca labels this "an angel." We encounter this combination again in *Libro de poemas,* in the verses of "Prólogo" when the young Lorca begs help from God, threatening Him that if He does not come to his aid, he would allow in his heart "a friend," none other than Satan, "my companion in an examination of lechery" (*O.C.,* pp. 240–243).

The two hands of the poet appear in *Perspectiva urbana con autorretrato* (Ap. 4), attempting to cover the visage. The disproportion, however, is considerable and the little hands, fetal-like, have no success in trying to cover the crude reality.[25] The urban perspective produces malaise and anguish anyway in the countenance of the poet, who is adorned with three black moons.[26]

A terrible hand emerges at the base of the column in *Columna y casa* (Ap., 5) as symbol of the human condition, trapped and submerged in worldly matters against its will.[27]

In *Sólo el misterio nos hace vivir, sólo el misterio* (Ap., 6), the hand searches for the heart (see note 34), seat of the mystery of man, while in *Bandolero* (Ap., 7), the being portrayed has lost his left hand (two rigid hooks have assumed its place) and his right hand has an appearance of total sterility. More than a hand, it looks like two chunks of wood attached to the arm.

In *Amor novo* (Ap., 8), the two hands are positioned possessively over the plain form from which the figure in sailor's costume emerges.[28] This impresses on the observer that above all, this "new love" is sensual. The moon, witness to the important moments of the life of man, has a testimonial presence in this drawing as it corresponds to the love/moon relation, so frequent in the history of literature.[29]

The hands acquire movement in *Figura* (Ap., 9) and this play of hands that poetically activates the quietness of the figure counterpoints the fixed expression that the sketch transmits. In this drawing the hands do not express drama as do the hands discussed before, but imply grace, animation and fluidity.

All of these characteristics mixed with singular intensity in the drawings, are encountered with even higher intensity in the poems, in which the erotic ("I will go with the No you gave /in the palm of my hand" (*[O.C.,* p. 396]) is united with the tragic ("the dead are concentrating on devouring their own hands" *[O.C.,* p. 486]) or with the lyric, the dreams of the poet, from the young Lorca of *Libro de poemas* (If my fingers only could / they would deflower the moon" *[O.C.,* p. 199]), to the adult of *Poet in New York* ("I seek the freed voice that leaks my hands" *[O.C.,* p. 499]).

4.2 The Eyes

"All the light of the world fits within an eye" *(O.C.,* p. 509). This verse from "Nocturno del hueco" *(Poet in New York),* acquires plastic reality in García Lorca's drawings in which the eyes either "shape" the sketch by casting, from the top of the drawing, a beam of light, or, by appearing without pupils, completely obscure the figures. The eye is a source of light and, since light is a symbol of intelligence, the act of seeing in the drawings of García Lorca symbolizes knowledge and understanding. The eyes with pupils are illuminators, *alumbradores,* while those in which the pupil is missing reflect ignorance and darkness.

In *Symbols of Transformation,* Jung considers the eye as symbol of the maternal womb, with the pupil as her daughter.[30] This is extremely valid for the works of Federico in which the woman without child, or sterile, is a dark woman, obscure, and without pupil. If we recall as well that the Spanish verb for "to give birth," *alumbrar,* or "to bring to light," mirrors this idea, we can accept with less uncertainty Jung's affirmation.

The lines of *La careta que cae* (Ap., 10) impress on the viewer the thematic rigor of movement by the way the neck and head are joined. The mask falls away from the face at a thirty degree angle, while the enormous clown's eyes gaze seriously back at us.

In *Pájaro y perro* (Ap., 11), the eye of the parrot casts a glance down at the tiny dog. The dog looks intently at the shadow or impression of the parrot, whose exaggerated plumage bears some similarity to a dog's tail.

The eyes of *Bandolero* (Ap., 7) express the sadness of a being who rejects society, but is forced to live, irremediably, as part of it. *Rostro con flechas* (Ap., 12) shows a face pierced by arrows. Because the face is dead, it has no eye to illuminate it. In *Nostalgia* (Ap., 13), one eye alone gives the drawing its luminous aspect. The roundness of the pupil radiates the equilibrium that balances the lines and curves which cut across from the top down and from right to left. The figure in *Amor novo* (Ap., 8) conceals his eyes, but the moon, witness to the novelty of that love, has the shape of an eye, because although love is blind, it is illuminated by the moon and the stars. In *Amor* (Ap., 14), the drawing is reduced to its essential strokes: two faces, two mouths united (the mouth is that which allows lovers to continue united) and four eyes: she, wearing a wide brim hat, has tender eyes;[31] he, wearing a beret with the inscription "AMOR," has startled eyes.

One of Lorca's most important compositions bears the title *El Ojo* (Ap., 15). In the center of the drawing there is a shapeless face with two arrows: the one on the left ends the line of the face; the second, in the middle, suggests the nose and the mouth (and the senses they represent.) It moves toward the lower part of the drawing and develops into a set of root-like lines. The right eye has been substituted by a series of dots connected to a filament. The left eye gives the drawings its title. From its upper meridian emerges a knot of threads, some of which develop into a set of dendrites which seem to go to the brain. On the right side of the drawing there is a dark window. Between the window and the eye there is a mirror from which departs a bundle of eight hands, all of them connected by the same stroke of the pen.

This drawing is García Lorca's depiction of his theory of poetry and the sense of sight. *El Ojo* shows a hierarchy of the senses, in this order: sight, touch, and hearing. These three are related to the upper part of man and are regarded as "superior" senses. The senses of smell and taste, the "inferior" senses, he connects with the lower part of the body. The eye, depicted realistically, reigns supreme above the organs of the other senses: the mouth, the nose, the hands, the ears. The hands state that many hands are needed to produce the effect that a single eye can produce. The dark window suggests that outside of the eye's kingdom there is only murk, and that the real can take shape only through the mirror-window of the eye. In the way that we discover ourselves in the image reflected in the mirror, so the eye is the first source of man's knowledge of his interior self.[32]

Ojo y vilanos reflects a similar approach (Ap., 16). In this drawing, the eye in the middle of the drawing, above a pot, gives a certain realism to the painting that, otherwise, would have remained in a level of total abstraction.

These visual games and the presence of the eye pass with great frequency from painting to poetry to theater. Consider, for instance, in *La casa de Bernarda Alba,* Adela's reply when la Poncia comments "How much you like that man!" Adela says: "How much! When I look into his eyes it seems that I'm drinking his blood slowly" (*O.C.*, p. 1482). *El maleficio de la mariposa,* García Lorca's first play, ends with the little male cockroach asking: "Who gave me these eyes that I don't want?" (*O.C.*, p. 721.) In *Libro de poemas,* the ant who had been mistreated by her companions in the poem "Los encuentros de un caracol aventurero" (*O.C.*, p. 179) says, referring to the stars:

> I climbed the highest tree
> of the poplar grove
> and I saw thousands of stars
> within my own darkness.

Dramatic tension becomes more pronounced as García Lorca's works mature. In *Poema del cante jondo,* when the narrator speaks of the one who fell in the streets, he announces the impossibility of giving light *(alumbrar)* when death dries the eye(*O.C.*, p. 304):

> No one
> was able to peep in at his eyes
> now open to the harsh air.

The poet repeated this idea almost identically in "Candil", when talking about the oil lamp (=candil). He compares it to a stork that peeps into the eyes of the dead Gypsy:

> Incandescent stork
> pecks from its nest
> at the thick shadows,
> and, trembling, it peeps in
> at the round eyes
> of the dead Gypsy. (*O.C.*, p. 326)

In "Narciso" (from *Canciones),* the boy drops his eyes into the water while admiring himself (*O.C.*, p. 386). The poet sees in the eyes of a girl "two crazy little trees" in "Al oído de una muchacha," (*O.C.*, p. 389), a motive that is intertwined with *Marinero* and with *Sólo el misterio,* in which a branch with leaves and a flower come out of the left eye first and the right eye second. Lastly, in "La monja gitana," out of the eyes of the Gypsy nun "gallop two horse riders" (*O.C.*, p. 433).

This dramatic ocular presence is a motive that stands out in *Poet in New York,* from which I extract this trio of examples: there are in the eyes of the poet "clothed creatures" *(O.C.,* p. 472); the king of Harlem "tore the eyes out of the crocodiles" with a spoon *(O.C.,* p. 478); and the statues "suffer in their eyes the obscurity of coffins" *(O.C.,* p. 504).

4.3 The Fish [33]

The fish as symbol of the sea provides a wealth of metaphor in the poetry of García Lorca. This symbol is made visually concrete in the drawings. Here, the fish is always accompanied by a round form that can be interpreted according to the Christian symbolism in which the fish is the sign of the Eucharist, according to the popularization of Jesus as IXTHUS among the early Christians.[34] In the second *Viñeta* (Ap., 17) and in *Naturaleza muerta* (Ap., 18) the fish supplies to both drawings a nuance of movement (do not forget the slippery character of the fish) and, as before, the eyes illuminate the entire scope of the picture. In the first *Viñeta* (Ap., 19), the fish fall from some twisted filaments. These filaments spring from the belly of the vase which is precisely where the water — the fish habitat — accumulates.

The connection between fish and water is encountered again in the imagination of the beaten Gypsy of *Poema del cante jondo.* The unfortunate Gypsy asks the Guardia Civil Caminera:

> Give me a few sips of water.
> Water with fish and ships.
> But water, water, water. *(O.C.,* p. 332).

These poetic lines are mirrored in *Florero* (Ap., 20), in which the vase contains water with a fish and a ship. A very similar metaphor is repeated in the song "Caracola" from the book *Canciones;*

> My heart
> is filled with water
> with little fish
> made of silver and shadows. *(O.C.,* p. 372)

Here the symbol exudes an air of eroticism. In art and culture the fish is a powerful phallic symbol because of its restless existence, its life in water, its lubricity and its capability to perpetuate life.[35] In another song, "Nocturnos de la ventana," in which they find "a child of the water" dead at the pool *(estanque),* the erotic is connected with the water and the fish in these terms:

> From her head to her thighs
> crosses a fish, calling her. *(O.C.,* p. 369.)

A similar image is used in "La casada infiel" of *Romancero Gitano:*

> Like startled fish
> her thighs slipped away from me. *(O.C.,* p. 435)

Without losing its erotic character, the fish acquires a dramatic level in the poem "Abandoned Church" from *Poet in New York.* This poem maintains a close relationship with the above examples:

> I found out that my daughter was a fish,
> a fish used by the wagons to recede.
> I had a daughter.
> I had a dead fish in the ashes of the censers. *(O.C.,* p. 483)

The dramatic sentiment is connected with ritual in the drawings, since almost every time the fish appears, it is visualized with a host-like image, round like a full moon, as if it were a knife cutting the bread, the bread of the Eucharist. This combination of ritual, moon, knife, and fish appears several times in the poems. A powerful example comes from the dialogue opening the drama *El público (O.C.,* p. 1146):

> FIGURA DE CASCABEL: What if I became a moon fish?
> FIGURA DE PAMPANO: I would become a knife.

Also, near the end of *Bodas de sangre,* the bride caresses the knife with which the groom has been killed:

> And this is a knife,
> a tiny knife
> that barely fits the hand;
> fish without scales or river. *(O.C.,* p. 1272)

5. Trees

Two drawings, very similar, bear the title of *Parque* (Ap., 21, 22). Sterility characterizes the foliage of these parks. In one of them there are various lips between the figures that symbolize trees, because the park is a meeting place for lovers who have come to it to consummate the rite of kissing. Also in *Perspectiva* (Ap., 4) there is a little garden, this time with a plant and leaves, which is somehow inconsistent with the city. As García Lorca's poetry is in many cases reduced to a *quintessential emotion,* here also the landscape has been reduced by leaving the image of the park almost bald, as the poet imagines it.

It would be tedious to detail how important landscape appears with its rows of olive trees amidst the uninhabited fields, throughout the writings of García Lorca. A few examples will suffice here.

From his first book *(Libro de poemas)* to his last play *(La casa de Bernarda Alba)*, García Lorca's writings reflect an affinity for open and desertic landscapes, many times filled with olive trees. The poem "Paisaje" from *Poema del cante jondo* describes what the eye sees from a moving train:

> The field
> of olive trees
> opens and closes
> like a fan.
> . . . .
> the olive trees
> are pregnant
> with cries. *(O.C.,* pp. 296–297)

In this landscape there might be water, there could be trees, but it is certainly inhabited by death and sterility. When the rider tells Amargo in *Poema del cante jondo* that the world is huge, the Gypsy replies: "That's why it is uninhabited." *(O.C.,* p. 340). In *Canciones,* the poem "Nocturno esquemático" does away with all trappings, and gives the reader not only a bare landscape, but a poem reduced to its absolute soul:

> Fennel, serpent and reed.
> Aroma, scent and shadows.
> Air, earth and solitude. *(O.C.,* p. 360)

Also in *Canciones,* the aged trees have a "dried verdancy" *(O.C.,* p. 381). One of the poet's most famous poems, "Romance sonámbulo" creates a mysterious atmosphere around the repetition of a symbolic "green" ("green wind, green branches /... /green flesh and hair of green") that is resolved with the death of the Gypsy girl. She dies "green," but it is a sterile greenness, since she died awaiting a love that never arrived. *(O.C.,* pp. 430–432) Yerma's name suggests absence of a symbolic verdancy, and no world could be as bare as the one represented in Bernarda's house. García Lorca's stage directions are specific:

> The walls in this room of Bernarda's house are thick and very
> white. There are arched doorways with jute curtains tied back with
> tassels and ruffles. There is a wicker chair. On the walls, pictures
> of unlikely landscapes full of nymphs or legendary kings. It is
> summer. A great brooding silence fills the stage. When the cur-
> tain rises, it is empty. *(O.C.,* p. 1439)

We know that the paintings of Poussin are the graphic representation of the literary generation of Racine; all of us know the pictorial-poetic work of Blake; the opinion is well-founded that the friendship of Baudelaire and Delacroix was maintained in the interrelation of the two artistic expressions; Doré is known above all for his illustrations of Dante, Rabelais, Cervantes, Balzac, and others; both the Pre-Raphaelites in England and the Surrealists in France stamped their seal in art as painters and poets, following the paths of their respective leaders Dante Gabriel Rossetti and André Breton; Juan Ramón Jiménez passes from Moguer to Seville to study painting; and Rafael Alberti cultivates parallelly his double vocation of poet and painter.

With the preceding paragraph I wanted to illustrate that the case of García Lorca is not unique in the history of the relation between poetry and painting. Our probing of this relationship has only scratched its surface; I only mentioned some few motives that appeared to me fundamental to the painting of the poet, and in searching for meaning, in no moment did I seek to weaken the sense of the drawings. They will remain inexhaustable, like the metaphors and symbols they are. I call them metaphors and symbols following Lorca's description of his own drawings:[36]

> Some drawings come out like that, like the most beautiful metaphors, and others by searching for them in the place *where one knows for sure* they're likely to be found. It's like fishing. Sometimes the fish goes into the basket by itself and other times one chooses the likeliest waters and throws in the best hook to catch it. The hook is called *reality*. I've thought about and produced these little drawings with a poetic-plastic or plastic-poetic criterion, in fitting union. ... I've tried to choose the essential features of form and emotion, or of super-reality or super-form, to turn them into a *symbol* that, like a magic key, might help us *better understand* the reality that they possess in the world.

Abhorring the fragmentation of language, García Lorca felt a need to paint, to sketch emotion itself. The works of Mallarmé show a similar yearning. Both artists sought to condense all possible discourse within the fragile density of the word, confining what we call reality, language, within the slim black, red or blue line traced by the hand in ink upon the paper.[37] Applying Mallarmé's conversation with Jules Huret to this discussion, we could conclude that all earthly existence must ultimately be contained in a sketch.[38]

Unlike the homosemanticism of the primitive man who painted the caves he inhabited in order to "see" the bison and "have" it with him, thereby confusing the thing with what it represents, García Lorca, in his drawings, avails himself of the symbolic and the metaphoric without confusing them with the real. The poet is aware that the uniform doesn't make the sailor. He hears the song of the sirens while the man of the street, as Foucault points out, only experiences resemblances.[39] García Lorca's sketches speak of a poetic experience in which, knowing how different from *the other* is each sign, the poet catches the *otherness* in each one of them. These drawings, at the same time, are pregnant with the same symbols and metaphors that made his poetic discourse so faithful to the reality he had dreamed. "I have and I feel I have my feet firmly on the ground in art," he would later write to Gasch, who seems to have told Lorca that his sketches were coming from a state of "perpetual dream."[40]

Delacroix took pleasure in repeating: "L'exactitude n'est pas la vérité," a phrase with which the romantic painter, opposing the neo-Classic precept of moderation and sensibility, stressed the absolute need of art to be spontaneous. A painting should be, he insisted, "a feast for the eye." Likewise, the same should be true for poetry, especially since poems are now more and more read than "heard." Delacroix's conception of painting was not far removed from the most fortunate statement of our correlation, Horace's *ut pictura poesis,* which has become one of the *loci classici* of mimetic representation.

In the case of García Lorca, this mimetic representation works in a two-directional way. His drawings are full of metaphors; they are signs, as Derrida would put it, that have a presence, a voice.[41] His poetry, on the other hand, is full of symbols, and avails itself of what Pierce called icons[42] or signs in which similarity prevails. Through his dual manifestation of symbol and metaphor, García Lorca, then, completes the circle of the sister arts. He is a poet with a pictoric diction; a painter with a poetic stance:

Ut pictor poeta; ut poeta pictor.

NOTES

1. Paul Klee, *The Diaries of Paul Klee: 1898–1918*. Ed. and Intr. by Felix Klee (Berkeley and Los Angeles: University of California Press, 1968), p. 60.

2. Since Aristotle's *Poetics*, the correlation of the sister arts has led many critics and philosophers on productive inquests into the functions of words, lines and colors. Since it is impossible to offer a complete list of works on this subject, I include here a few recent studies in which the reader will find extensive bibliography. Etienne Souriau, *La Correspondance des arts: éléments d'esthetique comparée* (Paris: Flammarion, 1969); Northrop Frye, *Fearful Symmetry: A Study of William Blake* (Princeton, N.J.: Princeton University Press, 1969), Ulrich Finke, ed., *French 19th Century Painting and Literature* (New York: Harper & Row, 1972), Wendy Steiner, *The Colors of Rhetoric* (Chicago, Ill.: The University of Chicago Press, 1982); Marianna Torgovnick, *The Visual Arts, Pictorialism, and the Novel (James, Lawrence, and Woolf)*, (Princeton, N.J.: Princeton University Press, 1985).

3. Although Plutarch mentions this "saying" several times in his *Moralia*, it is not until section 346F that he mentions Simonides as its author. (Vol. 4 of *Plutarch's Moralia*, from The Loeb Classical Library, Heinemann & Harvard, 1972, p. 501). The reason for giving this source here is purely scholarly: many times in the past, critics who have mentioned this statement have either ignored its source or attempted to quote it as common knowledge.

4. As much interested in visual characterization as García Lorca, Victor Hugo exercised the diversity of his genius with powerfully grotesque drawings. Through them, he searched for the metaphor that could best express "la bête humaine." (Cf. Jean-Bertrand Barrère, "Victor Hugo's Interest in the Grotesque in His Poetry and Drawings." Finke, pp. 258–279.)

5. Souriau, pp.7–8.

6. Roman Jakobson, "On the Verbal Art of William Blake and Other Poet-Painters," *Linguistic Inquiry*, 1 (January, 1970), 3–23.

7. Jorge Guillén begins his "Prólogo" to García Lorca's works by underlining not the adjective "extraordinaria," but rather the noun "criatura." (Cf. Federico García Lorca, *Obras Completas*, 7th ed. [Madrid: Aguilar, 1964], p. xvii.) Unless otherwise indicated, the translations from this work will be my own and will refer to this edition. *Obras Completas* will be abbreviated as *O.C.*

8. Federico García Lorca, *Selected Letters*, ed. and trans. David Gershator (New York: New Directions Books, 1983), p. 119. When quoted from, this book will be referred to as *Letters*.

9. The same could be said of Blake, the other extraordinary poet-painter I mentioned before. In fact, a comparative study between the English dramatic poet and the dramatic perspective of García Lorca's entire pictorial work would be of great interest.

10. *Letters*, pp. 115, 136, respectively.

11. Was García Lorca disappointed because *L'Amic* did not publish any of his drawings around this time (it had already done so in previous issues), or was it simply because shortly after this date the Catalonian magazine stopped publication?

In a letter prior to this one, dated in 1927, García Lorca communicated to Gasch his enthusiasm for an article that Gasch had written on him as a painter: "I like your article and thank you profusely for it. You already know what extraordinary pleasure I feel at being treated like a painter" *(Letters*, p. 115).

12. *Letters*, p. 101.

13. This interest is reflected in García Lorca's insistence. Besides the allusions already highlighted throughout this work, there is a sequence of other references that I have gathered from his letters to Gasch. "I'll take with me a collection of my drawings for you to see [them]" *(O.C.*, p. 1643); "I suppose you have already received my drawings" *(O.C.*, p. 1646); "I want to publish my drawings. What do you think? With a prologue of yours" *(O.C.*, p. 1650); "As for publishing my drawings, I'm quite decided. ... I'll intersperse some poems. ... You would compose a prologue or study, and we would try to see to it that the book circulates" *(Letters*, p. 125); "I'm definitely publishing my drawings. Do the prologue for them" *(Letters*, p. 127); "[You can keep] the drawings you publish; I give them to you, and so you can begin a collection of little silly things" *(O.C.*, p. 1655).

14. *Letters*, p. 121. I must call the attention of the reader to the parentheses of the first sentence: "I detest the art of dreams." This abominative remark seems to refer to the Surrealistic automatic writing, which García Lorca always rejected. He felt a need to disengage himself from any label, and whenever possible, he stated clearly that his work was very different from the Surrealists. (Cf. *Letters*, pp. 117, 119, 136, 138.) In Surrealism, dreams have a fundamental role not only as a source for artistic expression, but also as a technique in itself. On September 1928, a year after the date of this letter, commenting on two poems he had sent to Gasch from his new book *Poet in New York*, he states: "I enclose here two poems. I hope you like them. They answer to my *spiritualist* new manner, pure disembodied emotion, detached from all logical control — but careful! careful! — with a tremendous poetical logic. It is not surrealism, not at all! The clearest self-awareness illuminates them" *(O.C.*, p. 1654). For a more complete discussion on this subject see Angel del Río, "Introduction." Federico García Lorca, *Poet in New York*, trans. Ben Belitt (New York: Grove Press, 1955), pp. ix-xxxix.

15. In his lecture on Góngora's poetic image, he makes a detailed comparison between the act of creation and hunting: "The poet who is going to make a poem (I know it from personal experience) has the vague feeling that he is going to a hunting expedition at night in a remote forest. An inexplicable fear murmurs in his heart ... Delicate breezes chill the glass of his eyes. The moon, round like a horn made of a soft metal, sounds in the silence of the highest branches ... The poet must go out" *(O.C.*, p. 74).

16. Cf. J.E. Cirlot, "Introduction." *A Dictionary of Symbols,* 2nd ed., trans. Jack Sage (New York: Philosophical Library, 1983), pp. xli–xliv. T. Todorov and O. Ducrot bring as example of symbolization the word *flame* which "signifies flame, but also symbolizes love." This example could very well serve as an illustration of a metaphor. (Cf. *Encyclopedic Dictionary of the Sciences of Language* [Baltimore: Johns Hopkins University Press, 1979], pp. 101–103.) In his discussion on metaphor, Gérard Genette departs from Dumarsais' distinction between the literal and the figurative, and arrives at the consideration of the "equivalence" between the two terms. An equivalence that *stands for* in the symbolic and *is like* in the metaphoric. (Cf. Gérard Genette, *Figures of Literary Discourse,* trans. Alan Sheridan [New York: Columbia University Press, 1982], pp. 103–121.)

17. Cf. Mikhail M. Bakhtin, *Epopée et roman* (Paris: Recherches Internationales, 1973). A concise study of the "chronotopos" has been made by Roberto Salsano, *Estetica e "cronotopo" romanzesco* (Roma: Luciano Lucarini, 1981).

18. Cited by Christoph Eich, *Federico García Lorca, poeta de la intensidad* (Madrid: Gredos, 1958), p. 26. Notice also that the French dramatist was a contemporary of Claude Lorrain, the founder of the European landscape tradition. This verse by Racine has the same saturnianic nostalgia that the French painter reflects in his works.

19. Cirlot, p. 137.

20. Compare this graphic image of *Manos cortadas* with the speech of the Ama in *Doña Rosita la soltera* when the Ama comments to the Aunt on the departure of Rosita's man to Tucumán [Argentina]: "[We should] take a sword and cut off his head and crush it with two stones and cut off his false swearing hand and the lying writings of affection" *(O.C.,* p. 1414).

21. As can be seen on the bottom right, the drawing is from 1934. I call attention to this date because most of García Lorca's dramatic works, in which death plays a very important role, had already been staged. Perhaps the most notorious is *Blood Wedding,* which closes with the presence of the knife in hands of the Bride *(O.C.,* p. 1271 –1272). The knife as metaphor and symbol of death, so frequent in his poetry and plays, makes no appearance in the drawings.

22. Like a new Medusa who, in place of serpents, produces hands, Death shows a total of twelve hands. Six come out of her head; they are deprived of life and move with the dead figure in the direction of the wind. (Note that Death is in the posture of movement.) The other six hands are dispersed throughout the rest of the body but they all extend from the ribcage. Four are deprived of strength and are so connected to the first group while the other two show that they still possess life. The one on the right holds a truncated branch with two leaves and a flower; the hand on the left sustains another little branch. This branch has the particularity of bearing a leaf and an eye with pupil. (Notice that Death's eye sockets have no pupils, neither does the head of the dead figure, from which only the eyelashes are seen).

23. While in *Poema del cante jondo* "The ellipsis of a cry / goes from mountain / to mountain" *(O.C.*, p. 298), the cry has here a lineal expression, and can be seen in opposition to the final scene of *Así que pasen cinco años,* in which the echo is the only response to the youth's voice. (Cf. *O.C.*, p. 1144).

24. El Greco comes immediately to mind when we see this hand on the breast. According to Schneider, also, a hand on the breast symbolizes a posture of wisdom. (Cf. Cirlot, p. 137).

25. The young poet Miguel Hernández described a similar experience when he arrived in Madrid for the first time in December, 1931, and gave poetic diction to his impression of the city. (Cf. Miguel Hernández, "Silbo de afirmación en la aldea." *Obra poética completa* [Bilbao: Zero, 1978], pp. 199–204.

26. There seems to be a distinction between the black and the white moon. The white moon appears in *Marinero, Payaso llorando,* and *Amor novo* (Ap. 22). The three drawings are in one way or another connected to love and water. The black moon, on the other hand, appears in *Alcoba, La mujer del abanico* and *Perspectiva* (Ap. 9). In these three paintings the moon stands as a symbol of pain and confusion.

27. It is interesting to note that, among the Egyptians, the term with which one designated the hand was closely related to the term for pillar or column. (Cf. Cirlot, p. 137.)

28. In contrast, the figure *Marinero* (Ap., 21) has no hands; but as we examine the drawing, we discover two pillars that sustain the bust. If we relate this to that which is indicated in the preceding note, we can better understand the function of these two pillars that function as feet and hands at the same time. See also *Columna y casa* (Ap., 10), a drawing in which the hand/column relation is even more evident.

29. The moon was also present in *Perspectiva urbana con autorretrato* (Ap., 9), but it was a moon in the face (=dream) of the poet, it was "his moon." The city does not have it, it has lost it, or perhaps it is the moon that does not want the city, which perhaps causes the blackness of this moon and the one in *Amor novo.*

30. C.G. Jung, *Symbols of Transformation,* trans. R.F.C. Hull, 2nd ed. (Princeton, N.J.: Princeton University Press, 1967), p. 268.

31. In some children's songs the hat is associated with the desire of the woman to find a shadow [=husband] *(conseguir sombra)*

32. This union of eyes, hands, mirrors, and filaments can be connected with "Little Boy Stanton" from *Poet in New York.* In this poem García Lorca sees a reflection of society in the empty life of a little boy. (Cf. *O.C.*, p. 502.)

33. There is a distinction in Spanish between *pez* (a fish in the water) and *pescado* (a caught fish). García Lorca does not pay attention to this distinction. He always talks about *pez* or *peces* and supposes that, even if they are out of water, they are alive because they themselves symbolize water or life (including the one in *Naturaleza muerta* [Ap., 27]).

34. Because of its connection to the water, the fish was a symbol of Christian baptism. The fish became one of the most popular symbols for Christ in

early Christianity (in the Roman catacombs many graffiti depict Jesus in that form) because the letters of the Greek word for fish formed the initials of the words "Jesus Christ Saviour the Son of God." Those who believed were called *piscipuli* (little fishes). (Cf. James Hall, *Dictionary of Subjects and Symbols in Art*, rev. ed. (New York: Harper & Row, 1974), p. 122).

35. Cf. Cirlot, pp. 106-107; p. 253.

36. *Letters*, pp. 119-120.

37. See Michel Foucault, *The Order of Things* (New York: Vintage Books, 1973), pp. 303–307.

38. "Au fond ... le monde est fait pour aboutir à un beau livre." Stéphane Mallarmé, *Oeuvres Complètes*, eds. Henri Mondor and G. Jean-Aubry (Paris: Gallimard, 1945), p. 872.

39. Foucault, p. 49.

40. *Letters*, p. 117.

41. See Jacques Derrida, "Difference," *Speech and Phenomena and Other Essays on Husserl's Theory of Signs* (Evanston, Ill: Northwestern University Press, 1973).

42. See Charles S. Pierce, *Collected Papers*. Vol. 2 (Cambridge, Mass.: Harvard University Press, 1932), pp. 157–158.

K. M. SIBBALD
McGill University

Catoblepas and Putrefactos in Antofagasta, or Lorca and a Case of "Serio Ludere"

Much European art and literature produced in the early 1920s may well be described as "systematic comic nonsense."[1] The war to end all wars was finally over and a "sort of weed-world sprang up and flourished" which eclipsed for a time the daily realities of economic and spiritual bankruptcy "so that all that was unreal came into its own and ran riot for a season."[2] Thus, in the decade known variously as "The Roaring Twenties" or "Les années folles", the often desperate pursuit of fun can only be explained if seen as an attempt to compensate for the suffering, dislocation and annihilation caused by the first experience of the terrible potential of modern warfare. Although intellectuals and artists had kept faith with their individual allegiances, Spain had remained officially apart, neutral in the European struggle. Not so in peacetime. In a movement of integration forming part of the pendulum swing that so well describes the process of "europeization", and which in this cycle would bring her tragically full circle back to war, Spain entered wholeheartedly into the post-war cult of frivolity.

By 1925 a group of friends had come together; all were trying to write serious poetry, none were above cutting the most extravagant of poetic capers. Their base was the Residencia de Estudiantes in Madrid where every sort of clownery originated, fomented by a lively quintet composed of Lorca, Dalí, Buñuel, José Bello and Alberti. "Rebeldes" and "deportistas"[3], these young men had time and leisure enough both to plan the most ferocious of practical jokes or spend long hours composing nonsense rhymes or *anaglifos*[4] and contemporary satires or *jinojepas*[5], *and* to write the poetry which would make them famous. If Lorca's infectious gaiety and real charisma made him a natural leader, there was no shortage of willing participants in every adventure:

> Nuestra generación no era solemne. Ni hasta los más comedidos
> como Salinas, Guillén, Cernuda o Aleixandre.[6]

Neither individual nor institution was safe from attack in the group's *tertulias,* letters or reviews. Often the pranks were spontaneous, deriving from the combination of a particular situation and the dynamic of the group response. Inevitably, the tricentenary in 1927 of Góngora's death, the literary event of the decade — and the one which marks the historical moment of this generation's being — provoked a memorable series of high jinks.[7] For example, apart from the more serious acts of homage, these devotees of the Cordoban poet organized a mock trial by Inquisition, followed by an *auto-da-fe* in which some choice examples of work disparaging Góngora's poetry were consigned to the flames; headed up a football team, *Góngora F.C.,* in which each poet held a particular

position; and, in a "festejo muy Felipe IV", some of the more daring spirits decorated the walls of the Real Academia with "una armoniosa guirnalda de efímeros
surtidores amarillos".[8] At other times their games took the form of ingenious
word play, the spinning of a nonsense rhyme or jingle from a quotation or pro-
nouncement that, momentarily, took the group's fancy. Various examples of
these may be found in the little magazines which members of the generation
edited and published throughout Spain. Usually the work of various hands, and
according to Gerardo Diego "pongamos a Alberti, Lorca, Altolaguirre, Villalón y
Pepín Bello entre los que partearon las criaturitas"[9], these verses poked fun at
both established figures as well as the young poets themselves. Consequently,
quite typical on the one hand were the digs at Ortega, García Morente, Vela and
Eugenio d'Ors in the *letrilla,* "El espectorador y la saliva", signed by "Chiclet"[10],
or the "Aleluyas" against Ricardo Baeza for his unenlightened opinions:

> La muerte de la poesía
> profetiza cada día.
> A manos de las piruetas
> de los jóvenes poetas.
> Dice que plagian a Lorca
> Málaga, el Puerto y Menorca.[11]

as on the other hand were the "Declinación de Chabás"[12], the parodying of certain
verses of Fray Luis de León's "Profecía del Tajo" and his ode "A Santiago" to
carry on a lively war of words with Ernesto Giménez Caballero and his *Gaceta
Literaria*[13], the sonnet "a diez manos" in honor of the "joven erudito D. Isaías
Alonso, profesor de castellano en Barcelona"[14], and "la broma un tanto pesada"
played on Lorca in the form of a "Romance apócrifo."[15] Perhaps the best example of all may be found in *Lola* in the "Tontología", dedicated "en homenaje a
los sueñecitos del padre Homero" and composed of "algunos de los muchos res-
balones de los poetas capaces de escribir versos buenos".[16] If Juan Ramón
Jiménez was the particular butt[17], fun was had at the expense of both Machados,
Enrique Díez-Canedo, Ramón Pérez de Ayala, Salinas, Guillén, Altolaguirre,
Lorca, Dámaso Alonso and Alberti.

Thus, if we consider this succession of practical jokes, nonsense jingles and
elitist jargon words in vogue during much of the 1920s, Ernesto Giménez Caballero was quite correct in his assessment that this group of young poets were
"pro-cinema, sport, circus, gaiety and games", and that their *modus operandi*
was:

> Riqueza idiomática, tamizada, matizada, clarificada 1). Concepto y
> metáfora —como palancas levitadoras y esenciales 2). Berbiquíes de
> frases 3). Pinzas para las sonoridades 4). Algodones aseptizados
> 5). Nada de cloroformo 6). Escasísimo alcohol 7).[18]

His theorem did, however, postulate the existence of a "new literature." In retrospect it is true that the "revolutionary spirit" of this group brought about an important shift in sensibility. Our equation has two equal parts in "deportista" and "rebelde": from the habit of parody came the radical norms of a revolution in literary taste. Never was the game of poetry played more in earnest or for such high stakes. And at the center of the game, indeed one of its most expert players, is Lorca.

The aspect of *serio ludere* has, nevertheless, largely escaped attention. The aim here, therefore, is to examine three of the epithets invented by Lorca and his friends and used freely within the group to designate all manner of *kitsch*. From an understanding of their objects of scorn comes a sense of what they might venerate, the way back, as it were, from carnival to ritual:[19]

1. Catoblepa[20]:

The catoblepa or catoblepas is a fictitious animal with a most distinguished pedigree. Pliny (viii, 77) was the first to compare with the basilisk "this Ethiopian wild beast ... of moderate dimensions, except for a head so heavy that it hung down towards the ground — fortunately for the human race, because all who met its gaze expired immediately." Aelian (vii, 5) added that it was like "a bull or animal of the antelope kind (Gnu)", which led to some confusion in the medieval bestiaries with the Eale or Yale.[21] In 1607 Edward Topsell, translating Conrad Gesner's mammoth treatise *Historia Animalium* (Zurich, 1551-87), transformed the animal into the Gorgon or "beast all set over with scales like a Dragon, having no hair except on his head, great teeth like Swine, having wings to flie, hands to handle, in stature betwixt a Bull and a Calfe."[22] Flaubert, in *La Temptation de Saint Antoine,* resuscitated the catoblepas for the modern reader, incorporating in his description many of the confusions and attributes of previous authors:

> LE CATOBLEPAS, buffle noir, avec une tête de porc tombant jusqu'à terre, et rattachée à ses épaules par un cou mince, long et flasque comme un boyau vidé.
>
> Il est vautré tout à plat; et ses pieds disparaissent sous l'énorme crinière à poils durs qui lui couvre le visage.
>
> Gras, mélancolique, farouche, je reste continuellement à sentir sous mon ventre la chaleur de la boue. Mon crâne est tellement lourd qu'il m'est impossible de le porter. Je le roule autour de moi, lentement; et la mâchoire entrouverte, j'arrache avec ma langue les herbes vénéneuses arrosées de mon haleine. Une fois, je me suis dévoré les pattes sans m'en apercevoir.

> Personne, Antoine, n'a jamais vu mes yeux, ou ceux qui les ont
> vus sont morts. Si je relevais mes paupières-mes paupières roses
> et gonflées-tout de suite, tu mourrais.[23]

A consummate stylist, Flaubert was certainly an author known to many of this generation. In addition the centenary of his birth celebrated in 1921 had focused contemporary attention on the novelist.[24] Whilst it is possible, therefore, that Flaubert was the immediate source of their epithet, *catoblepa*, a less direct influence is most likely. Also from France came another and more strictly contemporaneous example of modern interest in the catoblepas which corresponds exactly to the use of this catch-word by the Guillén-Lorca generation. In *Le Potomak 1913-1914*, Jean Cocteau, an author read with pleasure by more of the young writers in Spain,[25] quotes the passage concerning the catoblepas from *La Temptation de Saint Antoine*.[26] The quotation is used by Cocteau to explain the genesis of his own creation, the *Eugène*, with which he satirized the chauvinism and militarism so prevalent in France before the First World War. Through Cocteau's intervention the possibilities of *catoblepa* not only as a mythical monster but also as a derogatory adjective were uncovered.

Curiously his discovery was made use of in both France and Spain by two elitist groups at roughly the same time: the first being composed of Simone de Beauvoir, J-P. Sartre, Pierre Clairaut and André Herbaud in Paris, and the second by Lorca, his friends at the Residencia, Guillén, Diego and Dámaso Alonso in Madrid. For Beauvoir and Sartre the *catoblepas* and the *catoboryx* were metaphysical animals of an inferior category, capable only of eating their own feet and expressing themselves in borborigmic rumbles. To this species they disdainfully consigned "Charles du Bos, Gabriel Marcel et la plupart des collaborateurs de la *N.R.F.*"[27] Lorca and his friends used the term to describe those crusty academicians and professors of poetry — and Justo García Soriano was a notable example — for whom Núñez de Arce and Ramón de Campoamor represented the acme of poetic achievement and who characterized as literary madness anything more adventurous or more modern.[28] In both cases the physical attributes of the animal, its short-sightedness and general heaviness, and the etymology of the word itself, from the Greek "that which looks downwards", lent vigor to the insult.

During the middle 1920s Lorca and company used the term *catoblepa* as a form of generational shorthand to describe the critics who lacked vision and poetic sensitivity. As tastes changed, the epithet lost much of its initial impact and one of the last recorded incidences of its use came in 1928. José Moreno Villa rightly sees the "sello lingüístico de la época por el uso del galimatías o la jerigonza, como 'jinojepa' o 'catoblepa'"[29]:

> En la catoblepa
> se encontró a Picasso

> y díjole: Paso.
> Europa es ya Eurepa.
> Y viva la Pepa.
> Ya no hay más poesía
> que la *Jinojepa*
> *de José María.*[30]

The implication is obvious: by 1928 Picasso, Lorca, Alberti, Aleixandre and others could no longer be dismissed as juvenile extremists. The *catoblepas* were undoubtedly still present in the literary Establishment but they no longer fashioned literary taste in their own image.

2. Antofagasta

Clearly such insensitive critics or *catoblepas* did not belong in the poets' republic envisaged by Lorca and his friends. The place to which they might be deported, however, was found as the result of one of Lorca's practical jokes. One day Lorca telephoned his friend Carlos Morla Lynch, a member of the Chilean diplomatic corps in Madrid, passing himself off as "'un señor don Pepe', de Tortosa, que deseaba obtener una recomendación para el Presidente de Chile con el fin de establecer en Antofagasta, la región más árida del país, en la que escasea el agua, un negocio de piscinas."[31] The joke enjoyed lasting success. Far distant from Spain and with a desert-like climate most propitious for spiritual renewal, Antofagasta was the ideal place to send unimaginative critics and pompous university professors. Used to denote cultural exile or a particular circle of Hell not envisaged by Dante, the term became part of the critical jargon of the whole generation. Like *catoblepa, Antofagasta* enjoyed currency during the 1920s, although as late as 1952 Dámaso Alonso was to remark, somewhat sadly, that those who lack literary taste and discernment "pueden vivir lo mismo en París que en la Puebla de Burón, en Nueva York que en Antofagasta."[32]

3. Putrefacto

Of all the epithets used in this decade *putrefacto* was the most important. It had immediate success and was for general use. As Alberti recalled, Lorca and his friends applied it to everything:

> a la literatura, a la pintura, a la moda, a las casas, a los objetos más variados, a cuanto olía a podrido, a cuanto molestaba e impedía el claro avance de nuestra época.[33]

There is, however, some disagreement over the identity of the inventor of the term. On the one hand, Alberti has insisted that the insult was first used by José

Bello[34] and then taken up by Salvador Dalí, who began to draw examples of the *putrefacto*:

> Dalí cazaba putrefactos al vuelo, dibujándolos de diferentes maneras. Los había con bufandas, llenos de toses, solitarios en los bancos de los paseos. Los había con bastón, elegantes, flor en el ojal, acompañados por la *bestie*. Había el putrefacto académico y el que sin serlo también. Los había de todos los géneros: masculinos, femeninos, neutros y epicenos. Y de todas las edades.[35]

On the other hand, Jorge Guillén has declared most emphatically that it was Lorca who gave new meaning to the word, using it first in Granada and then at the Residencia de Estudiantes in Madrid, thus passing it on to Dalí and Bello and, eventually, the whole generation:

> Vituperio que inventó Federico. Café de la Alameda, Granada. Los putrefactos: dibujos de figuras grotescas: "El cancro abrasador de los desiertos" ... El adjetivo pasa a Salvador Dalí, a Pepín Bello, y todos lo empleamos.[36]

What is certain is that Lorca, Dalí and Bello were intimate friends at the Residencia and that the term is most frequently associated with Lorca and Dalí.[37] Guillén is probably correct in his assumption that the origin of this as a generational insult lay in one of the more notorious of the student escapades of those habitual cronies, Lorca and Dalí, that is, the adventure of "la *Cabaña en el desierto*" which Lorca himself later singled out as memorable:

> Un día nos quedamos sin dinero Dalí y yo. Un día como tantos otros. Hicimos en nuestro cuarto de la "Residencia" un desierto. Con una cabaña y un ángel maravilloso (trípode fotográfico, cabeza angélica y alas de cuellos almidonados). Abrimos la ventana y pedimos socorro a las gentes, perdidos como estábamos en el desierto. Dos días sin afeitarnos, sin salir de la habitación. Medio Madrid desfiló por nuestra cabaña. También hemos encontrado nosostros eso de los "putrefactos", ya generalizado.[38]

Shortly after this incident, *putrefacto* began to appear as a frequent insult in letters written in and after 1926 by Lorca to his friends. In every case the term was used as an expression of exasperation or disgust occasioned by what Lorca viewed as particular examples of obtuseness. Gradually, recognition of the poetic talent of the generation had been won; the struggle against the prejudices and negative attitudes of the old guard and the public in general still continued, however, as Lorca's persistent use of this insult shows. Thus, Lorca praised Guillermo de Torre for his critique of Argentinian poetry published in *La Gaceta Literaria* as "una repulsa entre los 'putrefactos'".[39] A month later, in February

1927, he congratulated one friend, Melchor Fernández Almagro, on his new post on the paper *La Voz,* protesting his sincerity as opposed to the praise of "el putrefacto Lumbreras [quien] ha movido en tu honor su boca de culo"[40] and complained bitterly to another, Jorge Guillén, that he was being ignored in favor of "un putrefacto orteguista", Fernando Vela.[41] In each case the use of the term *putrefacto* underlined Lorca's angry, if unsustained, attacks on particular individuals who represented a whole aesthetic.

As the generation took up the term the list of *putrefactos* grew to include, according to Alberti, Azorín, Ricardo León, Emilio Carrere, Alfonso XIII and the Pope.[42] From the list it is possible to see two stages in the genesis of the epithet ("deportista" and "rebelde" like its users): first, the passage from practical joke to code word of a particular group to denote certain literary and cultural values of the group, and, secondly, the politicization of that code word as it came to express a deliberately radical, even revolutionary, point of view. *Putrefacción* implied the state of mental stagnation and decay of the *putrefactos* who denied progress whether in poetry or in politics. Such hide-bound attitudes threatened the intellectual health and well-being of the country. Thus, it was in all seriousness that, on receiving the *"putrefactísimo"* review of *Mariana Pineda,* a play with social overtones as well as artistic merit, Lorca articulated his fears for the future of the theater in Spain.[43] In 1921 Lorca had advocated an attack on "esta triste época de gentes mediocres y *gurrinicas"*[44] but, without the group dynamic, had achieved little. By the mid 1920s in an ambience "prodigiosa de poesía y putrefacción lírica",[45] the time had come for more drastic measures.

As a solution Lorca proposed to found a "Revista de alegría y juego literario"[46] which would be both *"epatante y alegre,"*[47] namely, the brilliant, if short-lived, *gallo.* In the pages of its first issue we find the best definition of *putrefacción,* given here by Dalí, who, in order that the species be readily recognized, appended a sketch of the *putrefacto.*[48] The important duality of "deportista" and "rebelde" is immediately obvious. In part Dalí's "poem" was one more elaborate joke played with juvenile enthusiasm and pomposity. However, there can be little doubt about the underlying seriousness of the artistic goals set out in the letter to Lorca which accompanied his text for *gallo:*

> se trata de algo muy orgánico y homogéneo. Creo haber logrado algo, aunque sea un poco de realidad, fuera del convencionalismo y estilización de la poesía corriente, es un poema meditadísimo y hecho con doble decímetro (y claro muy inspirado). Deseo que te guste — tenemos que desprendernos de la carroña poética histórica, antirreal, decorativa que hemos heredado, y evadirnos de nuestra confusión inventada, con el máximo aplomo y la máxima ligereza—. Por fin parece posible la poesía.[49]

At this stage, at least, both Lorca and Dalí shared a similar point of view. Thus the "kikirikiiis" of *gallo* were written expressly with K because, for the exquisite ear of Juan Ramón, K Q and X were the ugliest letters of the alphabet and the intention here was both to make mischief[50] and to reject the purist aesthetic of empty lyricism, or as Lorca put it, "la vaina decorativa."[51] For the same reason Dalí used *Putrefacción* only as a subtitle, giving instead poetry pride of place, albeit through another private allusion for those who understood his title, "San Sebastián". Lorca had defined true poetry as "amor, esfuerzo y *renunciamento*" in the image of and under the patronage of St. Sebastian.[52] Dalí's title and dedication to his friend well reflect the two levels of personal interest[53] and group aesthetic of all these poetic games.

Other members of the generation had little difficulty in deciphering Dalí's meaning, finding therein "toda una teoría estética".[54] To counteract the effects of *putrefacción* Dalí proposed *asepsia:*

> Pulcritud y euritmia del útil standartizado, espectáculos asépticos anti-artísticos, claridades concretas, humildes, vivas, alegres, reconfortantes, para oponer al arte sublime, delicuescente, amargo, putrefacto.

Dalí was continuing the play on words that, in its shorthand form "NO HAY CLARIDAD",[55] he and Lorca had imposed on their friends: he set medical precision against the inexactitude of lyrical sentimentality. The use of "asepsia", the disinfecting process, is complemented by the use of words like "eurythmy" signifying the harmonious combination of line and proportion in a work of art, "standards of utility" implying order, discipline and coherent form, and, finally, "deliquescent" meaning the property of liquefying, as by extension in tearful, sentimental verse. In a complex word play Dalí was outlining certain criteria; a definite preference for clarity and a certain mechanical precision rather than grandiloquence or refined sensibility. Ubiquitous sentimentality led to "angustia, obscuridad y ternura ... ternura, aún, por la exquisita ausencia de espíritu y naturalidad", in short, *putrefacción*. No saving grace was to be found in social class or higher education; to the *putrefactos* belonged "las familias que compran objetos artísticos para el piano, el empleado de obras públicas, el vocal asociado, el catedrático de psicología" and a great many more. In literature their ranks were swelled by "los artistas transcen dentales y llorosos lejos de toda claridad, cultivadores de todos los gérmenes, e ignorantes de la exactitud del doble-decímetro graduado."

Dalí ended his piece with a sketch of one type of *putrefacto*. As in the case of the *catoblepa,* it is perhaps possible to discern the distant influence of Cocteau. In *Le Potomak* Cocteau had made some sketches of the bourgeois *Mortimers*. Certainly a similar naming process lies behind both inventions. Cocteau's description:

mi-riant, mi-inquiet, j'inventai (je crus inventer) tout des Mor-
timer, et aussi leur nom qui ne cache rien, sinon que le mot "mort"
s'y incruste ...[56]

fits very well Alberti's summation:

> El *putrefacto,* como no es difícil deducir de su nombre, resumía
> todo lo caduco, todo lo muerto y anacrónico que representan mu-
> chos seres y cosas.[57]

With his white-collar worker's moustache and comfortable bourgeois hat, the
putrefacto was a first cousin of the *Mortimers* who slop about in a clear blue
sky, oblivious to their surroundings. Both creations were the vehicles of an ingenious attack mounted against the authority, self-importance, foolishness and
vulgarity of what was perceived as the unchanging, unsympathetic ranks of the
Establishment.

Following Dalí's definitions Lorca made the important editorial decision to
print in the second issue of *gallo* the "Manifiesto antiartístico catalán", signed by
Lluis Montanyá, Sebastiá Gasch and Dalí. Once again *putrefacto,* and its opposite *asepsia,* may be found, used liberally both in the document itself and in the
introductory statement written by Joaquín Amigo. The Manifiesto sounded a
radical profession of faith:

> proclama las que deben ser fuentes de inspiración y de auténtico
> placer artístico, denunciando la yerta caducidad de un orden que no
> satisface la urgente necesidad de alegre y objetiva belleza que siente
> la aséptica emotividad de nuestro tiempo.

The harshest words were reserved for "nuestros nuevos artistas reaccionarios"
whose elitist, alembicated literature constituted "el estado perfectamente pa-
tológico de la putrefacción." Thus, the self-erected triumvirate of Catalan art
eliminated all argument, literature, lyricism, and philosophy generated in "un
ambiente reducido y putrefacto", in order to herald "una época nueva, de una intensidad poetica imprevista" in which the machine would open up a whole new
vista of "jovial and joyful" possibilities that included the cinema, sport, the mo-
tor car and aeroplane, the jazz-band, camera and gramophone, newspapers and
modern architecture.

Much of the Manifiesto sounds like the irreverent dismissal of what has gone
before and the extravagant and sweeping enthusiasm for the new that characterized all the games of this generation. What is new is the ferocity of the
denunciation of part of the generation itself:

DENUNCIAMOS	la falta absoluta de juventud de nues-tros jóvenes
DENUNCIAMOS	la falta absoluta de decisión y audacia
DENUNCIAMOS	el miedo a los nuevos hechos, a las palabras, al riesgo del ridículo

The politicization of the code word meant, inevitably, literary fratricide.[58] As divisions deepened, *putrefacto* and *putrefacción* were finally to become synonymous with the *merde* and *pourriture* so persistently described by the French surrealists, with whom Dalí, Bello and Buñuel, particularly, wished to identify.

There is, however, a postscript to the games involving the *putrefactos*. The circulation of *gallo* certainly produced the scandal that Lorca had intended:

El *Gallo* en Granada ha sido un verdadero escandalazo. Granada es una ciudad literaria y nunca había pasado nada *nuevo* en ella. Así es que *Gallo* ha producido un ruido que no tienes idea. Se agotó la edición a los dos días y hoy se pagan los números a doble precio. En la Universidad hubo ayer una gran pelea entre gallistas y no gallistas, y en cafés, peñas y casas no se habla de otra cosa.[59]

Lorca had challenged the comfortable assumptions most dear to the hearts of the intellectual minority of the provincial capital but, as Antonina Rodrigo rightly points out:

Su grado de familiaridad con los temas tratados no era, en el fondo, el obstáculo principal. Lo grave era que la mayoría de ellos se negaba a hacer el menor esfuerzo no ya para intentar asimilar las sugestiones del juvenil movimiento estético granadino sino para tratar de comprenderlas.[60]

That Lorca knew how firmly entrenched was the opposition is clear from *PAVO* and the editorial of the second issue of *gallo*. A magazine of "cuatro páginas grisáceas de tosco papel de estraza"[61] appeared in March 1928, averring that:

Este perdiódico nace, el lector ha podido colegirlo por su título, como una réplica a cierta revista que se dice ella misma de Granada, pero no crean ciertos jóvenes que su sola importancia determina la aparición de este pavo. No sale *Pavo* a replicar únicamente a la aturdida revista, sino que ella es pié o por mejor decir, pretexto, a que gentes como nosotros, sensatas y razonables, se mofen de las modernas tendencias artísticas que un ave de corral defiende.[62]

The editors of *Pavo* offered to safeguard the national patrimony; to counteract *gallo*'s *kikirikíes:* "nos metemos el dedo en la boca y hacemos *glo-glo-glo*." With suitable pomp and circumstance they further offered a poetic canon:

Para hacer buena poesía
aunque sea putrefacta,
versos que rimen con garbo
o prosas sin camelancia,
es necesario señores
ser muy de la retaguardia,
tener ingenio de ley,
aprender bien la gramática,
hacer uso del cerebro,
expresar como Dios manda.

The "Romance no gallista" was, however, an acrostic in which the reader discovers that *PAVO* and *gallo,* rather like *Lola* and *Carmen,*[63] shared the same editorial board.[64] In the small drawings of a well-padded "butaca directora" [65] and of the top- and bowler- hats peeping over the pages; in the replication of just the right tone of patronage and pomposity for the front page editorial; and in the unmistakable provincialism of the stolid defense of "la vieja y honrada tradición española" in poetry, as exemplified by the fragment "El cruzado", Lorca parodied brilliantly the *putrefactos.*

The caricature was continued in the editorial on the "Recepción de *GALLO"* in that magazine's second issue published in April 1928. Here Lorca and his friends brought to life some conservative archetypes by "quoting" from *gallo's* supposed detractors.[66] Political, religious, intellectual and moral prejudices were ridiculed in the form of "un maestro nacional" who thought the publication to be of subversive nature "a lo mejor comunista, pues a mí no hay quien me quite de la cabeza que eso del punto rojo significa algo"; of the obtuse cleric who questioned the review's historical criteria "¿cómo han de escribir bien, muchachos que yo he visto con calcetines?"; and of the hard-line "woman's point of view" that "debían llevarlos a la cárcel, y que las autoridades no debían tolerar estos abusos." Collectively these were the *putrefactos* and much fun might be had at the expense of those

cuyas lecturas se reducen a las noticias del periódico y alguna novela de munición; su teatro, a las revistas, su música a la banda municipal, su escultura, a las estatuas de la plaza pública y su arquitectura, a la experiencia de un maestro de obras.

The life-span of epithets like *putrefacto, catoblepa* and *Antofagasta* was, however, drawing to a close. Their vogue had begun with the preparations for the Góngora tricentenary and their apogee would come with the surrealist mode in Spanish literature. In their attempt to reintegrate Góngora into the national tradition of good writing, Lorca and his friends had declared their own independence from and lack of respect for the established norms for poetry and criticism.

Their liberal use of these epithets formed part of this declaration. Thus, the critic who failed to perceive the luminous clarity of an *octava* by Góngora or a sonnet by Quevedo and/or he who denied the artistic value in Stravinsky's music, Picasso's art or Lorca's poetry, were *catoblepas* and/or *putrefactos* to be consigned collectively to *Antofagasta*. By the close of the decade, however, there was general recognition that "no todo ha de ser regocijo y tirarle de la barba al académico"[67] Books of poetry like *Romancero gitano, Sobre los ángeles, Cántico* and *Ambito* were receiving the critical acclaim they deserved and serious attention was being paid to the aspirations of the generation as a whole. In the 1930s there would be very little time for clownery as Lorca prepared *Poeta en Nueva York* and undertook his renewal of the Spanish theater. Notwithstanding, his practice of *serio ludere* was a game of enormous consequence: what started out as a practical joke or an ingame of elitist jargon led, in its most extreme form, to a disassociation with contemporary reality.[68]

NOTES

1. Edmund Wilson, *Axel's Castle* (New York: Charles Scribner's Sons, 1934), p. 253.

2. Wyndham Lewis, *Blasting and Bombadiering* (London: Eyre and Spottiswoode, 1937), p. 18.

3. "Vestía, creo recordar, traje oscuro, pero con toda claridad veo todavía el cuello bajo, ancho y blanco de la camisa y un gran nudo de corbata, detalles que yo creía eran entonces exclusiva propiedad de los señoritos que nos creíamos o éramos rebeldes y deportistas." Thus did Rafael Martínez Nadal record his first impression of Lorca in 1923, in *Cuatro lecciones sobre Federico García Lorca* (Madrid: Fundación Juan March-Cátedra, 1980), p. 16.

4. These were short nonsense verses consisting of three nouns, the second of which had to be "la gallina" and the third of which had to have no connection with the first as in "El té /el té, /la gallina /y el Teotocópuli." Cf. José Moreno Villa, *Vida en claro. Autobiografía* (Mexico: El Colegio de México, 1944), p. 114. As usual Lorca took a leading role in propagating the epidemic of *anaglifos* that swept through the Residencia, even to the point of inventing a variant longer last line: "Guillermo de Torre /Guillermo de Torre /la gallina / y por allí debe andar algún enjambre", quoted by Rafael Alberti in *La arboleda perdida. Libro I y II de memorias* (Buenos Aires: Fabril, 1959), p. 219.

5. "Las jinojepas son inexplicables. Las jinojepas son como las jitanjáforas, todo lo dicen con la palabra misma ... Una jinojepa no es exactamente una sátira, es más bien una broma, una burla de buen humor y sin veneno dentro. Si alguno cree lo contrario, piense en su condición y púrguese a sí mismo antes de aojar u ojerizar al prójimo. El buen jinojépico se jinojepa a sí mismo, como la caridad bien entendida." Gerardo Diego, "Prólogo," to *Carmen Revista chica de poesía española y Lola amiga y suplemento de Carmen,* rpt. (Madrid: Ediciones Turner, 1977), pp. 26–27.

6. Rafael Alberti, *La arboleda perdida,* p. 256.

7. For more details see C.B. Morris, "The Game of Poetry," in *A Generation of Spanish Poets 1920–1936* (Cambridge: Cambridge University Press, 1969), pp. 82-118.

8. "Crónica del Centenario de Góngora: Juegos de agua," *Lola* (Siguenza), 1 (December 1927), p. 8.

9. Diego, "Prólogo," p. 26.

10. *Lola,* 1 (December 1927), p. 3–6.

11. "Aleluyas y listeza del gran Ricardo Baeza'" *Lola,* 5 (April 1928), pp. 7–8. Signed "Jaime de Atarazanas", they were written by Gerardo Diego to vindicate the young poets, and especially Lorca, from Baeza's sharp attacks published in *El Sol.*

12. *Lola,* 2 (January 1928), p. 7.

13. Diego gives full details in his "Prólogo," pp. 27–29.

14. On the occasion of the nascent generation's visit to the Ateneo of Seville in December 1927, Dámaso Alonso was so described in the local press, much to the amusement of his companions who organized a triumphal dinner in his honor during which they made up the sonnet, beginning: "Nunca junto se vio tanto pandero /menendezpidalino y acueducto", see "Coronación de Dámaso Alonso," *Lola*, 5 (April 1928), pp. 1–3.

15. "Romance apócrifo de don Luis a caballo," *La Gaceta Literaria* (Madrid) 11 (June 1927), p. 1. Although the poem appears with Lorca's signature it was the work of several hands [probably Diego, Alberti and Dámaso Alonso] and was composed as part of the more frivolous celebrations of the Góngora tricentenary "en castigo de no presentarse a los actos de Madrid, ni enviar siquiera adhesión." It was for private reading only and Diego felt that its publication was a breach of friendship by Ernesto Giménez-Caballero, see "Crónica del Centenario de Góngora (1627–1927) II: Tarjeta, carta, esquela y otras cosas," *Lola*, 2 (January 1928), p. 2.

16. "Prólogo a la Tontología," *Lola*, 6–7 (June 1928), p.1.

17. Relations between Jiménez and the young poets, particularly Diego, had been strained since the first preparations for the celebrations in honor of Góngora, see "Esquela contra," *Lola*, 2 (January 1928), pp. 3–4. In revenge Diego not only chose excerpts from Jiménez's work for thee "Tontotología" but also quoted *his* version of the "*habanera*" "según la depuración de 1928" — a joke he later described as analogous to that played on Lorca (see note 15), see Diego, "Prólogo," p. 31.

18. Ernesto Giménez-Caballero, "Cartel de la nueva literatura," *La Gaceta Literaria*, 32 (April 1928), pp. 6–7. He further suggested that the generation were "PRO-pureza" 6) – matemática 7) – religiosidad 8) (en muchos casos católica.)"

19. Cf. "carnivalization made possible the creation of the *open* structure of the great dialog and allowed people's social interaction to be carried over into the sphere of the spirit and the intellect, which had always been primarily the sphere of a single, unified monological consciousness or of a unified and indivisible spirit, whose development took place within its own limits (as in Romanticism)." Mikhail Bakhtin, *Problems of Dostoevsky's Poetics*, trans. by R.W. Rotsel (US: Ardis, 1973), pp. 148–149.

20. Of all the authors noted in the text only the Spaniards favored the form *catoblepa*.

21. Quoted by T.H. White in *The Bestiary*. *A Book of Beasts* (New York: Capricorn, 1960), p. 55. See also Jorge Luis Borges, *El libro de los seres imaginarios* (Buenos Aires: Kier, 1967), pp. 51–52.

22. White, *The Bestiary*, pp. 265-266.

23. Gustave Flaubert, *La Temptation de Saint Antoine* (Lausanne: Editions Rencontre, 1965), pp. 165–166.

24. See, for example, the articles dedicated to Flaubert by Jorge Guillén "La risa en su centenario," *La Libertad,* (Madrid) 496 (6 July 1921), p. 4; "Flaubert y el académico," *La Libertad* 500 (10 July 1921), p.4; and "El gorro, la pipa y la pluma de Flaubert," *Indice,* (Madrid), 4 (1922), pp. 15–17, reprinted with some slight modifications in *El Norte de Castilla* (Valladolid), 33058 (11 January 1924), p. 4 and in *La Libertad,* 1460 (28 November 1924), pp. 1–2.

25. See, for example, Guillermo de Torre, "Del tema moderno: como 'número de fuerza'," *Mediodía* (Seville), 8 (1927), unp.; the references to Cocteau's popularity with Lorca and his generation in Carlos Morla Lynch, *En España con Federico García Lorca: páginas de un diario íntimo, 1928–1936* (Madrid: Aguilar, 1958), pp. 311-313; and some account of Cocteau's work as published in contemporary Spanish periodicals in Antonio Blanch, *La poesía pura española: conexiones con la cultura francesa* (Madrid: Gredos, 1976), pp. 138–185.

26. Jean Cocteau, *Le Potomak 1913-1914,* in *Oeuvres complétes* (Geneva: Editions Marguerat, 1947), p. 45.

27. Simone de Beauvoir, *Mémoires d'une jeune fille rangée* (Paris: Gallimard, 1958), p. 321. Beauvoir also records how all were enchanted by Cocteau's *Eugène,* for whom Herbaud had invented a new series of adventures in which "il utilisait ingénieusement son autorité contre la philosophie de la Sorbonne, contre l'ordre, la raison, l'importance, la bêtise et toutes les vulgarités."

28. Cf. "Nuñez de Arce el insípido, … Campoamor, poeta de estética periodística, bodas, bautizos, entierros, viajes en expreso, etcétera …" Federico García Lorca, "La imagen poética de Góngora," in *Obras completas,* I (Madrid: Aguilar, 1973), p. 1001. Justo García Soriano, Academician, was a noted "antigongorino" whose work on Góngora and Luis Carrillo Dámaso Alonso took pains to refute, see also, "Crónica del centenario de Góngora (1627–1927) II: Presto final," *Lola,* 2 (January 1928), pp. 6–7.

29. Moreno Villa, *La vida en claro*, p. 152.

30. *Lola,* 2 (January 1928), p. 5.

31. Morla Lynch, *En España con Federico García Lorca,* pp. 384–385.

32. Dámaso Alonso, *Poetas españoles contemporáneos* (Madrid: Gredos, 1952), p. 215.

33. Alberti, *La arboleda perdida*, p. 176.

34. Without being so specific, Martínez Nadal has also underlined the role of "Pepín Bello, el travieso genio de todo el grupo, alegre, eléctrico, hacedor-inventor de mil disparates y situaciones, luego atribuídas con frecuencia a Lorca, Dalí o Buñuel." See *Cuatro lecciones,* p. 22.

35. Alberti, *La arboleda perdida*, p. 176.

36. Jorge Guillén, "Federico en persona," in García Lorca, *Obras completas,* I, p. xxxiii.

37. Although both Lorca and Dalí were enrolled at the Residencia earlier, it seems most likely that they met some time in February or March 1923. Their

friendship was at its most intense during and just after Lorca's first visit to Cadaqués in 1925. According to Antonina Rodrigo, in that year the friends took over the descriptive word *putrefacto* from the Figueras journalist Carlos Costa y Pujol, who used it as a synonym for *pintoresco*. This may have been the meaning intended by poet and painter in the first instance as they planned an illustrated text entitled *Libro de los putrefactos,* advertised as forthcoming in *La Verdad* in June 1926, but which, in the end, was never published. In early 1926 Dalí had distinguished between the "social" caricatures of Georg Grosz and their own interpretation of "la *lírica de la estupidez humana*" which embodied "un cariño y una ternura tan sincera hacia esa estupidez casi franciscana", see Antonina Rodrigo, *Lorca-Dalí. Una amistad traicionada* (Barcelona: Planeta, 1981), p. 82. However, if *putrefacto* is freely used in the letters exchanged between Dalí and Lorca between 1925–1928, its meaning gradually assumes a harsher significance than that supposed by Dalí's initial references to the charm of his *"pequeños* putrefactitos". What seems to have happened is that Lorca used *putrefacto* in his Granada circle immediately after his return from Cadaqués (thereby associating himself with the epithet); and that both Dalí and Lorca brought *putrefacto* (possibly at first with their private meaning) back to the Residencia, where very soon it became fashionable (almost certainly with a more negative connotation than *pintoresco*). Hence both Alberti and Guillén are in some measure correct. Cf. "Recuerdo que para Federico todos los poetas anteriores a él, o los que mi padre le nombraba, como Espronceda, Campoamor, Gabriel y Galán etc., eran 'putrefactos'", quoted in Eulalia-Dolores de la Higuera Rojas *Mujeres en la vida de García Lorca* (Granada: Editorial Nacional, 1980), p. 38. Certainly such sentiments fit the generational use of the epithet. Gloria Ibáñez is, however, vague about when such conversations took place, although she implies some time before her marriage in 1919. There is insufficient evidence here to note more than corroboration for the fact that, in Granada, the epithet was closely associated with Lorca.

    38. First reported in an interview with Ernesto Giménez Caballero which appeared in "Itinerario jóvenes de España: Federico García Lorca," *La Gaceta Literaria* (15 December 1928); see also García Lorca, *Obras completas,* II, p. 889.

    39. Letter dated January, 1927, García Lorca, *Obras completas,* II, p. 1175.

    40. Federico García Lorca, *Cartas, postales, poemas y dibujos,* ed. Antonio Gallego Morell (Madrid: Editorial Moneda y Crédito, 1968), p. 91.

    41. García Lorca, *Obras completas,* II, p. 1159.

    42. Alberti, *La arboleda perdida,* p. 244.

    43. In a letter to Melchor Fernández Almagro dated 4 March 1927, García Lorca, *Cartas, postales, poemas y dibujos,* p. 94.

    44. Letter to Melchor Fernández Almagro dated Spring 1921, García Lorca, *Cartas, postales, poemas y dibujos,* p. 39. *Gurrinica* was another of these jargon words invented by Lorca for use among the initiated. Like *catoblepa,* it designated mediocrity, but referred to the literary ambiance full of envy, gossip and

calumny; however, like *carnuzo,* engendered and used particularly by José Bello, it was less popular with the generation as a whole.

45. Thus Lorca described Granada to Ana María Dalí in a letter which contains a sketch of "Vatis capiliferus. Putrefacto artístico," García Lorca, *Obras completas,* II, p. 1197.

46. This was the subtitle Lorca proposed in a letter to Jorge Guillén dated 3 March 1926, see *Obras completas,* II, p. 1139. When it finally appeared, *gallo* was, in fact, subtitled *Revista de Granada.*

47. Lorca's own description in a letter to Guillermo de Torre dated January 1927, in *Obras completas,* II, p. 1177.

48. Written originally in Catalan and published in *L'Amic de les Arts* (Sitges) 16 (31 July 1927), pp. 52–54, this "poem" was translated into Spanish in Granada and reappeared in *gallo,* 1 (March 1928), pp. 9–12. The sketch that accompanied the piece probably belonged to the "cuaderno" that Dalí and Lorca had begun to assemble in 1926 in which they catalogued certain types of *putrefactos* like "Siluetas", "Temperas", "Freturosos" and "Caratones", see Rodrigo, *Lorca-Dalí,* pp. 82–83. Lorca was to write the prologue and Dalí had even had some of the sketches printed in Figueras. This "cuaderno" had provoked much merriment in the Residencia and was, presumably, the draft of the *Libro de los putrefactos* announced in *La Verdad* in 1926 (see note 37).

49. Quoted in Rodrigo, *Lorca–Dalí,* pp. 187. Some measure of the effect on Lorca of Dalí's aesthetic of "Santa Objetividad" may be seen in his prose poems "Santa Lucía y San Lázaro" published soon after in *Revista de Occidente,* XVIII (December 1927), pp. 145-155; the parody "Elogio del bisturí o San Cosme y San Damián" signed "Enrique Solí, mataor de marranos, La Rábita" in *PAVO,* 1 (March 1928), unp.; and Lorca's sketches, completed in the summer of 1927, including "Ireso sevillano", "Sirena" and "San Sebastián", of which he wrote to Sebastián Gasch: "Yo he pensado y hecho estos dibujitos con un criterio poéticoplástico o plástico-poético, en justa unión. Y muchas son metáforas lineales o tópicos sublimados, como el 'San Sebastián' … He procurado escoger los rasgos esenciales de emoción y de forma, o de super-realidad y super-forma, para hacer de ellos un *signo,* que, como llave mágica nos lleve a *comprender mejor* la realidad que tienen en el mundo," see García Lorca, *Obras completas,* II, p. 1223.

50. Reported in Alberti, *La arboleda perdida,* p. 254. See also the letter signed K[uan] Q[amón] X[iménez] reprinted in "Crónica del centenario de Góngora (1627–1927) II: Tarjeta, carta, esquela y otras cosas," *Lola,* 2 (January 1928), pp. 3–4 (see also note 17). Certainly relations between Jiménez and his former protégés had become embittered on both the private and the aesthetic levels. Dalí was, perhaps, more outspoken than most in his letters, defining Juan Ramón as "el jefe máximo de la putrefacción poética", quoted in Rodrigo, *Lorca-Dalí,* p. 207.

51. Cf. "¡Ay!", querido Jorge, vamos por dos caminos falsos: uno que va al romanticismo y otro que va a la piel de culebra y a la *cigarra* vacía. ¡Ay! ¡Cuánta trampa! Es triste. Pero tengo que callar. Hablar sería un *escándalo*. Pero yo estoy estos días que leo *poesía vacía* o vaina decorativa, como recién bautizado", quoted in a letter to Guillén dated 27 March 1927, see *Obras completas*, II, p. 1165.

52. Letter to Jorge Guillén dated 9 September 1926, *Obras completas*, II, p. 1145.

53. Although related to the use of *putrefacto*, this obsession with St. Sebastian shared by Dalí and Lorca in the period 1925–1928 is more esoteric. References to the saint first made privately later spilled over into public manifestations such as Dalí's prose poem, Lorca's sketches of the saint and his project to give three lectures on this theme. The many secret allusions in the correspondence range from the frankly scabrous to the genuinely aesthetic. For examples and some discussion, see Gibson, *Federico García Lorca*, pp. 425–426; 467–468; and 489–500; and Rodrigo, *Lorca-Dalí*, pp. 93–100. In this context the homosexual connotations of this particular saint cannot be ignored, see for example J.M. Saslow, "The Tenderest Lover: Saint Sebastian in Renaissance Painting," *Gai Saber*, 1 (Spring 1977), pp. 58–66. Others of this generation were also fascinated by the image of St. Sebastian and some germane comments may be found on Juan Larrea, Diego, and Guillén in E. Cordero de Ciria, "A propósito de un poema inédito de Juan Larrea: la figura de San Sebastián," *Insula*, 462 (1985), p. 4.

54. The opinion of Lluis Muntanyá who reviewed favorably for *L'Amic de les Arts* (31 March 1928) all of *gallo;* whilst privately in a letter to Lorca written about the same time, Sebastiá Gasch confessed that "me parece de lo mejor que ha hecho Dalí." See Rodrigo, *García Lorca en Cataluña* (Barcelona: Planeta, 1975), pp. 245 and 247.

55. Like many other catch-words and phrases this, too, came from Lydia Noguer Sava, was taken up by Dalí and Lorca, and may be found, usually written with capital letters, in letters from different members of their circle. Cf. "La frase: 'No hay claridad', desde que la acuñaron el poeta y el pintor había alcanzado carta de naturaleza, como *putrefacto*, y se aplicaba en serio y en broma." See Rodrigo, *García Lorca en Cataluña*, pp. 170; p. 173 and 238.

56. Cocteau, *Le Potomak*, p. 48.

57. Alberti, *La arboleda perdida*, p. 176.

58. By 1928 Dalí's feelings towards Lorca had cooled noticeably; in questions of art and poetry, too, Dalí identified himself with the surrealists and so broke with what he considered important earlier. As a result his critiques of Lorca's work acquired an increasingly harsher tone. Seeing Lorca's poems in the July and August 1927 issues of *Verso y Prosa*, he bemoaned "el marasmo putrefacto en que se mueve toda esa promoción de Prados, Altolaguirre ... y en el fondo de sus seudointelectualismos, qué roñoso sentimentalismo, me da pena tus

cosas tan UNICAS y verdaderas confundidas entre todo esto"; he described *gallo* as "de una putrefacción intolerable"; and, finally, in September 1928, found it "imposible coincidir en nada en la opinión de los grandes puercos putrefactos" who had reviewed *Romancero gitano* favorably, because "Tu poesía actual cae de lleno dentro *de la tradicional,* en ella advierto la substancia *poética más gorda que ha existido* ... ligada de pies y brazos a la poesía vieja ... se mueve dentro de la *ilustración* de los lugares comunes más estereotipados i más conformistas ... putrefactamente ... antipoesía." See unedited letters from Dalí to Lorca reproduced in Rodrigo, *García Lorca en Cataluña,* pp. 260–264; the last quotation is, however, quoted in the form reproduced in Gibson, *Federico García Lorca,* pp. 566–567, which would seem to be a more correct rendering of the letter in the García Lorca Archives.

59. Letter from Lorca to Sebastiá Gasch dated March 1928, García Lorca, *Obras completas,* II, p. 1215.

60. Rodrigo, *García Lorca en Cataluña,* p. 244.

61. *Ibid,* p. 251.

62. "Nuestro objeto," *PAVO,* 1 (March 1928), unp.

63. Lorca may have been inspired by Diego — or may have inspired Diego. Diego recalls that Lorca was visiting him in Santander when the idea of founding not one but two magazines germinated, see Diego, "Prólogo", p. 10.

64. In the issue of *PAVO* consulted, in Lorca's handwriting the "Ejemplar de lujo dedicado a Melchor [Fernández Almagro]", Lorca also indicated the "acróstico" which reads "Pavo está hecho por la redacción de gallo."

65. The words appear, again in Lorca's handwriting, under a sketch of an armchair, presumably for the use of an equally well-padded editor.

66. Perhaps Lorca was making fun of real people, recognizable to a select audience. As likely is the hypothesis that he was creating archetypes from a recognizable body of opinion. T.S. Eliot played much the same kind of joke when he concocted five outrageous "Letters to the Editor" for *The Egoist.* Purporting to come from the "Rev. Charles James Grimble, The Vicarage, Leays"; "J.A.D. Spence, Thridlingston Grammar School"; "Charles Augustus Conybeare, The Carlton Club, Liverpool"; and "Helen B. Trundlett, Batton, Kent" the letters are remarkbably similar in tone, theme and evident prejudice as those supposedly received by *gallo.* See T.S. Eliot, "Correspondence," *The Egoist,* 4 (December 1917),.p. 165.

67. Dámaso Alonso, "Ascálafo y Góngora," *La Gaceta Literaria,* 11 (June 1927), p. 2.

68. I am grateful to Jorge Guillén, Dámaso Alonso and Gerardo Diego for having explained to me on different occasions how members of their generation used the epithets commented upon here. I also thank the Social Sciences and Humanities Research Council of Canada for granting me a leave fellowship in 1984–85 during which this article was written.

MORAIMA DONAHUE
Howard University

Lorca: the Man, the Poet, the Dramatist, As Seen Through His Lectures, Letters, and Interviews

In order to facilitate a critical study of any work of art, one would do well to learn as much as possible of the person responsible for the work. It is particularly true of writers who, in many cases, readily admit the subjectivity of their writings. This is evident in the case of Federico García Lorca who, as Manuel Durán states: "... was a great human being before he became a poet."[1] Lorca also said of himself:

> ... I entered the kingdom of Poetry, and finished by annointing myself with love for everything. I am a good man, ... who opens his heart to everyone ... I feel nothing except an immense desire for Humanity. Why do battle with the flesh when the problem of the spirit is still there?[2]

In another instance he stated that: "My poetry is a pastime. /My life is a pastime. /But I am not a pastime."[3] It is also true that writing poetry was for him a form of communication and a need for affection: "I do it so people will love me; only for this love have I written my plays and my poems, and I will go on writing them because I need everybody's love."[4]

The critic must be independent, true. He must arrive at critical conclusions primarily based on the text itself; we don't deny this premise. In fact we concur with Darío Villanueva when he writes: "One of the worst errors that ... a critic can make is to become, so to speak a 'valet de chambre,' or if we prefer, an author's butler," but we are not in total agreement with his further observation:

> This domestication of criticism can be arrived at from different directions: from the critic who relies on an author to unlock his work by revealing clues the critic should have figured out on his own to the opposite extreme, namely the critic who in studying the work from a distance transforms his dedication to the work into a cult worship of its author.[5]

We fear that often enough there is too much critical independence, that we have gone to an extreme where the author, when alive, upon reading the criticism of his works, cannot agree with anything the critic has written about him.

Juan Goytisolo, speaking in his dual role as an author and a critic in a lecture he gave in 1976 at York College, is aware of the need for a variety of critical systems — each with its own methodology and objectives. Each critical approach may operate and be accepted *not just on its own terms, but as a complement to the other systems*. He adds, ... "the critic must adopt a certain margin of freedom with respect to his own methodology — this freedom is required not only because of the particular nature of the text, but also in order to liberate his analysis from any dogmatic burden ... the description or analysis of a given work will never be complete unless it refers to the dynamic totality of its internal elements and extra-textual relationships."[6]

Granted, the critic's job of filtering all available information is arduous. In many cases, statements may seem contradictory or changeable. Furthermore, the artist may opt to confuse us by concealing his true feelings about what he writes. The critic should not, however, be put off by this; warned, perhaps. For instance, we know that Lorca was once quoted as saying that the poet does not care for "the applause (nor) the admiration of the people who pass you in the street."[7] We know this is not generally true. Nevertheless, in his case we also know he was a very reserved poet quite unwilling to publish his poetry. In a letter written in January of 1927 he tells Jorge Guillén: "I am not interested in seeing my poems dead ..., that is to say published" (1277, Vol. II). Since these two men were intimate friends and respected each other completely, we can accept what Lorca confided to Guillén as genuine.

A few years later, in an interview conducted in Buenos Aires, probably in 1934 when Lorca was in Argentina — neither the interviewer, nor the exact date are identified —, Lorca states that:

> The last thing I am interested in is literature. Besides I never intended to 'do literature.' Sometimes I have this irresistible attraction to write ... When I am so inclined, I thoroughly enjoy it, but I do not enjoy publishing my work. On the contrary. Everything I have published has been wrenched from me by editors or friends. I like to give a reading of my poems, to read my things. But I am dreadfully afraid of publishing. (1027, Volume II).

Perhaps one of the most revealing of all the assertions Lorca made was his annoyance and concern at having been labeled the "gypsy poet." The success of his *Romancero gitano* and *Poemas del cante jondo* had produced a series of articles and comments which praised his excellent understanding of these people from Andalusia. However, and this is what infuriated Lorca the most, the public seemed to limit recognition of his poetic artistry to this subject only.

Lorca continually insisted that his gypsy theme was one among many in his poetry. He thought the critics, the general public, and the intellectuals, had diminished the artistic value of his work by limiting its scope to one theme only. In fact, because he was Andalusian, he was also irritated at the folkloric accent this public had given to his poetry and to his people. In his famous lecture on the "cante jondo" (1004, Vol. I), a song style of the gypsies, he notes that the clumsy interpretation ordinarily given to all gypsy ballads is due to ignorance and the persistent habit of labeling everything we do not understand, nor are willing to investigate:

> It is inconceivable that some of the songs which carry the most feeling of our mysterious soul we criticized by being labeled as dirty, only belonging in taverns ... It is time for the voices of musicians, poets and Spanish artists to unite and be heard... in order to define and exalt the beautiful clarity and suggestiveness of these songs.

In a letter to Guillén he explains further that:

> The myth of my gypsy-like style bothers me somewhat. They confuse my life and my character. The gypsies are only a theme, nothing more. I could be a poet of sewing needles or hydraulic landscapes. Besides, this gypsy idea suggests a lack of culture, a lack of education, of being an uncivilized poet, which you know full well I am not (1277, Vol. II)

Less known is a statement he made in 1931 to Gil Benumeya commenting on his Gypsy Ballads again:

> The Gypsy Ballads are only gypsy in the beginning and only in some parts ... They are Andalusian songs in which the gypsies serve as a refrain, I have gathered all the local poetic elements and I place on them the most common label possible. They appear to be the ballads of several characters, but the characters are only vehicles for the unique and essential character: Granada (976, Volume II).

In another instance, he adds a new element to this observation by declaring that the main theme of the book is "la Pena," the sorrow that "has nothing to do with melancholy nor nostalgia, nor any other affliction or ailment ...; the Andalusian sorrow which is a conflict of the intelligence of love with the mystery that surrounds it and which it cannot understand" (1114, Vol. I). Anyone who has read this collection of poems cannot ignore this commentary.

We therefore must never lose sight of Lorca's fear of not being taken seriously as an artist. He was keenly aware of how much his personality enchanted all those who knew him, but this otherwise desirable asset became a serious problem inasmuch as his work might only be understood in relation to his outward charm. In another letter written to Jorge Guillén he announces to his friend the publication of his "Canciones" in book form. He is pleased to know that his friends are planning a party to celebrate its publication; however, he is concerned because he thinks that "deep down they are not accepting my poetry ... they are accepting me."[8] This simply would not satisfy him. Without denying his longing for affection, admiration and camaraderie, he nonetheless wrote later:

My feeling is always joyful and this dreaming of mine presents no danger to me, I always have defenses; it is dangerous for those who allow themselves to be fascinated by the large dark mirror of their ravine. I AM AND FEEL ENTIRELY CONFIDENT IN MY ART. I FEAR the abyss and the dream in the reality of my life, in love, in the daily encounter with others.[9]

It is true that there are certain human beings who seem to embody poetry. Lorca was one of them. He saw the artist's work in everything around him, particularly in nature and people. He recalls that when he was a child he used to be very much attuned to nature. Often he would personify objects, listen to the wind as it whistled through the trees. This particular habit resulted in his imagining voices which he thought were pronouncing his name as if inviting a response. In spite of this deep relationship with nature, he was even closer to people. In fact, he was once quoted as saying that he was more interested "in people that live in the landscape than in the landscape itself." To this he added:

I may contemplate a mountain range for fifteen minutes; but after, I run to speak to the shepherd or the woodsman. Later, when I write, I remember these dialogues and the authentic speech patterns come out. I have a large archive of childhood remembrances of listening to people. It is this poetic memory that I hold to... Poetic schools and credos do not worry me. I am not interested in being old fashioned or modern, only in being natural, in being myself (1082, Vol. II).

In another interview given to Felipe Morales in 1936 Lorca insisted that:

Poetry is something that walks the streets ... Everything has its mystery, and poetry is the mystery that all things have. You pass a man on the street, you look at a woman, you glance at the slanting walk of a dog, and in all these objects you find poetry ... Therefore I don't conceive poetry as an abstraction, but as a thing that really exists, that has gone by me. All the people in my poems have existed. The main thing is to discover the key to poetry ..., and the poem will come forth in all its glitter (1117, Vol. II).

He wrote to Carlos Morla Lynch: "... I have a great desire to write, an irrepressible love of poetry, for the pure verse that fills my soul shaken still as a small antelope is by the last brutal arrows."[10]

Lorca's summation of poetry is quite simple: "The poet finds himself confronted with something that jumps out at him ... One must interpret it, decipher its deep secret and out comes poetry! ... Poetry is simply this: 'something that the poets do'" (997, Vol. II).

A few commentaries about Lorca's theater, specifically *Yerma,* are in order: Over the years the most common interpretation of the play's main theme was the frustration and despair occasioned by the sterility of the woman protagonist. The prevalent critical opinion was that, in effect, the heroine was portrayed as not being able to conceive and this in turn constituted the basis for the plot of the tragedy: the suffering of a woman who thinks of herself as but a shadow of womanhood since she is convinced she cannot fulfill her role in society inasmuch as she cannot bear children.

The reason most critics used to arrive at this conclusion was twofold: one, that when reading the play it is easy to see the main theme of frustration and grief mentioned above. The other comes from statements Lorca made when interviewed by José S. Serna in 1933 where he told the interviewer he was working on a "dramatic trilogy," *Blood Wedding* was the first, the second, without a title yet, dealt with "Women's sterility" (999, Vol. II). In 1934, again Lorca referred to this same play, but this time by name, "Yerma" (1059, Vol. II). Once more this same year he made a similar statement to a newspaperman, Juan Chabás: *"Yerma* will be the tragedy of a sterile woman" (1064, Vol. II). Obviously all these statements contributed to this general opinion, which has prevailed over the years. However, without contradicting the poet, we believe that Yerma, — the play was named after the protagonist — cannot conceive children not because she is sterile in the clinical sense, but because she cannot be made pregnant by her husband Juan, who is the sterile one. She must therefore renounce motherhood or violate accepted social morality in which, without exception, a married woman must not have sexual relationships with any partner outside of her husband. Yerma feels she has to renounce motherhood, believing her only choice in life is to remain exclusively with her husband. When speaking of him she says: "I don't love him ... however he is my only salvation because I am honor bound and because I am chaste" (723, Vol. II).

Perhaps the most important of Lorca's observation concerning this play was given to Alfredo Muñiz in 1934: "Yerma, the embodiment of a typical Greek tragedy which I have dressed up in modern clothing is, primarily, the image of fecundity punished by sterility. A soul chosen and baited by Destiny to become the victim of infertility" (1075 – 6, Vol. II).

At first glance it seems as if we are defeating ourselves by showing García Lorca in statements about his work to be essentially in line with an interpretation we think misses the point. As a matter of fact what we are doing is quite the opposite. We are listening very carefully to what the poet said and at the same time analyzing the words in the context of the dramatic forces at work within the play. Lorca stated that the play was "the image of fecundity punished by sterility," thus Yerma can be, and in fact is, sterile. She is the "victim" to whom Lorca referred.

He was not trying to confuse his public. He was challenging it. For further corroboration, examine what the adjective "yermo" means — interestingly enough, it can also be a noun in the masculine gender, but not in the feminine —: uninhabited, uncultivated, barren land, and so forth. It does not necessarily mean it cannot bear fruit. Therefore this woman Yerma — the protagonist — is barren only in the strict sense of the word, because no seed has been planted in her. In fact, a knowing old woman in the play tells her clearly: "It is your husband's fault" (738, Vol. II). Even more pointedly, Yerma asks Juan if she can expect a child from him. Without hesitation, he answers, "No" (743, Vol. II).

In the prologue to his edition of Lorca's "Suites,"[11] some of which had never been published together, André Belamich explains why his research was so important. He indicates that, not only are some of these poems exceedingly beautiful and therefore worthy of publication, but that they give as well a clear indication as to what direction Lorca's work was taking by providing some intimate thoughts of the poet which we would do well to keep in mind when analyzing his more familiar published literary art. Among the observations made by Belamich, one in particular lends itself quite well to what now concerns us. He says that one of the prevalent themes of some of these poems deals with the "increado," as he names it, that which has not been created as yet. He further claims that they "offer a clue to almost all of the Lorcan theater of the impossible." He goes on to say that in order to shorten his explanation he wants to limit himself to the example of *Así que pasen cinco años* insisting that "the whole work has its inception in the 'Suites.' The young man in the 'legend of time,' resembles the poet of the 'Suites' as if they were brothers. Both relate to a woman who is successively offered to them and then taken away ... as in the ideal fiancée of the poem 'Encuentro,' he would also like to have children: 'Yes, my sons run inside of me, as a lonely ant confined within a closed box ... '" Specifically the female mannequin in the play says:

> ... It is your fault
> You could have been for me
> a colt of lead and foam ...
> ...but you are a sleeping lagoon,
> with dry leaves and moss
> where my clothes rot.

Belamich cites these verses in his prologue and finishes by saying: "Yerma's husband is equally at fault, he alone is responsible for her sterility."[12] By "equally at fault" we are to understand that the young man in the "legend of time" and Juan in *Yerma* are similar in their relationships to the women involved. Another example can be found in the "Arco de lunas:" "My children who have not been born /persecute me."[13]

García Lorca wrote constantly on the theme of unborn children, not only in his poetry and plays, but also in a letter written in July of 1923 to José de Ciria y Escalante; he talks about working feverishly on a poem "El jardín de las toronjas de luna" informing his friend that,

> The landscapes in the poem are absolutely still, without any wind,
> any rhythm. I could tell that my verses were running away from

my hands, that the actual poem was static and somnambulant. My *garden* is the garden of possibilities, the garden of what is not, but could (and sometimes) should have been; the garden of theories that went by without being seen and of children that were not born (1249, Vol. II).

Continuing in this same vein, we find yet another example of Lorca's obsession with this theme: the longing for the birth of a child and the tragedy of being unable to have children. The following verses can be found in Belamich's book. They had not been printed before:

A child has just been born
A star has told me.

. . . .
The child is my lamb,
But I am very far from its dream.
I sing in the fog,
Absorbed with my own sadness
Blurred melancholy of old silver.[14]

Returning to Lorca's theater, perhaps one of the best and most concrete statements he gave us concerning the theater is one that Felipe Morales cites as part of a literary conversation he had with the poet in 1936: "The theater was always my vocation ... The theater is the poetry that rises from the book and becomes human. And when it does, it speaks and screams, cries, and despairs ..." (1119, Vol. II). Here Lorca joins his poetry with his drama insisting that the theater "has always been in the hands of the poets ... not the lyric poet, but the dramatic poet" (1087, Vol. II).

Without negating what has been discussed up to this point, it is important to recall briefly a suggestion made at the beginning of this essay which implied that, since no author always means everything he says, nor says everything he means to say, we should be ready to treat the statements made by artists, even though essential, with caution. In the case of Federico García Lorca, he was quite often quoted as saying he wrote for everyone, that poetry belonged to the people, that art for art's sake did not make sense, especially in Spain during the turbulent years of the thirties. He declared that:

In this dramatic time of the world, the artist must cry and laugh with his people. You must set aside the bouquet of lilies and immerse yourself to the waist in mud to help those who are looking for the lilies. I am particularly anxious to communicate with others. That's why I write plays and I consecrate to the stage all my sensitivity (1124, Vol. II).

In spite of these explicit and apparently sincere words, we know perfectly well that a large portion of Lorca's work is only intelligible to a minority: "My first plays are impossible to stage ..." In reference to *Así que pasen cinco años,* he further stated: "My real purpose lies within these impossible plays. But in order to convey a certain type of personality and to earn due respect, I have written others ..." (1120, Vol. II), plays such as *Doña Rosita la soltera* and *Mariana Pineda*. We consider the former a case of "deep social dramatism." This is to be understood not from the literary point of view of what would eventually become the social theater and novel of the fifties in Spain, but as the theme of the imposition of rules of conduct expected of people in the late 19th and beginning of the 20th centuries. Although the protagonist of *Doña Rosita* is a woman and the principal victim of this society, Lorca's central dramatic interest is the Spanish middle class as a whole, whose members infect each other with the microbe of stern, narrow behavior. Lacking the understanding and willingness necessary to change their environment, they statically wait for happenings which will alter their lives, but they never try to overcome any social obstacle which would help achieve a happiness they had once thought possible.

Lorca was a very imaginative and restless author and as such was in constant need of creating new styles, new themes. As an example, when he was interviewed in 1927 by Juan González Olmedilla, he told the interviewer that he had written the play *Mariana Pineda* "as a fun thing to do." He goes on to explain how he knows that there have been many legendary Mariana Pinedas based on the historical character, a Granadian woman who died on the scaffold rather than betray her lover and the cause of freedom. The character he created, he stated, represents not the liberal cause, but personifies personal freedom, becomes its symbol. She is a real person, not a legend. He suggested that perhaps the Mariana Pineda of his play may not have the symbolic greatness of the legendary figure, but that she embodies the epitome of freedom: "When she is apprehended by Pedrosa — ... my Mariana ... cries out 'I am imprisoned ... Now I have started to die!'" (966, Vol. II). In the same interview he made his intentions regarding his theater very clear:

> ... the course of my dramatic work follows the classical style of Lope, and my poetry, the classical — in its two directions: the cultivated and the popular—, of Góngora (966 and 967, Vol. II).

A further observation to support our approach. One of the great advantages in being attentive to the words of the literary creators is that quite often when they speak they do so in a very original manner. It would almost seem as if they were continuing their artistic endeavors. In one of the most interesting interviews García Lorca granted to the press, entitled "I will go to Santiago ...," probably remembering the line so many times repeated in the poem "Son de negros en Cuba," the poet responded in the following manner to a question asked in reference to his New York experience:

> Extra-human architecture and furious rhythm, geometry and anguish ... The spires climb to the heavens without the will of

clouds, without the will to glory. Nothing more poetic and terrible than the war waged by the skyscrapers with the heavens that cover them...

Snow, rain and fog ... underline, soak, cover the immense towers; but they, blind to any game, express their cold determination, enemies of mystery, who clip the hair of the rains or make their thousand swords invisible through the swanlike softness of dawn (986, Vol. II).

He concluded, "...Wall Street. Impressive in its coldness and cruelty. The rivers bring the gold from every corner of the earth and death comes with it" (988, Vol. II). These words recall some lines in *Poet in New York*.

Even in his letters to friends he could be very lyrical: "Between two people there are small spider webs that become wire mesh, or even more, bars of steel. When death separates us, a bloody wound remains in place of each spider web."[15]

Federico García Lorca was a man of many facets, a writer of many styles and as such we must read his works. Those who knew him well have commented, among other things, about his childlike qualities, as did Guillén: "Childhood throbbed within the man. He was never a lost adolescent, his childlike personality prevented it ... And he played, he played the games of a young man and a poet. With things, with phrases ..." (XXXI, Vol. I).

It is also evident he thought of himself as a man who wanted to remain in many ways a child. In a letter written to his friend, Adriano del Valle, he said: "My personality and my poems give the impression of something extremely passionate ... however, in the profoundest depths of my soul there is an enormous desire to be very much a child, very poor, very much hidden.[16] And in 1927 he wrote to Sebastián Gasch in reference to some drawings he was forwarding to him: "These drawings are pure poetry or pure plastic poetry as well. When I create them, I feel cleansed, comforted, happy, *a child*." [17]

Guillén and others were known to have remarked that he was a cheerful person, always looking for a good time, in whose company one had no choice but to be merry. He once said to a newspaperman that he did not want to talk about his art, that he had come to Buenos Aires to enjoy himself "... I don't worry about anything. I want to have fun, to enjoy life, to live!" (1030, Vol. II).

Yet there is another Lorca, the sad unhappy poet who spent all night writing feverishly, at times tragedies, at other times obscure and difficult verse where turmoil and death, blood and knives are common symbols of human existence. This Lorca was known for the most part only to his intimate friends and family. The man whom Vicente Aleixandre first described as, "... the powerful charmer, banishing sadness with his presence, casting a spell of happiness around him, an exorcist of joy of living, master of shadows which he banished with his presence ..." and later, "... the noble Federico of sadness, the man of loneliness and passion who at the verge of a life of triumph could hardly be visualized (X, Vol. II). Inasmuch as the poet, the writer and the man were but one, the critics should study his work and listen to his remarks even though they might be uttered in what is often considered a flippant way: "... the last thing in the world I am interested in is literature. Sometimes I have an irresistible urge to write, then I write feverishly for a few months, but soon I go back to living." (1027, Vol. II).

No one statement of the artist should be taken in isolation. The Lorca obsessed with blood, knives, death and sorrow was also the man of the *joie de vivre,* the Lorca of social concern, the acute critic who realized that he did not "have a very definite appraisal of (his) work," who claimed "... If I were to write it again I would do it a different way, in one of a thousand possible ways. I therefore think that all critics may be correct when judging it, each from their own point of view" (966–967, Vol. II). We can infer from this that Lorca understood the difficulties encountered in critical analysis.

Two statements of Francisco Ayala, who also attended the York colloquium referred to earlier, come to mind that we feel, together with Goytisolo's views, illustrate our premise that there are many paths to the study of literature and all are good provided their approach is an honest one: "... I believe that, far from the dogmatic arrogance of those who think they possess the only method, it would be advisable for the critic to assume, in relation to the work of art, ... the humble attitude of one who tries to find out which methods are best suited to its evaluation." Later he dictated: "We should accept the premise that biographical circumstances and, within them, the author's personality, will significantly help to clarify the conscious intentions as well as the unconscious impulses that went into the writing of his work ..."[18]

The fundamental statement that illustrates the thesis suggested by the title of this essay is, that if we want to do a thorough and objective critical analysis of a work of literature, we must consider what the author is trying to tell us not only in his writings, but, also whenever possible, in interviews, lectures and letters.

I am fully aware that the followers of Formalist Criticism or the Structuralists will frown at my statement. Nonetheless I do insist on my thesis. In much the same way in which we analyze the brainchild of the imagination and reach conclusions mostly based on study and interpretation of the work itself, we must undertake as well a thorough investigation of what the author has been telling us outside of his writings, especially with a writer such as Lorca who, very often, gave us clues to interpreting and otherwise enjoying his work.

NOTES

1. "Lorca: from Child to Poet," Unpublished at this writing, p. 2, Christopher Maurer, ed.

2. *Federico García Lorca Epistolario,* Alianza Editorial (S.A.: Madrid, 1983), Vol. I, p. 18.

3. Christopher Maurer, ed. p. 101.

4. J.B. Trend, "Lorca," in *Lorca. A Collection of Critical Essays.* ed. Manuel Durán. (Englewood Cliffs, N.J.: Prentice-Hall, 1962), p. 29.

5. Darío Villanueva, "Crítica literaria y literatura española del siglo XX." In: *Siglo XX/20th Century* 1,2 (Spring 1984):13. (Newsletter of the Twentieth Century Spanish Association of America). Translated from Spanish by the author.

6. Juan Goytisolo, "Escritores, críticos y gendarmes." In: *The Analysis of Hispanic Texts: Current Trends in Methodology* (First York College Colloquium. Jamaica, N.Y.: Bilingual Press, York College, CUNY, 1976), pp. 11–12.

7. Most of Lorca's quotes have been taken from: García Lorca, Federico. *Obras completas.* (Madrid: Aguilar, 1980). For the sake of simplification, the page number in which they appear will be entered in our text. If a change occurs, it will be duly footnoted. The quotes and poetry have been translated from the Spanish by the author. In this particular case the quote comes from the 1966 edition of *Obras completas,* page 1685.

8. Maurer, II, p. 38.

9. Maurer, II, p. 80.

10. Maurer, II, p. 127.

11. Federico García Lorca, *Suites.* André Belamich, ed. (Barcelona: Editorial Ariel, S.A., 1983. pp. 22–23. These quotes and those that follow have been translated by the author.

12. F. García Lorca, p. 23.

13. F. García Lorca, p. 198.

14. F. García Lorca, p. 288–289.

15. Maurer, II, p. 145.

16. Maurer, I, p. 17.

17. Maurer, II, p. 81.

18. Francisco Ayala, "La disputa de las escuelas literarias." In: *The Analysis of Hispanic Texts,* Jamaica, N.Y.: Bilingual Press (York College, CUNY), 1976, pp. 4–5. These quotes have been translated from the Spanish by the author.

II. Towards the Main Subjects: Nature, Love, Death

GUSTAVO CORREA
Yale University

Nature and Symbol in the Poetry of Federico García Lorca

Federico García Lorca was a poet of Nature. The first contact that the poet had with nature will always be present through his poetry, whether he is exploring the mystery of his own self or of the universe, or delving into the dark forces of nature and man, or trying to face the enigma of human destiny. From the very beginning, nature acted for Lorca as a primary code in the awakening of his poetic consciousness. It constituted a path for the structuring of his mental development and set the trajectory for the formulation of his emotional life. This absorption of nature by the poetic consciousness in its formative years is no doubt a key to the powerful appeal that the poetry of Lorca always has for us. He speaks to us with a vocabulary which is directly related to the soil, the mother earth, to a simple rural society and to the cosmic universe.

It will be important to note, on the other hand, that the objects of nature with which the poet was able to converse when he was a child and that continued to give him hints and suggestions in his adult and creative life will actually become a repertory of symbols underlying the texture of his poetry. The sun, the moon, the wind, the water, trees, grass, mountains, rivers, brooks, horses, bulls, cows, fish, birds, different kinds of plants and fruits, oleander, jasmine, pomegranate, lemons, oranges, rocks, pebbles, all of these enter into his poetry with powerful calls pointing to concrete experiences and coherent structures of meaning. In *Deep Song,* one of Lorca's earlier books, the wind that blows through the olive trees carries all kinds of mysterious sounds, and is intermingled in a single experience with the green color of the groves, the neighing of the horses and the passionate shouts of people singing their songs of tormented love, out into the distant horizons of dark nights. The air vibrations at night and in the dawn are the same vibrations of the guitar strings, which, in turn, put in motion the foliage of the trees and the hair and skirts of the gypsy girls. The sound waves are reflected on the undulations of the dry earth, the "undulated desert." The long shadows at dusk fuse with the burning grape vines and with the olive trees to form the labyrinthine maze within which man's destiny is being determined. Black and dreamy horses take men with inescapable fatality to a final labyrinth of crosses. Grief and dark premonitions permeate the landscape. Also, in his book *Gypsy Ballads,* the fate of man can be read in solidarity with the manifestations of nature. The death of a child and the drowning of a girl occur under the malignant influence of the moonlight, at the moment when dawn is beginning to appear in the horizon. Men kill each other in a senseless fight ("Reyerta") in the midst of ill auguring signs in the sky (clouds, lightning and rain). The gypsy outlaw, who has to appear before the authorities ("El emplazado") can read his destiny in the hard and metal-like light of the nearby rocky hills. The black horses of the Civil Guard are, on the other hand, the carriers of bad omens for the city of the gypsies. Things and phenomena of nature acquire, thus, a symbolic significance in relation to human destiny and the realization of the self.

This compact solidarity of man and nature is expressed in a dramatic web of interrelations that gives rise to the texture of myth. If myth is fundamentally a fable, an archetypal story, in which the deep impulses of the subconscious and the representational world of primitive mentality are projected, then the whole spectacle of nature and man's actions and cognitions can be seen in the perspective of myth. We can observe three different levels in the presentation of myth in the poetry of Lorca. First, a spectacle of nature is seen in an anthropomorphic context of mutually interrelated movements. Second, a spectacle of nature is woven into an integrated story, in which man is an active participant. Third, a spectacle of nature is seen objectively as a mythical story, but it is one that has an avowed and direct relationship to the inner life of the poet. All of these levels of mythical representation come through the individual mind of the poet, since the poetic consciousness acts as the center of the interrelated movements, whether the mythical story is being played out in the external world, or whether there is an active participation between man and the universe. The mythical story conveys clarification to the content of the poetic consciousness.

Let us give concrete examples of the three levels of mythical patterns that appear in the poetry of Lorca. At the first level, a poem like the one entitled "Fable" from his book *Canciones* (1921–1924)[1] presents the well-known mythological figures of the Cyclops and the Unicorns in deadly confrontation with one another, in a hurried stampeding against the cliffs at the water's edge. There is no doubt that the cyclops, with their green eyes, are the projected figures of the green waves of sea water, while the unicorns appear as the embodiment of the reflections of light over the water:

> Unicornios y cíclopes
>
>   Una pupila
> y una potencia.
> ¿Quién duda de la eficacia
> terrible de esos cuernos?
> ¡Oculta tus blancos,
> Naturaleza!
> (p. 365)

The last words of the poem are a warning to Nature by the poet, in view of the efficacious power of the unicorns: "Nature, Hide your targets." The dramatic confrontation of the two sets of physical phenomena in the world of nature, that is, light and waves, which becomes a struggle of the unicorns and cyclops at the level of myth, can certainly be symbolically referred to the creative forces of the artist. The unicorns, with their objective referent to light, point to the conscious and, therefore, ordering aspect of artistic creation. On the other hand, the bare forces of the cyclops, with their referent to the onrushing waves of the sea, represent the tumultuous and chaotic forces of the subconscious and of poetic inspiration. In the end, the sea waves are hit by the horns of light.

The ballad "Precious and the Wind" exemplifies the second level of mythification of nature, that in which man is an active participant. The anthropomorphizing impulses start in the mind of the gypsy girl, who gives to a sudden gush of wind the attributes of an aggressive lover ("viento hombrón"). The latter, in turn, threatens her with the loss of her virginity. The wind unleashes a real storm, which is then accompanied by lightning and rain and continues the persecution of the girl with its hot sword ("espada caliente") and its shining tongues. The frightened, terrified girl runs and takes refuge in a nearby house, while the masculine wind keeps on biting at the roof of the house. It is clear that in this story, the cosmic forces of the wind and storm act at the level of human configurations establishing, thereby, an uninterrupted continuum between man and nature. This makes possible the creation of a plot of an aggressive masculine figure pursuing the panicky helpless girl. Such structure of meaning is magically enhanced by the presence of powerful images of light and fire and wind, and by the cosmic orchestration of sounds, colors and the phenomena of temperature. The *Duende* makes its appearance here, radiating its power into the projections of a well-constructed and primitive story.

At the third level of mythical configuration, we find the enactment of a mythical story which is played out in a spectacle of nature, and which has a direct relationship to the inner life of the poet. Here, myth is an objectivization of subjective and unconscious states of mind, with a strong emotional content. Lorca builds up a trajectory of mythical representation related not only to human destiny, but also to his career as an artist, and to a broader context of the realization of the self. The poem "Adam" from his early book *Primeras canciones, 1922,* reveals the structure of a mythical plot concerning the birth of a new son of the cosmic parents, the sun as the father and the moon as the mother of the newly-born day. The sun father feverishly dreams of the new child that in a rush gallops over the pulsating beat of his two cheeks. This happens after the birth has taken in a bloody spectacle ("Arbol de sangre moja la mañana"), and the bewailing mother, with no blood left in her veins, is forced to flee in emaciating paleness ("y un gráfico de hueso en la ventana"). Nevertheless, the poet contemplates this renewed story of the birth of the day and the presence of the energizing forces of nature with a feeling of utter helplessness and frustration. He sees himself, in effect, as another "Adam", who will be able only to father a son who will burn out into nothingness, since he lacks the energizing power of the cosmic sun. The last tercet of the sonnet establishes the connection between the archetypal cosmic spectacle and the degraded personal story of a birth which is doomed to failure:

> Pero otro Adán oscuro está soñando
> neutra luna de piedra sin semilla
> donde el niño de luz se irá quemando.
> (p. 353)

The obscure Adam (the poet) can only dream of images of sterility ("a sexless stone moon without any seed"), which no doubt have to do with the feeling of lack of artistic potency.

The cosmic plot of the archetypal family and the birth of the day will soon expand in Lorca's poetry into a wide context of symbolization. In fact, the end of the day will constitute the continuation of the myth, since the red coloration of the sky at the moment of the sunset is seen as another bloody spectacle that marks the death of the powerful mythical figure. The death of the sun, makes possible, in turn, the appearance of the moon, whose full dominance in the horizon has a portentous influence on the life of man. If the sun implies vitality and the full realization of the self, the moon acts as an evil omen on man's trajectory. The two symbols are, thus, interrelated not only by their mutual position in the mythical story (man, wife and son), but also by the fact that their movements are determined by astronomical laws, including the succession of day and night. Their location in the sky, particularly at the moment of dawn and dusk and during the night, and also their coloration and shape, or even their full presence or absence, will reflect variations in their mythical representation, and, ultimately, in their manner of signification. The poetic structure, will, thus, present definable signals, which will guide us in the process of decodifying its own meaning. The mythical story allows for the fusion of the obscure with the clear, of the shapeless with the schematic, of the undefinable with that which is plastically projected in figures, color and contrasts of light and darkness, all this within the texture of cosmic events.

It is to be noted, on the other hand, that the original plot of the birth and death of the day, marked by the appearance and disappearance of the sun and the counterpart movement of the disappearance and then the appearance of the moon in the horizon, is intertwined in Lorca's poetry with the presence of the bull and cow, in correlation with the figures of the cosmic father and mother. In Egyptian mythology, the solar god Osiris, the father, is identified with the bull Apis, and the moon goddess Isis, the mother, with the cow. Out of the union of the two parents the child Horus is born. In fact, we can infer that Lorca found the correlation of the cosmic father, mother and son from some knowledge of Egyptian mythology.[2] On the other hand, the sunset will constitute for Lorca the enactment of the killing of the mythical figure, an event which will be associated with the killing of the bull in the bullfight arena.

Moreover, the killing of the bull, that is, the sunset, will also be associated in Lorca with the myth of Saint John the Baptist, as it appears in Mallarmé's poem "Hérodiade." The last part of Mallarmé's poem is titled "Canticle of Saint John", and has as its theme the decapitation of Saint John, which, in the poem, is also the beheading of the sun, although in reference to the summer's solstice, rather than to the sunset. This cosmic event coincides with the day of Saint John the Baptist, which takes place on the twenty-fourth of June.[3] All these correlations appear in Lorca's prose poem "The Beheading of the Baptist", written around 1928, the same year in which he gave his lecture on "Imagination, Inspiration and Evasion." The poem presents masses of people, lined up as observers of a great spectacle, in which the actual participants in the confrontation are divided in two teams, the Reds and the Blacks, hence the reference to a large stadium, rather than specifically to the bullfight arena. The two colors allude, nevertheless, to the sun and shade areas in the disposition of the seats around the arena or the stadium, according to which the various locations are termed "Sol y Sambra" or "Blanco y Negro," and in our poem "Rojos y Negros." The two colors appear here, nevertheless, as the actual name of the confronting teams. On the other hand, the division into Reds and Blacks alludes to the colorations of red in the horizon and the approaching darkness of late afternoon. The spectacle of the "Degollación del Bautista" re-enacts, thus, the decapitation of Saint John, with implications to the killing of the bull in the sky and in the arena, in unison with the setting of the sun. The last part of the poem refers to the actual moment of the beheading of the mythical figure, in the midst of shouting crowds:

El griterío del Estadium hizo que las vacas mugieran en todos los establos de Palestina. La cabeza del luchador celeste estaba en medio de la arena. Las jovencitas se teñian las mejillas de rojo y los jóvenes pintaban sus corbatas en el cañón estremecido de la yugular desgarrada.

La cabeza de Bautista:	¡Luz!
Los rojos:	Filo
La cabeza de Bautista:	¡Luz! ¡Luz!
Los rojos:	Filo filo
La cabeza de Bautista:	Luz luz luz
Los rojos:	Filo filo filo filo (p. 28)

In addition to the figures of the cow and the bull, the figure of the horse appears in the poetry of Lorca as one of the essential components of the mythical plot. The horse is of paramount importance in Andalusian culture and plays a constant role in the life of the gypsies. In the *Romancero gitano,* the horse allows man to move from one place to another and eventually leads him to meet his own destiny of death. In the context of the cosmic story, in Lorca's vision, the horse is identified with the rounded horizon, the celestial abode, which becomes the rump of the horse, and which keeps moving in order to let the protagonists appear in the sky and have their encounters. The image of the horizon as the rump of a shiny colt occurs in the ballad "Predimiento de Antoñito el Camborio" (p. 445), at the moment when Antoñito is taken to prison to be executed later:

Y a las nueve de la noche
le cierran el calabozo,
mientras el cielo reluce
como la grupa de un potro.

In the ballad "Martirio de Santa Olalla" (p. 458), the dark night appears as a long tailed horse that runs and jumps among the streets of Mérida, while Roman soldiers await sleepily the hour of the execution of Saint Eulalia:

> Por la calle brinca y corre
> caballo de larga cola,
> mientras juegan o dormitan
> viejos soldados de Roma.

We should remember that in the poem "Adam," the newly born creature appears galloping along a horse: "Adán sueña en la fiebre de arcilla /un niño que se acerca galopando /por el doble latir de su mejilla" (p. 353). The horse is, thus, the dynamic impulse that sets in motion the other figures of the mythical story. Man's destiny is tied up to the inevitability of their movements and their encounters. As the sun, the primeval Adam, inexorably moves toward its own beheading, so is man's destiny essentially a tragic one. At night, the moon, in turn, radiates its own evil influence from which there is no escaping. Man is a participant in this mythical story, together with the other figures that move on their trajectory in the cosmic universe. The mythical plot helps to clarify man's destiny, and to give the mysterious and dark impulses of life a symbolic representation in an ordered pattern.

Although Lorca absorbed early into his poetry some of the components of his mythic vision, it is in the years 1927–1928, the period of composition of his prose poems, when he seems to have developed fully the mythic plot into a tight structure of mutual interrelations. This can be seen in the "Beheading of the Baptist," but also in some of his other prose poems. In his letter to Sebastián Gasch, he alludes to the fact that he is sending him the two "degollaciones," out of three that he intends to write. We might surmise that the "Degollación del Bautista" was one of them. A second one could very well be the "Degollación de los inocentes" (pp.29–30), whose very title alludes to the act of beheading. In this latter prose poem, the end of the massacre of the innocent children takes place at the end of the day, when blood is being splashed on all clocks at six in the afternoon:

> A las seis de la tarde ya no quedaban más que seis niños por dego-
> llar. Los relojes de arena seguían sangrando, pero ya estaban secas
> todas las heridas.

In another prose poem, "Santa Lucía y San Lázaro" (pp. 13–19), there appear images of physical violence, since Saint Lucía's martyrdom consisted of the gouging of her eyes. Saint Lazarus, the other protagonist, suffered death, was buried and then miraculously resurrected. According to the biblical story, the narrator in the poem travels to a town where he takes lodging and board at midnight in Saint Lucía's Inn (Posada de Santa Lucía). The next day, he goes around watching all activities, and in the afternoon he is able to observe that the showcases in the stores are full of optical lenses and prisms, and that monstrous eyes ("ojos terribles") are dangling from their pupils in the horizon. There is here, no doubt, a reference to Saint Lucía's eyes, but also to the particular kind of light that now filters in the atmosphere. The moment finally approaches for the red coloration of the sky, which announces the beheading of the Baptist:

> Gafas y vidrios ahumados buscaban la inmensa mano cortada de la guantería, poema en el aire, que suena, sangra y borbotea como la cabeza del Bautista.
> (p. 15)

Concurrently, religious services are being conducted in the cathedral in honor of Saint Lucía. It is the moment in which horror prevails, on account of the impending blood-spout outside:

> Con el miedo al latido y el horror al chorro de sangre, se pedía la tranquilidad de loas ágatas y la desnudez sin sombra de la medusa.
> (p. 16).

It is with *Poet in New York,* nevertheless, that the full implications of the myth are revealed to Lorca's tragic vision, in the perspective of his own personal life. Lorca's trip to New York in the summer of 1929 brings him, in effect, to the alien atmosphere of a technologically advanced city culture, basically deprived of a direct communication with nature. There is, in fact, no rural landscape in New York and whatever is left of nature is diminished by the presence of the tall skyscrapers along the narrow streets and the absence of daylight in the dark subway tunnels. Moreover, with the approach of fall and winter, with their cloudy skies, the sun and the moon rarely appear in the horizon. Also, the trees are without leaves and snow and slush cover the ground. Within this landscape, man's life is not fully integrated with the pulsations of nature, and so, his destiny is marked by the signs of sterility. The mythical figures have been mutilated and appear totally degraded. In the poem "Cow" ("Vaca," p. 503), one of the earliest of the collection, the feminine figure has been mortally wounded at dawn ("se tendió la vaca herida"), and its body has been cut into pieces, with its four hooves left trembling in the air ("Cuatro pezuñas tieblan en el aire"). In a later poem "Dawn" ("La aurora," p. 497), the dawn in New York collapses over its four pillars of mud, while a storm of black doves splash from the rotten waters. The early risers who come out of their homes know that they will drown in the mud. Others walk along, half asleep, as if coming from a bloody shipwreck. In the poem "The Birth of Christ" ("Nacimiento de Cristo, p. 496), the bull can only dream of a bull full of holes and water, and the child weeps with the number three on his forehead. The birth of the Christ child is thus frustrated by the ominous portents of rain in the sky. On the other hand, the symbol of the dead child, or of the utterly fragile creature who will die while being born, is one of the prevailing ones in the poems of *Poet in New York*. A dying child is bemoaned by the barking dogs in the poem "Unsleeping City"

("Ciudad sin sueño"): "y el niño que enterraron esta mañana lloraba tanto / que hubo necesidad de llamar a los perros para que callase" (p. 493). Similarly, the moon appears in the horizon without its fertilizing attributes, as if it were a stone without seeds, or is identified with the skull of a horse, as in the poem "Ruin" ("Ruina"): "Pronto se vió que la luna /era una calavera de caballo / y el aire una manzana oscuza (p. 511).

This degradation of the mythical figures in *Poet in New York* is, no doubt, a symbolic projection of the poet's lack of emotional and artistic self-realization. Love here never reaches fulfillment, or strangles in the initial process of its manifestation. On the other hand, the poet has to wrestle with the chaotic impulses of his creative power. Hence, the accumulation of negative signs and the ominous presence of the dead child. In the poem "Nocturne of the Void" ("Nocturno del hueco"), the power mythical figure has been beheaded at dawn over the empty square: "En la gran plaza desierta /mugía la cabeza recién cortada." This event coincides with a love that has withered away and only offers empty gloves and hollow dresses. The gyrating voids are projected from the inner soul of the poet into the sky and on the face of the wounded moon:

> Ruedan los huecos puros, por mí, por ti en el alba conservando las
> huellas de las ramas de sangre y algún perfil de yeso tranquilo que
> dibuja instantáneo dolor de luna apuntillada.
> (p. 508)

In the second part of the "Nocturne of the Void" (p. 507), the poet finds himself in complete solitude, inside empty space and with only the company of the very white void of a horse, which has ashes in its mane. The horizon at dawn has thus been emptied of the mythical presence of the horse, and does not even show any imprints of blood:

> Yo.
> Con el hueco blanquísimo de un caballo.
> Rodeado de espectadores que tienen hormigas en las palabras.
>
> En el circo del frío sin perfil mutilado.
> Por los capiteles rotos de las mejillas desangradas
> (p. 509)

The poet's life has been anchored, with no feeling of movement: "Ecuestre por mi vida definitivamente anclada."

The poem "Crucifixion" (p. 532) fuses the cosmic impact of a dark and rainy day with the religious symbols of the crucifixion of Christ. The moon appears at dawn on the very white curve of a horse, although the child is already dead at the very moment of the circumcision. The weeping that can be heard coming from the south reflects the fact that the moon has been burning the phallus of horses in candle fire. A skull appears in the sky and the three Holy Virgins look at it through the window. The galaxies are rusty and have been nailed down with thorns. Rain begins to fall drenching hearts and streets. At this point the pharisees accurse the moon for the milk and birdshots she is sending down to earth. In the afternoon, the sun has not yet appeared in the horizon, although as soon as the moon has bathed with water drops the blistering horse-flesh, the moment of redemption will be revealed. When night time comes, the pharisees withdraw to their houses in the midst of bloody taints in the sky. They accurse the moon for not letting them sleep. The poem ends with a parodic biblical allusion:

Fue entonces
y la tierra despertó arrojando temblorosos ríos de polilla.

Man's destiny has, thus, lost all meaning in this vision of New York, where the mythical figures have been emasculated and degraded. There is no hope of salvation for man deprived of a real participation with nature and the cosmic universe.

It is significant that after his New York experience, Lorca's poetic vision reaches the full strength of man's participation in the mythical plot. Man's destiny is indeed a tragic one, but his life is enhanced and made meaningful by his solidarity with the forces of nature. In *Blood Wedding* (1933), the passionate lovers, Leonardo and the Bride, flee from the scene of the wedding following the dictates of their innermost, dark impulses. In the end, the killing of the lover and the bridegroom takes place in the open spaces at night, under the ominous influence of the red moonlight. In *Lament for Ignacio Sánchez Mejías* (1935), the death of the bullfighter occurs when he is facing the real gull in the arena, and at the moment when the other bull in the sky is close to its own beheading. The blood of the bullfighter's sacrifice is subsequently drunk by the thirsty ancient cow ("vaca del Viejo Mundo"), the cow of the Old World, the mythical figure which now appears in the sky with its unequivocal signs of evil omen. The bullfighter's strength and vitality have been broken down by fate, but his life has been made significant by the full presence of the mythical figures. The bullfighter's blood drenches the arena and filters through the earth in a ritual sacrifice that fulfills the solidarity of man and cosmos. Lorca saw in nature not only man's way to self-fulfillment, but also the inevitability of his own tragic destiny.

NOTES

1. Federico García Lorca, *Obras completas* (fourteenth edition), Madrid: Aguilar, 1968. All of our quotations and translations are from this edition.

2. See my article, "El simbolismo del sol en la poesía de Federico García Lorca," NRFH XIV (1960): pp. 110–119.

3. See: Wallace Fowlie, *Mallarmé,* Chicago, 1953, p. 140.

ALLEN JOSEPHS
University of West Florida

"Don Perlimplín": Lorca's *amante-para-la-muerte*

Shortly before he stabs himself, Perlimplín tells Belisa: "Esto que yo hago no lo hizo nadie jamás."[1] Whether he is speaking for himself as a character or as spokesman for the playwright, Perlimplín is right: *no lo hizo nadie jamás*. Don Perlimplín, Lorca's *amante-para-la-muerte*, is a unique character in every sense of the word. To understand what he is about is to understand one of the primary mysteries of theater and to appreciate the extent to which Lorca's technical and innovative genius — much like Picasso's — was unerringly returning us to the beginnings of art.

On the technical level, *Amor de Don Perlimplín con Belisa en su jardín: aleluya erótica en cuatro cuadros y un prólogo: versión de cámara*, to give the play its entire title (there are actually only three *cuadros*), presents us with an unusual theatrical phenomenon through which Lorca portrays symbolically and historically the obscure, ancient custom of ritual sacrifice from which we suspect theater began. Much of Lorca's theater is concerned precisely with the nature of theater itself. *La zapatera prodigiosa*, to choose a closely related example, shows us a fine use of the play within the play in which Lorca cleverly goes beyond Shakespeare's use of that device in *Hamlet* and presents us with a model treatment of the interchangeability of reality and illusion.[2] However, in *Amor de don Perlimplín* he goes beyond theater within theater and creates character within character. In the process, he delves deeper, by a dimension or so, into the shifting planes of perspective between what seems to be and what is.

Perlimplín, basically an eighteenth-century character, a child of the Enlightenment and an "illustrated" man who lives by his reason, upon his sudden confrontation with Belisa's sea of eroticism and his consequent cuckolding by the respresentatives of the five races of the earth, converts himself into a Romantic hero. The figure wrapped in the red cape who steals Belisa's heart is, of course, none other than Perlimplín himself. By his extravagant and unprecedented split, Perlimplín reveals himself, to the audience's and Belisa's immense surprise, to be her new lover and her old husband — both cuckold and cuckolder, Don Juan and his prey, the romantic hero and the villain. But he is more than that. He kills himself with a *puñal de esmeraldas*, with a *ramo ardiente de piedras preciosas*. He is both high priest and sacrificial victim.

What undercuts the intentionally mythic dimension of the play is the fact that Lorca has written it as a farce. Yet it is no ordinary example of the genre. *La zapatera prodigiosa* was a sixteenth-century farce staged with twentieth-century techniques in a style that Lorca called a *farsa violenta*. *Amor de don Perlimplín* is even more unusual. We could call it a ritual farce that seems in style to be a transitional work, half eighteenth-century and half Romantic, a contrived and intentionally theatrical mixture best described by Francis Fergusson in his well-known essay, "'Don Perlimplín': Lorca's Theater Poetry".

But just because the farce and its people seem so ancient, it strikes us as not only farcical but also sinister. Lorca, while keeping the cynical old tale, with its neoclassic stagy glitter, also views it in the perspective of a later, gloomier, and more romantic age; he transposes it to bring out also the love-death theme. That theme also is traditional in European literature, as Denis de Rougemont explained in his book, *Love in the Western World.* He traces the terrible aspiration beyond physical love to some of the Provençal poets, and he thinks that the love-death theme which re-echoes through the nineteenth-century literature obscurely revives the heretical cult of the Cathari. Lorca certainly seems to echo the theme here with a full sense of its deep roots, especially in Don Perlimplín's lyric on the mortal wound of love, and in the final scene in the garden, which has the ceremoniousness of a dark old erotic rite.

As Francis Fergusson states, "It is an extravagant notion to combine farce and *Liebestod,* but Lorca knew it was extravagant. It is by means of the *style* of the piece that he makes an acceptable fusion of such disparate elements: for a knowing style implies the limitations of mood and viewpoint which the author has accepted in advance, and thus makes them acceptable and comprehensible to the audience. Lorca indicates the style of his play in its subtitle: "An Erotic Alleluya." An alleluya is something like a valentine: a love poem decorated with pictures, gilt cutouts, lace paper, and the like: something heroic, overdone, absurd: an *extravagant* offering to the beloved. All the elements of the production, music, sets, costumes, acting, should obey the requirements of this style. And one must remember that it is a Spanish style, akin perhaps to those drawings and paintings of Goya's — wounded cavaliers, frightening mustachioed old women, greedy young women in discreet mantillas — in which the remains of the eighteenth-century elegance are seen in a somber light.[3]

Fergusson understands that this farce is perplexing, enigmatic, and unlike any other in modern theater. He has also understood perfectly the grotesque combination of elements, the extravagant style Lorca creates in order to treat his theme. However, Fergusson thinks Lorca uses the style to create the work. I believe Lorca uses that style to disguise, or at least partially to mask, what he was really portraying.

Perlimplín, the neo-classical man who becomes a Romantic hero, is the first man sacrificed in Lorca's theater. He is both sacrificed and sacrificer, the first true bearer of the *Liebestod* theme, although that love-death connection is hinted at strongly in his earlier plays. Fergusson has evaluated perfectly the extraordinary significance of this theme in modern theater: thus he sees "Perlimplín" — unlike anything written in English — as "an authentic modern poetic drama" (p. 97).

Perlimplín, however, is not merely a man who realizes himself in death (I am thinking here of Heidegger's *Sein zum tod);* he is something I call *amante-para-la-muerte,* one of the most familiar figures, in one guise or another, in Lorca's work.[4] Fergusson has seen this and related the love-death theme with courtly love as explained by Rougemont. He is quite correct in relating the figure of Perlimplín to ancient rites. Rather than "the heretical cult of the Cathari," I believe Perlimplín should be related to rites far older and more obscure, something of which the most heretical parts of courtly love may well have been a medieval reflection. Fergusson was not incorrect, he just did not carry his conclusion far enough.

Angel Alvarez de Miranda, the late religious historian whose specialty was ancient religion, did. Alvarez de Miranda was the first to understand fully the nature of ancient religion, the nature of Lorca's work, and the striking similarity between the two. As a result, his thin volume called *La metáfora y el mito* is, in my mind, the single most essential item in the enormous bibliography dedicated to Lorca. Here is his only discussion of Perlimplín:

> No es casualidad que a lo largo de la obra lorquiana sean varones los protagonistas del morir, como tampoco era casual el protagonismo de la mujer en los otros aspectos. Muere el varón, muere sobre todo *para* la mujer; se trata de muertes que están sentidas — como la sexualidad, como la sangre — *desde* la mujer, desde la madre, la esposa o la amante. Muere el salvador. Pero el salvador es siempre el varón. Hace falta siempre que el salvador muera, y toda religiosidad mistérica, hipersensible al tema soteriológico, predica siempre una pasión y muerte masculinas como la de Dionysos y la de Atis, como la de Adonis, Osiris y Tamuz. A su manera, los héroes lorquianos reproducen ese misterio y pasión de "El dios que muere": ya hemos vislumbrado en *Bodas de sangre* el significado victimario del doble sacrificio varonil. En *Amor de don Perlimplín* el varón se inmolará por la mujer hundiéndose el puñal en el pecho, y el poeta nos hará saber que, gracias a esta muerte, la mujer quedará para siempre "vestida de la sangre gloriosísima" del sacrificado.[5]

It may seem difficult to accept that Alvarez de Miranda says essentially that a very great part of Lorca's work recapitulates ancient religion. Nonetheless if biologically ontogeny restates phylogeny, then why, speaking analogically, artistically, Jungianly, should poetry and theater, both essentially atavistic activities, not be able to reiterate the religions from which we think they began?

Part of our problem is ignorance. The Church worked so hard to eradicate rival religions that it turned any divergent belief into witchcraft. Yet from Mohenjo-Daro to Los Millares, or as Juvenal put it, "omnibus in terris quae sunt a Gadibus usque/Auroram et Gangem," 'In all the lands which reach from Gades to the Ganges and the dawn,'[6] and from the Ice Age Venus figures of 15,000-20,000 years ago, down through the earth-mother spirals at Catal-Hüyük, and in Andalucía vestigially right up to modern time, our religions — and art — have celebrated the fecundity of the female. Organized religion, from the first traces we have of it, has provided a sacrificial masculine death in connection with the female divinity — Dionysus, Attis, Adonis, Osiris, Tamuz. And from the rites of Dionysus and similar earlier festivities we believe — some more literally than others — that tragedy, the song of the goat who was slain in lieu of the god, originated.[7] Why, when this ancient world was constantly being rediscovered by the Romantics and their modern-day followers, should we doubt that Lorca was aware of it and, in fact, not intentionally using it?

Fergusson seemed to know the source. He tells us Eliot experimented with Greek myth and concludes that "it is very difficult to reincarnate a myth in our time. Myths as we read them in learned collections tempt us with their suggestion of deep poetic insight; but the crucial labor of the dramatic poet, faced with the modern stage and the modern crowd, only begins at that point".[8] Yet with "Perlimplín" he stops short since he thinks "the story is not strictly a myth," and so only connects it to a medieval heresy.[9]

On the first page of his essay on "Perlimplín", Rupert Allen observes perceptively that "to study the work of Lorca is nearly the same thing as to study myth and folklore; and to study myth and folklore is to see Lorca's significance at the proper level." Unfortunately, instead of pursuing the mythic significance of "Perlimplín," he then studies, for one hundred eight pages, the play's phallic implications, as he sees them.[10]

One problem with the criticism is that we have been persuaded to believe that myth is myth, that it is something no longer valid except archetypally as some remote echo in whatever Jungian chambers still exist in whatever collective unconscious we may still have vestigially intact, and, more significantly, that myth is something we can analyze rationally. Not many critics have wanted to look at the extent of the mythic in Lorca.

Robert Bly, the poet, is one who has. In *Leaping Poetry* he traces the ways the Christian ethic and rationality have, in his mind, all but destroyed modern poetry:

> By the eighteenth century the European intellectual was no longer interested in imagination really. He was trying to develop the "masculine" mental powers he sensed Socrates stood for — a de-mythologized intelligence ... an intelligence dominated by linked facts rather than "irrational" feelings....

> Nevertheless, this careful routing of psychic energy, first done in obedience to Christian ethics, and later in obedience to commercial needs, had a crippling effect upon the psychic life....

> Blake took the first step [to correction]: he abducted the thought of poetry and took it off to some obscure psychic woods. Those woods were real woods, occult ceremonies took place in them, as they had in ancient woods.... All over Europe energy in poetry began to come more and more from the unconscious, from the black side of intelligence.[11]

The best example of that black side — Bly cites the essay on *duende* — is Lorca himself.

It is interesting to note that Bly starts with the Earth Mother mysteries and works through Blake and the Romantics up to Lorca. In *Perlímplin,* we have precisely the same progression working the other way. Lorca shows us that Perlímplin, the perfect man of reason who has had no experience with women, is afraid of anything erotic and is reminded of the sea by Belisa. Belisa is the perfect incarnation of a chthonian goddess, insatiably erotic, beautiful, ever undecipherable to Perlímplin, and mortally dangerous. When she deceives Perlímplin on their wedding night, it is with no less than the "Representantes de las cinco razas de la tierra" — a detail which assures we understand her "goddess" stature. Perlímplin changes because of this cosmic cuckoldery. He finds himself with a great pair of golden horns and the one thing he had lacked: an imagination. He tells his servant, "Feliz como no tienes idea. He aprendido muchas cosas, y sobre todo puedo imaginarlas." He tells Belisa "Quiero sacrificarme por ti … Esto que yo hago no lo hizo nadie jamás." What he has done is to invent with his new imagination the Romantic hero he could never be. Belisa falls for the trick to the extent that she tells him: "¡Me parece que soy otra mujer¡" Perlímplin replies, "Ese es mi triunfo. El triunfo de mi imaginación."

Once Perlímplin has become the romantic hero he takes on his sacrificial aspects, which up to the end have not been apparent. Perlímplin describes his cape, as he pulls out his dagger, as "Roja como su sangre." And when he wants Belisa to look for the new lover he has created for her, he tells Belisa, "Míralo por dónde viene," an unmistakable religious reference straight out of the *saetas* of Semana Santa used to point out the arrival of the figure of Christ on his *paso* (cf. "Saeta" from *Poema del Cante Jondo:* Cristo moreno/pasa/de lirio de Judea/a clavel de España./¡Miradlo por dónde viene!)[12]

Finally, if any doubt remains about the sacrificial stature of Perlímplin and what that sacrifice means, after stabbing himself with an emerald dagger, he says "Belisa ya tiene un alma." As he dies, *"la escena adquiere una luz mágica."* Marcolfa, the *criada,* will put a "corona de flores como un sol de mediodía" on him. Belisa becomes "vestida por la sangre gloriosa de mi señor." And as the curtain falls, *"suenan las campanas."*

Obviously, the entire play is symbolic, not merely in the sense that all theater is symbolic, but on a deeper level. Perlímplin is modern man being led grotesquely astray by pseudo-Socratic pure reason and blinding enlightenment. He tells Belisa: "Yo no había podido imaginarme tu cuerpo hasta que lo vi por el ojo de la cerradura cuando te vestías de novia. Y entonces fue cuando sentí el amor. ¡Entonces! Como un hondo corte de lanceta en mi garganta." As he had spied on her, he had remarked to himself: "Belisa, con tantos encajes pareces una ola y me das el mismo miedo que de niño tuve al mar." Not since childhood — his state of grace prior to reason — could he *feel.* But his confrontation with her body and his cuckoldry release his imagination. His romantic half will be able to love her "con el amor infinito de los difuntos," but old Perlímplin himself can only escape her mystery through death: "Yo quedaré libre de esta oscura pesadilla de tu cuerpo grandioso ... ¡Tu cuerpo¡ ..., ¡¡¡ que nunca podría descifrar!!!" The man of reason cannot face her elemental nature. Only through imagination can he deal with her. But in the end, regardless of that momentarily triumphant instant, the old man of reason murders the young romantic hero.

Amor de don Perlimplín is a sort of irreverent, sacrilegious and grotesque morality play. Belisa represents the "old religions," the "goddess," the "earth mother," the *Magna mater,* Astarte herself, the Ashtoreth of the Old Testament, the Babylonian Ishtar, the whole "undiscovered" female fertility principle.[13] She is precisely that whole aspect of humanity which is incomprehensible to reason. The moral of this morality play is that reason is impotent. Since the Romantics were precisely the ones who began to lead us out of the modern labyrinth of the *sin razón de la razón,* if I may turn that phrase around, it is entirely appropriate that Lorca conceive of the play as a farce *a caballo* between the age of reason and the Romantic period.

Pure reason, the reason of the original Perlimplín, is impotent. But the pure sexuality of Belisa is mindless. Thus Perlimplín says in his last line, after he has sacrificed himself: "Yo soy mi alma y tú eres tu cuerpo. Déjame en este último instante, puesto que tanto me has querido, morir abrazado a él." In death, his sacrifice for her, they are joined, become complete, complement each other. Perlimplín triumphs, regains his honor, and controls his destiny, but only through his death. He is not just being-for-death, he is also loving-for-death. As such he is both the archetypal Spanish hero and the recapitulator of the oldest mystery we know. He is simultaneously a unique figure in modern theater and Everyman, the protagonist not of an *auto sacramental* but of an *auto sacrificial.* Lorca knew, as Euripides did in his last play, that the most fascinating mystery of the theater was precisely the mystery with which it had begun.

Perlimplín's triumph is the triumph of his imagination and *Perlimplín* is the triumph of Lorca's imagination. But it is no mere fantasy: it is the conscious and deliberate reconstruction of one of our most essential myths. This ritual farce is written as though Lorca had privileged access to the inner meaning and hidden structure of the human mind. Perlimplín is right: *Esto que yo hago no lo hizo nadie jamás.* But our old gods did, over and again.

We can still observe a symbolic representation of such a sacrifice in the night air thick with incense and orange blossoms, candlewax and torch smoke, of *Semana santa* in Sevilla, in Málaga, in Granada. The modern rationalist who attends Holy Week in Andalusia may not fully understand that he is watching religious spectacle, street theater at its most poignant, a reenactment of the passion of Christ, the Virgin's lamentation for a crucified, dying, and resurrecting God, and the final inexplicable, and urgent mystery of restoration in all its ancient seasonal glory. He probably will not realize that the raw and perfect emotion of the *saeta* he hears rending the night is an echo of the ululation of the women wailing for Adonis or that the whole spectacle harks back thousands of years, not merely two thousand years, but beyond to the rituals from which Greek tragedy developed and beyond that, to the Canaanite and Babylonian rituals that are the earliest theater we have.[14]

But Lorca knew it to perfection. Consider again the beginning of "Saeta" from *Poema del Cante Jondo* in which the poeta addresses the *paso:*

> Cristo moreno
> pasa
> de lirio de Judea
> a clavel de España
> ¡miradlo por dónde viene!
> De España. (I, 184)

Lirio de Judea/a clavel de España: the lily, we must remember, was not only sacred to the Virgin who weeps for her Son but also — and long before — to Astarte who wept for Adonis. That *lirio* becomes the *clavel de España*. By the same token, Perlimplín becomes and echoes all the gods who must die, and the mystery of Perlimplín's love is consummated in the ultimate mystery of sacrifice.

NOTES

1. Federico García Lorca, *Obras Completas*. Madrid: Aguilar, 1977. II, pp. 323–360. Since the play is so short, I see no need for further citations.

2. For a discussion of the play within the play, see my "The Violent Technique in *La Zapatera Prodigiosa.*" *García Lorca Review* V, 1 (Spring 1977): pp. 53–60.

3. Francis Fergusson. *The Human Image in Dramatic Literature*. Garden City, NY: Doubleday, 1957. pp. 89–90.

4. I first used the term *amante-para-la muerte* in Juan Caballero's and my edition of *La casa de Bernarda Alba*. Madrid: Cátedra, 1976. p. 35. I was expanding on Pedro Salinas, who used Heidegger's terms, *ser-para-la-muerte (Sein zum Tod)*, to describe Lorca in: *Ensayos de literatura hispánica*. Madrid: Aguilar, 1961. p. 393. See also my introduction to: *Federico García Lorca: antología poética*. Barcelona: Plaza & Janés, 1981. p. 58, for a discussion of Lorca's *amante/poeta-para-la-muerte*.

5. Alvarez de Miranda, Alvaro. *La metáfora y el mito*. Madrid: Taurus, 1963. p. 35.

6. Juvenal. *Satires* 10, 1–2. My translation.

7. Francis Fergusson. op. cit., p. 92.

8. Francis Fergusson. op. cit., p. 93.

9. See, for example, the works of Theodor H. Gaster, René Girard, Benjamin Hunningher, and Jan Kott.

10. Rupert Allen. *Psyche and Symbol in the Theater of Federico García Lorca*. Austin and London: University of Texas Press, 1974. pp. 3–112.

11. Robert Bly. *Leaping Poetry*. Boston: Beacon, 1975. pp. 5–6.

12. García Lorca. op. cit., I, p. 184.

13. The old goddesses had been around Andalusia for at least four or five hundred years. For a discussion see especially chapter five, "Goddess," of my study: *White Wall of Spain: The Mysteries of Andalusian Culture*. Ames, Iowa: The Iowa State University Press, 1983.

14. Paraphrased from *White Wall of Spain*, p. 129.

CHRISTOPHER MAURER
Vanderbilt University

Bach and *Bodas de sangre*

Late in the summer of 1932, García Lorca was working in the Huerta San Vicente, nearing completion of *Bodas de sangre*. His sister Isabel remembers him listening, day and night, to records of the *cantaor* Tomás Pavón and of Johann Sebastian Bach.[1] The affinity of Bach and *cante jondo* probably seems less obvious to us than it did to García Lorca, two of whose lectures contain revealing references to the Baroque composer. In "Juego y teoría del duende" (1933), the "vieja bailarina gitana *La Malena*" hears Alexander Brailowsky play a fragment of Bach and exclaims, "¡Olé! ¡Eso tiene duende!" as though to confirm that all great art, both popular and learned, springs from the same dark and unmistakable source.[2] The other mention of Bach occurs in "Arquitectura del cante jondo" (1932): it is a comparison of the melody of the *siguiriya* gitana with that of Bach:

> La *siguiriya* gitana comienza por un grito terrible. Un grito que divide el paisaje en dos hemisferios iguales; después la voz se detiene para dejar paso a un silencio impresionante y medido. Un silencio en el cual fulgura el rastro de lirio caliente que ha dejado la voz por el cielo. Después comienza la melodía ondulante e inacabable en sentido distinto de Bach. La melodía infinita de Bach es redonda. La frase podría repetirse eternamente en un sentido circular; pero la melodía de la *siguiriva* se pierde en el sentido horizontal, se nos escapa de las manos y la vemos alejarse hacia un punto de aspiración común y pasión perfecta donde el alma no logra desembarcar.[3]

What *cante jondo* and Bach have in common, then, is their "melodía ondulante e inacabable," "melodía infinita." Lorca thought that Bach's melody is "redonda", "circular." I wonder if the poet was right: perhaps Bach's melody too is "horizontal." Leonard Bernstein writes of the admiration jazz musicians feel for Bach:

> all primitive music, like Oriental folk music today, is made of *lines,* just as present-day jazz is also primarily involved with line ... [For jazzmen, Bach] is the great model of the continuously running melody, and this is natural, because Bach and the jazz player both feel music in terms of line — that is, horizontally.[4]

One can only guess at the aesthetic qualities Federico must have admired in Bach, and no two readers will agree on them. Was it the austerity, the lack of sentimentality common to Bach and to *cante jondo* which he wanted to emulate?

Years before, in *Impresiones y paisajes,* he had admired the same phenomenon of "less is more," the same illusion of infinity, in the architecture of Gregorian chant, with its "melodía de severidad monumental":

> La melodía, como enorme columna de mármol negro que se
> perdiera entre las nubes, no tiene solución ... Hay jadeares enormes
> en los cuales un sílaba va recorriendo notas y notas, que no tiene la
> resolución que se espera.[5]

Impresiones y paisajes reveals the struggle of a gifted adolescent to reconcile his two vocations of music and literature. Nowhere else in his works are visual phenomena compared so often, and so unconvincingly, to musical ones. Everywhere he looks, he hears "modulaciones" and "acordes" that tell us less of the Spanish landscape than of his own aesthetic emotion.[6] Musical genres are often turned to descriptive use: the bells of Granada form a symphony (169), as do the fields ("inmensa sinfonía en sangre reseca", p. 18). The rustling of leaves reminds the author of a "romanza" (157), and the wind of "solemnes marchas" (38). The silence "reza su canto gregoriano y pasional" (52) and the night seems a "preludio" (27). Naively, the author evokes his favorite composers to characterize an atmosphere or to describe his emotions: "El sollozo de una canción de tarde de Schumann ... pasa dolorosamente por mi alma" (61). "¡Ciudades de Castilla, al contemplaros, tan severas, los labios dicen algo de Haendel!" (21) There is, of course, no attempt to make the prose of *Impresiones y paisajes* emulate that severity. The author's faith in the expressiveness of musical terms and his addiction to synesthesia lead him to the brink of incoherence, or worse:

> En los parajes de intenso sonido como son las sierras, los bosques,
> las llanuras, la gama musical del paisaje tiene casi siempre el mis-
> mo acorde que domina a las demás modulaciones. (166)[7]

In his later works, such imagery grows less frequent, and the relation between music and literature grows complex and interesting. By the early 1930's, he speaks of having written some of his poems in musical time: the same year that *Bodas de sangre* is performed he announces that he has finished a book entitled *Porque te quiero a ti solamente (tanda de valses):* "Eso libro está escrito en tiempo de vals ... Así, dulce, amable, vaporoso."[8]

Notwithstanding the abundant musical imagery of his earliest works, his later experimentation with musical rhythms, and his abiding use of musical titles for poems and even books of poetry, it is in *Bodas de sangre* that García Lorca came closest to endowing a literary text with musical structure, and it is to *Bodas* that we now turn.

Lorca once remarked that it was in Act II, Scene I of *Bodas* (the "¡Despierte la novia!" scene) that he first experimented, timidly, with a dramatic chorus.[9] He seems to have believed that the revival of the chorus, as used in ancient drama, was indispensable to the revival of tragedy in 20th century Spain. There was, however, an equally important generic model for that epithalamium, a model that, to my knowledge, no critic has ever studied, one much more pertinent than the wedding songs in Lope de Vega's *Peribáñez,* so often mentioned in connection with *Bodas de sangre;* and that was the unidentified cantata of Bach to which he listened so insistently as he wrote the play. It is tempting to suppose that the "¡Despierte la novia!" scene is indebted to cantata 140, "Wachet auf, ruft uns die Stimme," a joyful celebration of the symbolic marriage of the daughters of Jerusalem with Christ the bridegroom:

> Wachet auf, ruft uns die Stimme
> Der Wächter sehr hoch auf der Zinne,
> Wach auf, du Stadt Jerusalem!
> Mitternacht heisst diese Stunde;
> Sie rufen uns mit hellem Munde:
> Wo seid ihr klugen Jungfrauen?
> Wohl auf, der Bräutgam kömmt,
> Steht auf, die Lampen nehmt!
> Alleluja!
> Macht euch bereit
> Zu der Hochzeit,
> Ihr müsset ihm entgegengehn!

> "Awake," the voice of watchmen
> calls us from high on the tower,
> "awake, you town Jerusalem!"
> Midnight is this (very) hour;
> they call to us with bright voices:
> "where are you, wise virgins?
> Take cheer, the Bridegroom comes,
> arise, take your lamps!
> Alleluja!
> Prepare yourselves
> for the wedding,
> you must go forth to meet him."[10]

What we hear, Whittaker writes lovingly, is "an amazing scene of excitement and confusion, people rushing to and fro, sounds of voices coming from all quarters of the streets, while the serene and divine announcement of the coming of the Bridegroom peals above the melée."[11] The idea of choral singing cannot have been far from his mind as García Lorca rehearsed *Bodas de sangre* in Madrid (1933). His brother has remembered how difficult it was to bring to life:

> el cuadro de las despedida de la novia, fragmentado en numerosas entradas de personajes desde diferentes y escalonadas alturas, con el juego alterno de voces femeninas y masculinas que se expresan en

versos de extremada riqueza rítmica ... En los ensayos Federico interrumpía innumerables veces el curso de las escena, diciendo: "¡Tiene que ser matemático!"[12]

The actress Josefina Díaz Artigas, who played the Novia, has written:

> [el cuadro de la mañana de la boda,] que decían varias personas distintas, él lo puso como un concertante, que no hubiera una voz que no encajara con la otra ...[13]
> Asoció las voces, su timbre, su fuerza, como un músico asocia los sonidos. Fue un trabajo extraordinario. Gritaba: "¡Tú no! ¡Tienes una voz demasiado aguda! ¡Prueba tú! Me hace falta una voz grave ... Necesito una voz fresca."[14]

In fact, it is not so much thematically as it is structurally that the scene resembles the Bach cantata. For Lorca and Bach are working with the same basic components: aria, recitativo and chorale: in Act II, Scene I of *Bodas,* we find choral and individual singing, as well as short, spoken prose passages. In the first movement of cantata 140, the sopranos' call "Wachet auf" is imitated by the altos, tenors and basses; García Lorca's use of the *estribillo* "¡Despierte la novia!", both sung and spoken by different men, women and children, is akin to Bach's use of "imitative entry." Not surprisingly, the cantata has been compared to a theatrical work:

> The accompanying voices are lively, psychologically apt — and, at one point ... even impatient with the slow pace of the hymn tune. The accompanying voices will do most of their energetic urging-on in carefully-spaced bursts of fervor. As if this were a mass scene on the theater stage, Bach changes the order of their mostly imitative entrances as often as possible.[15]

The preceding observations are meant to invite analysis of the internal "musical" structure of the entire play. But that analysis would have to begin with research on the songs, dances and background music which accompany, and interact with, the written text. The musical texture of *Bodas de sangre* is far more complex than has ever been supposed.

Very little is known of the music Lorca used in his plays, but there exist several excellent sources of information on the music of *Bodas:* various drafts of the English translation *(Bitter Oleander)* made by José Weissberger under Lorca's supervision; the notes taken by Weissberger during Lorca's consultations with Weissberger and Rafael Martínez Nadal in Madrid in June of 1933; the prompt-book of the Neighborhood Playhouse production of *Bitter Oleander* in New York in February, 1935; and the music which Lorca sent to Irene Lewisohn, director of the Playhouse, for that production.[16] The latter was published by Angel del Río in 1941, and has often been reprinted.[17] The other documents have not been consulted until now by students of Lorca's theatre.

That García Lorca took much interest in the New York production is corroborated by newspaper interviews and by the diary of his friend Carlos Morla Lynch.[18] That he himself selected at least some of the music used in New York is proven by an unpublished letter from Irene Lewisohn, who writes Federico, during a return voyage from Spain to New York (in 1934?):

> I have the music carefully stored away, and will put it straight to work when I land the day after tomorrow. It's beautifully arranged, and I am sure will help the atmosphere tremendously. One song, or rather the words are missing; the original song of the horse you sang for me the other day. We spoke of using it before the second scene of Act I. If you can possibly send it to me, I would be most grateful.[19]

Because the manuscripts of the Spanish text contain so few indications regarding the music, its importance is easily forgotten.[20] For example, in the New York production, background music is supplied for almost the whole of Act II, Scene II, the preparations for the wedding feast. The music ceases abruptly with the announcement of the flight of Leonardo and the Bride ("¡Han huido!").

The scene begins with guitar music, as accompaniment to the Criada, who partly speaks and partly sings the long, markedly rhythmical poem "Giraba, / giraba la rueda ... ".[21] The wedding guests and bridal pair enter to the tune of "Los cuatro muleros." A note in the New York prompt-book, in Irene Lewisohn's handwriting, says: "Spanish dance #3. Los muleros. Music Forte." Three more songs which cannot easily be identified are heard before the scene is over. The prompt-book contains only numerical references, e.g. "Andalusian dance [?] No. 6. Music. Lorca'." The mention of "Los muleros" and a reference to "No. 4 Argentinita ..." suggest that these songs may have been selected from the ones García Lorca recorded with Encarnación López Júlvez in 1931. Whether the author himself suggested that they be used is uncertain.

One of the typescripts of *Bitter Oleander,* which Weissberger covered with corrections and notes during his consultations with García Lorca, reminds us of the playwright's belief in the importance of the chorus and his frustration with the actors he had had to work with in Madrid. Lorca had thought of ending the tragedy itself with a choral chant. The bitter, final dialogue between the Bride and the Mother ends on this exchange:

NOVIA: Déjame llorar contigo.
MADRE: Llora, pero en la puerta.

Weissberger notes that, "While mother and novia speak, more women come in, one by one, dressed in black against white walls."[22] The lines that follow, the last ones in the play, were assigned to different characters in the two known versions of the original.[23] In Weissberger's rough draft, as revised by Lorca, the distribution is as follows:

A woman (neighbor)	There was a beautiful horseman and now he is a heap of snow. From fair to fair he cantered and at every fair a woman. Now his brows will be burdened with dark moss of the night.	GIRLS CHANT
Another woman:	Sunflower of your mother, mirror of the earth. Let them put on your breast A cross of bitter adelphas.	
Another woman:	Let them wrap you in a shroud of shining silk. Let the water weep between your quiet hands.	CHANT STOPS
Another woman:	Oh, see the four youths coming with tired shoulders.	
Novia:	Oh, see the four lovers bring death through the air.	
Mother:	Women!	
Little girl:	They bring them. *(In the doorway)*	
Mother:	It does not matter. The cross. (Looking upward with hands to her breast and all the women kneel down weeping.)	
The oldest of all women, with religious gesture:	May the cross protect the living and the dead.	
Mother:	Neighbors, with a knife, with a little knife, on a destined day between two and three, two men killed one another for love. With a knife, with a little knife that hardly fills your hand, but that penetrates finely the astonished flesh	CHANT

and stops on the spot
where trembles, deeply embedded,
the dark root of a scream.

Novia: And this is a knife,
a tiny knife
that hardly fills your hand,
a fish without scales or river.
On a destined day between two and three,
through that same knife
two hardy men
lie here with pallid lips.

(The women on their knees weep)

THE END[24]

There are no directions in the Spanish original as to how these lines are to be spoken, and this makes Weissberger's marginal note, after the words "Sunflower of your mother" (originally assigned to the Bride), an extremely valuable one:

> Federico thinks that instead of Novia the womenfolk like a choir
> should speak these words. But he did not dare to do so in Madrid
> on acct. of poor work of 2nd hand artists.[25]

Much of this final section was to be spoken against the background of the "Viejo romance infantil" published by Del Río: the prompt-book tells us that the chanting began and ended at the place indicated. A note in the Lorca archive, in Weissberger's handwriting, indicates that the only music in the third act is "3 hilanderas" and "cuatro mujeres llorando."[26]

There is another valuable annotation at the beginning of Act III, before the woodcutters' scene, a scene which was especially dear to Lorca for here "el realismo que preside hasta ese instante la tragedia se quiebra y desaparece para dar paso a la fantasía poética, donde es natural que yo me encuentre como pez en el agua."[27] Although the Spanish texts of *Bodas* tell us that the Moon is "un leñador joven con las cara blanca," it is known that in performances in Madrid and Buenos Aires, the moon was played by a girl.[28] In Weissberger's rough draft, before the moon's soliloquy, we find the following note:

> Federico proposed not to personify the moon. Proposes to have
> the verse spoken by an invisible actor, and the light playing on the
> scene with different shades, as if to represent a breathing breast,
> representing with colours and rhythms of light the song of the
> moon. Fears that this solution would not be quite satisfactory, as
> this cliff of personification continues to exist.[29]

It appears that Irene Lewisohn asked Lorca to shorten the Moon's poem. In the end, she persuaded him to delete the character altogether. For some, this long, densely metaphorical poem would be an unwelcome interruption of the action, standing in impossibly sharp contrast to the more realistic tone of the two preceding acts.

"Federico understands the danger," Weissberger writes, "but if victorious it would be a triumph."[30]

García Lorca relied on music to prepare his audience for the strangeness of that poem and for all of Act III. What he said of the music in *La zapatera prodigiosa* is equally true of *Bodas:* "La intervención de la música ... me sirve para desrealizar la escena y quitar a la gente la idea de que aquello 'está pasando de veras,' así como también para elevar el plano poético."[31] The stage directions for Act III, Scene I read as follows: "Bosque. Es de noche. Grandes troncos húmedos. Ambiente oscuro. Se oyen dos violines." It is not known what music those two violins were playing. I have, however, ascertained what the Madrid audience listened to as it waited for that act to begin:

Weissberger's annotation reads: "andante of Brandenburg concerto of Bach. They used a disk in Madrid. It has to sound from afar. When curtain rises, the three woodcutters are on stage, without moving."[32] It is the andante from the second, the best known, of Bach's Brandenburg concerti.[33]

Which brings us back to Bach. Every artist, Lorca remarked in 1934, has a "círculo mágico," a region of the imagination into which he withdraws in order to create.

> ... Va trayendo lo que uno quiere atrapar. Te lo trae. Voces que te dicen: sigue por aquí, escribe esto, di lo otro. *Bodas de sangre,* por ejemplo, está sacada de Bach ... No tiene nada que ver, pero ese tercer acto, eso de la luna, eso del bosque, eso de la muerte rondando, todo eso está en la Cantata de Bach que yo tenía. Donde trabajo, tiene que haber música.[34]

That he mentions Act III, Scene I, rather than Act II, Scene I (¡Despierte la novia!) as having been "taken from" Bach's cantata should remind us of the double influence, both structural and emotional, of the Baroque composer on Lorca's work. Though their structural affinities can, and should, be further explored, we cannot hope to penetrate that "círculo mágico," nor ever find words for what Bach meant to García Lorca. Those who love both of them will rejoice, for now, in the coincidence: Bach and *Bodas de sangre.*   1984

1. García Lorca, Federico. *Bodas de sangre*. Mario Hernández, ed. Madrid: Alianza Editorial, 1984 pp. 20–21 hereafter referred to as *Bodas*.

This lecture was read at the special session on "García Lorca and Music" chaired by Dr. Roger Tinnell at the 1984 convention of the Southern Atlantic Modern Language Association.

2. García Lorca, Federico. *Conferencias* (Vol II). (Christopher Maurer, ed.) Madrid: Alianza Editorial, 1984 — pp. 90–91. The Spanish poet Francisco Giner de Los Ríos has told me that when Lorca took him to see the Albaicín in 1935, Lorca played some records of Bach for a group of Gypsies and heard the same reaction: "¡Olé! ¡Eso tiene duende!" Giner alludes to this incident in his response to "Preguntas sobre Federico García Lorca" in: *Trece de Nieve*. NS 1–2 (1976):225.

3. Maurer, Christopher. op cit. (Vol. I), p. 53, note 4.

4. Bernstein, Leonard. *The Joy of Music*. New York: Simon and Schuster, 1965. p. 233.

5. García Lorca, Federico. *Impresiones y paisajes*. Granada, 1918. pp. 95–96. I have used the facsimile edition published by "Los Libros de Don Alvaro Tarfe" (Granada, 1981). In the quotes that follow, page numbers are given in parentheses.

6. "Acorde" is one of the most overworked images in the book: it is applied to cathedrals, sunsets, light, the landscape, smoke and vegetation, mountains and clouds, villages, olive groves, the "Vega" of Granada, and the howling of dogs.

7. *Impresiones y paisajes*, p. 97.

8. García Lorca, Federico. *Bodas*, p. 196.

9. García Lorca, Federico. *Yerma. Poema trágico*. (Mario Hernández, ed.) Madrid: Alianza Editorial, 1984. p. 142.

10. Bach, J.S. Cantata No. 140, *Wachet auf, ruft uns die Stimme*. (Gerhard Herz, ed.) New York: W.W. Norton & Co., 1972. p. 113.

11. Whittaker, W.G., *The Cantatas of Johann Sebastian Bach: Sacred and Secular*. London: Tocome: 1959.

12. García Lorca, Francisco. *Federico y su mundo*. (Mario Hernandez, ed.) Madrid: Alianza Editorial, 1981. p. 335.

13. García Lorca, Federico. *Bodas de sangre*. (José Monleón, ed.). Barcelona: Aymá, 1971. p. 66, quoted in *Bodas*, pp. 33–34.

14. Auclair, Marcelle. *Vida y muerte de García Lorca*. (Aitana Alberti, tr.) Mexico, Era, 1972. p. 275.

15. Herz, op. cit., p. 118.

16. Using these manuscripts, I am preparing a full study of the translation and New York production of *Bodas*. They are in the Billy Rose Theatre Collection of the New York Public Library (call Nos. NCOF p.v. 359; NCOF p.v. 431; and MWEZ n.c. 10, 238) and in the archives of the Neighborhood Play-

house School of the Theatre, New York. I must thank Miss Alice Owen, the School's Librarian, for her gracious help.

17. Del Río, Angel. *Federico García Lorca (1899–1936). Vida y obra.* New York. Hispanic Institute, 1941. pp. 146–149. The manuscript from which del Río copied the music is now in the Billy Rose Collection (MWEZ n.c. 10, 238). Del Rio published the songs in the wrong order ("Viejo romance infantil" is last in the series).

18. *Bodas,* pp. 203–24, 214–215; and Morla Lynch, Carlos. *En España con Federico García Lorca (Páginas de un diario íntimo. 1928–1936),* Madrid: Aguilar, 1958. p. 363.

19. Archives of the Fundación Federico García Lorca, Madrid. The letter was uncatalogued at time of writing. I am grateful to Isabel García Lorca and to Manuel Fernández Montesinos for permission to consult it. Lewisohn seems to be referring to the "Canción de cuna" found in Del Río, op. cit., p. 149.

20. The musical indications found in the Neighborhood Playhouse promptbook are listed here, in the hope they will be of interest to some future director of *Bodas de sangre.* (Numerical references are to page and line in the M. Hernández edition of *Bodas:* "fb" means "from the bottom"):

Act I, Scene II
80,12 to 89,7fb: directions on when MUJER and SUEGRA should "hush" (i.e. hush the baby) and when they should "hum."

Act II, Scene I
107,14: novia [sic] starts to dance.
109,10: Song [begins]
110,3: [after "Un poco"]: Stop song
113,2: Song coming up. No castanettes.
113,5fb: ser. swings 1st g[irl] round
113,1fb: girls dance around servant taking her by hands
116,1: speaks as girls gather round her. Great movement
116,15: stop music
117,11fb: Song, Music
117,5fb: castanets stop
118,2: Music Estrale [="Acuérdate que sales / como una estrella"?]
       Enter musicians. forte music
119,12–16: Music playing *piano*
119,17: 2nd wedding [song — "Al salir de tu casa"?] guitars
119,1fb: Music *piano*
120,10fb: music [stops] forte.
122,4fb: guitars playing
123,1: sings

123,3: speaks
123,1fb: music stop
126,3fb: Music. Spanish dance #. Los Mularos [sic] music *forte*
130,9fb: Nº 4 Argentinita Tango [partly erased]
131,1fb: music stop
132,10fb: Nº 5 music Andalusia
135,8fb: music stop
136,17: [illegible: Andalusian dance?] No 6 music Lorca's swell
    castanets
137,8fb: Crowd. Music *forte* swell
139,4fb: Swell music
141,4: music stop

Act III, Scene II
160,11fb: girls chant
161,6: chant
161,9fb: chant
161,7fb: chant stops
169ff: as shown on pp. 100–09, below.

21. The preliminary budget for *Bodas* (Nov. 16, 1934), a copy of which is in the NPST archives, allocates money for two musicians.

22. NPST, "English script, copy 3. Bodas de sangre, Federico García Lorca," Act III, p. 30.

23. *Bodas,* p. 221 ff.

24. "English script, copy 3," Act III, pp. 31–33. In the right-hand margin I have copied the musical directions from the prompt-book in the NYPL.

25. "English script, copy 3," Act III, p. 4.

26. For Act II, the note mentions: "Boda, Despierte la novia," "Al salir de tu casa," "Campanilleros [?]," "Nana," and "Criada (1ª escena, 2º acto)."

27. *Bodas,* p. 184.

28. *Bodas,* pp. 218–219.

29. "English script, copy 3," Act III, p. 4.

30. *Ibid.*

31. García Lorca, Federico. *La zapatera prodigiosa.* (Mario Hernández, ed.) Madrid: Alianza Editorial, 1982. p. 141.

32. NCOF p.v. 431, Act III, p. 1.

33. Another movement entitled "Andante" occurs in the fourth concerto, but would hardly provide the right atmosphere for Act III, Scene I.

34. Quoted by Andrew A. Anderson in: "García Lorca en Montevideo: Un testimonio desconocido y más evidencia sobre la evolución de *Poeta en Nueva York." Bulletin Hispanique* LXXXIII (1981): p. 156.

ROBERT LIMA
Pennsylvania State University

Towards the Dionysiac: Pagan Elements and Rites in *Yerma*

> "What a terrible loss not to be able to
> feel the teachings of the ancients!"[1]
>
> F.G.L., *Yerma*

Second in García Lorca's trilogy of rural tragedies, which includes *Bodas de sangre* and *La casa de Bernarda Alba, Yerma* examines human sexuality in a perspective differentiated from that of its companion works. In *Yerma,* Lorca assesses the nulliparal state of his titular protagonist, the attendant frustration brought about by her unfulfilled desire for a child of her own, and the tragic consequences of her despair.[2]

But the play is not only a study of maternal instinct gone awry. It is also a powerful statement on two polarities that govern the characters' lives and effect massive changes thereof when the contrasting systems are placed in direct and open conflict.

Yerma's is a distinctive struggle between two diametrically opposed aspects of European life in general and Spanish life in particular — the veneer of the Christian ethos and the substratum of pagan tradition. Lorca's protagonist is victimized by the social and religious codes of a Christian milieu, codes which frustrate human drives and are, therefore, *contra natura* in the eyes of the play-wright. In sharp contrast is the naturalness of those who follow the old pagan ways, especially in instinctual and sexual matters: theirs is a holistic state, a wellness both of body and spirit, as Lorca sees it, for they have attained a state of integration in which the Apollonian and the Dionysiac modes are in harmony.[3] Out of this cohesiveness comes the fullness of human potential.

Throughout *Yerma,* Lorca focuses on the contrasting forces at work on the protagonist, as well as on the means towards their resolution. He does so by introducing natural factors that are in obvious opposition to the unnatural state of affairs in Yerma's relationship with each of the three men in her life — her husband Juan, her dream man Victor, and her potential lover (the son of La Vieja). Simply put, Yerma rejects all three in one manner or another: she views Juan only as a means to an end — procreation legitimized — and never as a man to be desired for himself; Victor, the only man to have aroused her sexual instinct, was not chosen by her father as her husband and she neither protested nor sought him as a lover; and the virile young man who awaits her, meaningfully behind the church, is never given the opportunity to make love to her. For Yerma, only that which is socially and morally legitimate can be considered as a potential cure for her barrenness. Thus, she spends herself berating Juan for his callous indifference to her maternal need, or envisioning Victor with a child that might have been theirs had she been given to the shepherd in marriage,[4] or indignantly rejecting La Vieja's celestinesque pandering on her son's behalf. The temptation of that which is illict cannot overcome her resolve to live within the social and moral bounds of her Christian upbringing.

Yerma comes closest to crossing that barrier when she makes a desperate visit to Dolores the Conjurer. The old crone, who services the more esoteric needs of the villagers, leads Yerma to the nearby cemetery, where prayers are offered and conjurations performed to cure her infertility. This, Yerma's first inclination towards the pagan, is the result of the inevitable surfacing of instincts long suppressed; these emanate from her pagan substratum and threaten to erode the protagonist's Christian bulwarks. Put in other terms, the primal forces of Dionysus are arrayed against the cilivized minions of Apollo, and Yerma is to be the battleground.[5]

The most pervasive and, therefore, notable factors that Lorca marshalls against the Christian ethos and its Apollonian counterpart are the four cardinal Elements: Earth, Water, Air and Fire. The lore of the Elements has its origin in antiquity and manifests itself in all inhabited continents of the world, having various and diverse associations with the four seasons of the year, the four "humors" that characterize human temperament, the four points of the compass, as well as colors, gender, signs of the Zodiac, deities, totems and the ages of humanity.[6] Wherever they appear, the four Elements constitute the foundation of all that exists. So pervasive was this belief, that it survived in Europe in Hermeticism, Alchemy and rudimentary sciences until the Apollonian "Age of Reason" caused the demise of many of the ancient world's concepts. And yet, the Elements survived, if metamorphosed into symbols of lesser impact.

The four Elements begin to appear in the very first scene of *Yerma,* either singly or in combinations, and continue to be a major frame of reference in the rest of the play. Through the Elements, Lorca is able to create a symbolic pattern that is both ironic (in that it is Yerma who most frequently and intuitively refers to the pagan Elements, yet cannot assimilate them) and portentous (in that they build towards the full manifestation of the Dionysiac in the final scene of the play).

Earth is the first Element introduced. It is manifested, if somewhat indirectly, in an off-stage lullaby at the very beginning of the play:

> For the baby, baby, baby,
> for the baby we will make
> a cute little hut in the field
> and refuge in it we'll take. (11)

"El campo," the field, is the manifestation of the Element Earth. As such, it is the foundation for "una chocita," a hut which will shelter the child and the singer of the lullaby. If the singer is the mother, then Earth, child and woman are immediately bound together. This relationship demonstrates the traditional view of this Element's association with birthing and nurture, of Earth as the Great Mother out of whose womb came many living things. Earth is, therefore, a female Element in ancient systems of belief.[7]

Just as many living things originate in this Element, Lorca's drama begins with "el campo" and goes on to establish Yerma's relationship to Earth. Early in the play, Yerma herself makes the significant connection when she explains to her friend María: "Often at night I go barefoot into the patio to feel the earth without knowing why." (20) Although she does not know what motivates her, she follows the instinct that prompts her to tread the ground with bare feet. Yerma senses that she must be in physical contact with the soil underfoot, thus identifying with Earth.

Yerma's husband, Juan, also has an association with the soil. His longstanding commitment to it is evident in the time that he devotes to farming and in the way that he speaks of the fields: "My life is in the fields." (55) But Juan fails to recognize in Yerma the other soil that he must fertilize towards her personal fruition as a mother. He desires in her only the pleasures of sexual union, abhorring the thought of procreation. Juan also experiences the soil in a physical manner, but his involvement with it culminates in its fecundity.

The attention that Juan gives his wife pales in comparison. Unlike the soil that he perpetually tills, plants and sleeps on, Yerma is uncared for, has not been impregnated, and is frequently left to sleep alone. Thus, she must find a way to attract Juan as much as the soil that he farms if she too is to become fertile. Since Juan is seldom at home, Yerma must go where that productive life is lived, to the fields.

Yerma trudges daily to those fields to fulfill her obligation of bringing her husband his food. What she has yet to learn is that she must also feed his other appetite — for the lover that he craves to find in her. But she must give herself wholly, like the earth to the farmer, in order to attain the fulfillment of her potential as a woman. Like La Vieja, who tells her "I've lain on my back and started to sing." (27), Yerma must willingly lie prone on the earth and let its chthonian powers arouse her senses towards the sexual enjoyment of her husband as a man. For that end to be realized, Yerma must undergo a major transformation: only with her rebirth as an earthy woman capable of satisfying her husband's passion for her earthy body will she find herself as productive as the fields that Juan farms. Only then will Victor's words to Yerma at the end of the first scene — "¡que ahonde!" — be fulfilled by Juan. The verb *ahondar* means to dig, to deepen, to go deep into, to penetrate: Victor is telling Yerma that Juan must enter her deeply, tilling her into fecundity, as he does the earth. Yerma repeats his words passionately — "Yes! Let him penetrate!" (24) — but immediately returns to the thoughts she had expressed in an earlier soliloquy:

> Oh yes, I would say, my child,
> for you I'd be severed and torn.
> How painful this waist has become
> where first your cradle will be!
> When, child of mine, will you come?
> When jasmine has perfumed your flesh!(24)

Yerma has clearly misinterpreted the intent of Victor's words. Instead of comprehending the strongly sexual connotation of the phrase, which he had underscored with a knowing smile, Yermas has taken it to signify a means to quite a different end — the fulfillment of her maternal desire. What she has failed to recognize is that she must put aside her fixation and yield to Juan; she must become "tronchada y rota" for her husband, not for the dream child that the "tí" addresses. She must become lover before she can become mother. Only when she abandons her egocentricity and accepts this natural state will she possess that scent of jasmine that will herald her body's fecundity. She will only become like the earth when she opens herself to the Dionysiac.

Even so, other factors must come to bear before the natural course of events can follow. Despite Juan's intense attention to the fields, it has been very difficult for him to make them productive. But even if his labor takes its toll on his body, as Yerma reminds him, Juan sees strength rather than weakness in his situation: "When men are (enjutos) dried up, they become as strong as steel." (12) Yet, if the condition of steel is improved by its dryness, the state of man is not. The word "enjuto" means wizened, shrivelled up, arid, dry; when applied to Juan, "enjuto" indicates a serious lack in his constitution.

What Juan lacks is symbolized by the second Element, Water. The soil that Juan works so diligently must be irrigated by the scant water allotted to him by a community cursed with little precipitation and few rivers. As Juan tells Yerma: "I'll spend the whole night irrigating. What little water there is belongs to me until the sun comes up and I have to keep watch for thieves." (40) Just as he has minimal amounts of water to give the parched soil, so too is he unable to quench the thirst of his wife. It is a situation that Yerma herself brings to the fore when she expresses her concern and proposes a solution to Juan: "I would like to see you go to the river and swim, see you go to the roof when the rain drenches our house." (12) Yerma's invocation of two types of water — the river water and the rain — harkens back to an ancient conception of the Element's dualistic nature. The water of the river, like all water present on the surface or in the innards of the planet, was referred to in antiquity as "Lower Water" and symbolized actuality; the water that came down in the form of rain or dew was thought of as "Upper Water" and symbolized potentiality.[8] Dew, furthermore, was symbolic of semen.[9]

Intuitively, Yerma wants these symbols of what exists and what could be to come together in her husband. She wants Juan to swim in the river so that its water may reinforce what is already in his being; she wants him to be exposed to the rain so that its water may stimulate a new vitality in his body. The respective activity and receptivity would construe beneficial rites of passage. Swimming in the river (an immersion) and being sprinkled by the rain (an aspersion) represent two forms of initiation. They also signify both an annihilation (or "death") of the old indentity by a symbolic drowning in the water of reality and a regeneration (or "rebirth") of the life force by a symbolic reemergence through the water of potentiality, as that of the womb. Exposed to these aspects of Water, Juan would no longer be "enjuto;" rather, as Yerma believes, he would be able to impregnate her. Just as lower and upper waters work together to stimulate seeds to take root and thrive, so too would Juan's revitalized semen instigate growth in Yerma's womb.

Victor, the dream man in Yerma's life, needs no such rite of passage. His association with Water is consistent and positive, as evident in Yerma's encounters with his virility in their youth. This is established in the first scene when Yerma tells La Vieja of her reactions to Victor's exuberance: "He took me (*me cogió*) by the waist and I couldn't say anything to him because I couldn't speak. Another time when I was fourteen, that same Victor (who was very big) took me (*me cogió*) in his arms to jump over a water ditch; I was shaking so much that my teeth rattled." (28) The symbolism that attaches to his jumping over the irrigation ditch with Yerma in his arms clearly associates Victor with Water — his is the fluid that could flow through the channel that is Yerma, just as water is intended to flow through the irrigation ditch. Furthermore, the use of "me cogió" in Yerma's narration of both incidents may refer to the sexual possession implicit in Victor's embraces if the verb *coger* is given the prurient interpretation that it has in some areas;[10] to do so would reinforce the symbolism of Victor's fluid flowing through Yerma.

Unlike the Earth-Water axis in the Yerma-Juan relationship, the symbolic union of these Elements when Victor carried Yerma over the irrigation ditch was positive, highly charged and potentially fruitful. That these factors are still evident years later is attested by the encounter of Yerma and Victor in the second scene of the first act. There, having heard a man singing off-stage, Yerma listens intently to his words, but when the singer emerges, she is surprised to find that it was Victor who sang so movingly: "How well you sing! I had never heard you ... And what a gushing voice. It's as if a torrent of water fills your mouth." (36) Her association of Victor with water, and in particular with a torrent of water emanating from his mouth, reinforces the image that La Vieja had stated earlier: "We have to have men we like, girl. They have to undo our tresses and give us water to drink from their own mouths." (29) It was also La Vieja who had told her that "Children come like water." (27) But it is now too late for Yerma to drink the water from Victor's mouth. Because she is married, her mores will not permit an illicit dalliance even though her need to quench her maternal thirst might be thought of as justifying the means, particularly when her husband "Has an arid nature." (36) and Victor is aquaeousness personified. So great is Victor's affiliation with life-giving Water, that the intense silent struggle between him and Yerma over their natural but impossible love culminates in the crying of a child that only she hears, a child that very close by "was crying as if drowned" (38). The child that could have been theirs must forever be drowned in that water that Victor symbolizes.

Since it is impossible for Yerma to become the conduit for his fluid, the natural flow is impeded. Thus, in the opening scene of the following act, Victor's torrent of water is replaced by "the cold brook" (43) in which gossiping women wash the laundry — water having become only a means to a routine end. Significantly, the very first item referred to in their laundering song is "tu cinta," the sash associated with pregnancy ("Estar encinta" means to be pregnant), but here it is being washed in the "arroyo frío" that represents both Victor's inaccessibility and Juan's cold aloofness.

In Yerma's encounters with both men, Water has been dealt with as a male-oriented Element. However, Water is traditionally, with Earth, a female Element in most ancient religions and mythological systems because of its capacity to bear life. This is encapsulated in a saying attributed to Moses: "Only Earth and Water bring forth a living soul."[11] Earth and Water are also female procreative Elements in the *Corpus Hermeticum*[12] and numerous other esoteric writings, where they are frequently interlaced: Water is the fluid of the Earth Mother's womb and the substance of the Sea, in both of which life is nurtured: Water is the sustaining life-fluid (sap, milk, blood) of all Nature: Water in springs, fountains and wells is the sacred emanation of the female numen resident in Mother Earth. Seen in the female orientation, the river water and the rain by which Yerma wishes Juan to be bathed are meant to infuse in her husband the feminine Element as a complement to his masculinity. But whereas Juan's present state makes him incomplete, Victor's condition is one of wholeness for he contains the fecundizing fluid which could engender Yerma's child.

Unable to motivate Juan to perform the ablutions she desires, Yerma must bring the sacred water to him. Her daily task of going to the fountain for water is, therefore, of larger import than that of a mere household task. In her role as water-bearer, Yerma daily recreates the ancient pagan custom of pilgrimage to places where water rises from the earth; in this case, she goes to the fountain at the center of the village (Water is at the center of life). When Yerma fills the earthen jars with water, the vessels become female symbols of plenitude for they hold the numinous emanation of the deep, the Water of Mother Earth. Quite in contrast, the same jars filled with the same water become symbols of sterility in the hands of Juan's spinster sisters.

But Yerma's daily rite is to no personal avail because the water in the earthen jars remains only a symbol of potentiality. Earth and Water may be the only Elements capable of bearing life, but in reality the female must be impregnated by the male if procreation is to occur. Yerma may, despairingly, see men negatively — "They are stones that stand before me. But the don't know that if I wanted it, I could become the rushing water that would carry them." (64) — but she cannot conceive without the semen of the male; thus, the water that she says she could become would be as that of the "arroyo frío," unsuitable for anything more than the menial task of laundering. Similarly, the process of completion cannot occur without the co-joining of the male Elements.

In those cosmogonies which consider it the primary Element, Air is held to be male and active because of its association with the "breath of life" (as in the Old Testament, when Yahweh performs the ultimate act of creation by breathing life into Adamic Man),[13] with the dynamics of storms and winds, and with the concept of flight (into the male dominion of a god, such as Saturn or the Gnostic's Unknowable God). Furthermore, Air is the medium through which movement occurs, as well as the Element which surrounds all things in Nature, envelopment being suggestive of the male's sexual embrace of the female.

There are many and varied references to Air in the play. In the first scene, Yerma bemoans the irony that even worthless plants are caressed by the pollen-bearing air, flaunting "their yellow flowers in the air" (14), and that "the wind sings in the trees" (15), agitating the numerous leaves. Seeking the same plenitude, Yerma "raises her arms in a beautiful yawn" (15), a ritualistic deep inhalation of the air that has made nature fertile. But Yerma fails to recognize the fact that she cannot be passive, like the flowers and trees; in order for her own fruition to take place, she must actively manifest her sexuality. This is the lesson that La Vieja tries to instill in her through example: "I have always been a woman with her skirt in the air" (26); her "free as air" attitude has fulfilled her as a lover, having had two husbands, and as a mother, having given birth to fourteen children. But Yerma finds it impossible to follow her lead for she lives by one code and La Vieja "lives on the other side of the river" (26), where the pagan way of life thrives. Nonetheless, when La Vieja tries to end the fruitless conversation, Yerma makes a last effort to arouse the old woman into answering her searching questions — "and you, knowing everything, leave with your mighty airs" (30) — but to no avail.

When, in time, Yerma's unwillingness to change brings increased frustration over her barren condition, Air is cast in a negative role. In a dreamy soliloquy, after an encounter with Juan, Yerma bemoans the fact "I ask to suffer with child, and the air / offers me dahlias of a sleeping moon." (61) After a later heated conversation with her husband, she alludes to herself as the victim of "the evil airs" (83), comparing her state to that of the good wheat that bad winds have blown to the ground. Ultimately fed up with her lamentations, Juan turns on her and berates her for the fixation "with things that drift in the air." (98)

But the most telling function of Air in *Yerma* is described in one of the early stage directions. After a conversation with Victor at the end of the first scene, Yerma "goes to the spot where Victor has stood and breathes deeply, as if inhaling mountain air" (24). This ritualized breathing of air is very distinct from the earlier generalized inhaling of the air that fertilized the flora. It is Victor's specific virility, symbolized in the breath he has exhaled and in the air that has surrounded him, that Yerma inhales so fervently, as if taking into her being the air that touched him could in itself make her fecund.

It is appropriate for Yerma to associate the male Element with Victor because he is the embodiment of maleness in the play; as such, Yerma realizes, if too late, that he has always had the potential to satisfy her fully. Such is the power latent in Victor. To breathe in the air of a potent man is, therefore an action full of sexual significance; furthermore, the stage direction refers to Yerma as inhaling "aire de montaña," the cold, hard-edged and penetrating mountain air that Nietzsche has termed phallic.[14] This sexual connotation is reinforced by one of the washerwomen, who sings: "And the tents of the wind cover the mountains." (52) The coursing wind covers the mountains just as potent men cover women during coition. Such is the role of any male worthy of the name in the context of the work, as another washerwoman gleefully sings: "Through the air is coming / my husband to sleep." (51) "Sleep" (dormir) is the lightly veiled reference to sexual intercourse, and Air is the Element that conveys the male's potency.

But, as with the sterile union of Earth and Water, the joining of Earth and Air is ineffectual. Yerma may be symbolically united to Victor in their respective associations with Earth and Air, female and male Elements, but there is nothing to change their inert status into an interaction towards procreation. As in the mixture placed in the athanor, the alchemical furnace, there must be present an agent of transmutation. That catalyst is the final Element, Fire.

Fire is the other male Element. In esoteric traditions, it functioned as an agent of purgation (the purifying fire of the ascetic), of transmutation (the alchemical fire that changed base metals into gold), and of regeneration (the consuming fire out of whose ashes rises the Phoenix). Fire also has a traditional association with well-being or ill-health, depending on the fluctuations of body heat between normalcy and extremes beyond or under it. Its relationship to the Sun in ancient religions and mythologies is universal, often being considered as worthy of deification itself as an emanation of the heavenly body.[15] Sometimes, as in Celtic Europe, fire was the focus of major rituals in which bonfires, torches and hearth fires were lit to propitiate ancestor spirits, to stimulate the fertility of fields, animals and humans, or to attempt magically to forestall the Sun's departure in winter (as in the festival of Samhaim), or to herald the Sun's return in spring and welcome all its blessings (as in the festival of Beltane). In Christian times, many pagan symbols were taken over and adapted, among them Fire, both in its negative aspect (reinterpreted as the fires of Hell) and in its positive aspect (visualized as the inspirational fire-tongues of Pentecost).

Many such symbolic uses of Fire appear in *Yerma*. Passion, of course, is symbolized by this Element, and the lack of passion is an early concern of the protagonist when she addresses her husband: "Now your face is as white as if the sun hadn't shone on it." (12) Juan's face lacks the color of life — the ruddiness of blood — of passion, of fire. He is pale and morose. In contrast, when Yerma sees Victor, she notices a mark on his face that is "like a burn" (37) and he explains "It must be from the sun." Victor's passionate nature is symbolically evident on his face, as if an inner fire was burning through in an attempt to manifest itself outwardly. Victor possesses the signs of a sanguine personality — the ruddiness, cheerfulness and hopeful spirit which in early physiology were the outward signs of abundant, healthy blood and an active circulation. Again, Victor epitomizes the potentiality of an Element, in this case, Fire.

Yerma is also involved with the Element, but not in the positive context of Fire's basic symbolism. Her capricious embrace of her husband, "she taking the initiative" (14), is not expressive of the fiery passion of sexual desire: rather, it represents her ardent quest to become pregnant, with copulation considered only as the means to that end. Because of Juan's antagonism, Yerma's maternal drive has no proper outlet. Her fixation with fecundization is a flame that sears her very being, as she admits: "I don't think it's fair for me to be consumed here." (20) Yerma's association with Fire, therefore, is as a victim. As one of the washerwomen says of her situation: "With every hour that passes the hell in that house increases ... for the greater the dazzle of the household, the greatere the burning inside." (47) Yerma would like to exchange that victimizing fire for one that would enliven her womb: "I sense that those who have given birth recently possess something like an inner glow." (76)

The possibility that Yermas has decided to pursue the illicit Fire that would fulfill her maternal need becomes plausible when, at the end of the second act, one of Juan's spinster sisters searches for her with a large candle, itself an ironic symbol of maleness in her hand. When the bells of Victor's flock of sheep are heard off-stage, it would appear that Yerma has indeed gone to seek out Victor.

But Yerma has not taken that course. What she has done is steal away in pursuit of another Fire, that of esoteric knowledge. Yerma has taken a direction which, if not illicit, is certainly borderline in terms of her moral stance: she has gone in search of Dolores the Conjurer, the village wise-woman. The ritual to which the hag subjects Yerma in the cemetery is not shown but subsequent references to it indicate that it contained a syncretic mixture of pagan incantations — "The laurel petition twice" (79) — and Christian prayers — "and the prayer to Saint Ann at midday" — which Yerma is to continue daily. The need to placate the pagan gods is emphasized more than the need to pray to the Christian saint. The greater efficacy of the Dionysiac is thus underscored.

After the ritual, Yerma explains how the hope of having a child is kept aglow in her being: "Sometimes, when I'm certain that it'll never happen ... something like a surge of fire goes through my feet" (77) But such feelings occur only when she is alone; in bed with Juan, matters are very different: "When he lies on me, he's doing his duty; yet, his waist is cold against me, as if his body were dead. And I, who have always been disgusted by passionate women, would like to be a mountain of fire at that moment." (78) Juan's lack of passion is pitted against Yerma's flaming desire; the consumption implicit here will be effected in the climax of the tragedy.

Yerma's words unify two of the Elements — Earth ("montaña") and Fire ("fuego"); earlier, she had similarly brought together in herself Water ("I could be rushing watet") and Air ("and breathes deeply, as if inhaling mountain air"). This need to have all the Elements coalesce in her being proceeds from Yerma's view of men as useless in her life and from her subsequent desire to be self-sufficient in the context of child-bearing: "Oh, if only I could have them by myself!" (78) But Yerma's androgynous daydream cannot be and so she must continue to weigh her need against the social and religious constraints that she has chosen to honor. The presence of Victor is ever a reminder of what might have been; it is also a temptation.

First associated with Air and now with Fire, the male Elements, Victor combines the maleness requisite to interact with Yerma's femaleness. The natural conjunction Earth-Fire, which the union of Yerma and Victor would represent on one plane, would be enhanced on another level by the conjunction Water-Air, their other axis, thus bringing about that tetralogical unification of the Elements necessary for fecundity. Yerma had longed for this very union in the first scene

of the play where, threading a needle (a symbol of sexual integration), she solil-
oquized in an imagined dialogue with her child:

> O child, what is it you seek from afar?
> White mountains that lie on your breast.
> Let branches wave wildly in sunlight
> and fountains leap high all around! (16)

The soliloquy unifies the Elements — "montes" and "ramas" (Earth), "agiten"
and "salten" (Air), "sol" (Fire) and "fuentes" (Water) — but only in Yerma's
dream dialogue. In her reality, the integration of the Elements is not actualized
because Yerma cannot give herself to the natural course, the Dionysiac, that
would end her distress. The Fire of Victor is never permitted to burn in the
Earth of Yerma, nor is his Air allowed to permeate her Water.

Having erected the structure and developed the symbolic interaction of the
four Elements in the lives of his principal characters, Lorca proceeds to show the
contrasting pattern in the lives of those who follow the pagan, that is, the natural way, by having the Elements cohese in the last scene of the play, where the
Dionysiac is dominant in its encounter with the Apollonian.

Whereas the pagan substratum of the society in *Yerma* is viewed
intermittently during the rest of the play, and primarily through dialogue rather
than action, the "Romería" scene is the enactment of a pagan fertility rite within
the setting of a Christian pilgrimage. Yearly, the barren women of the vicinity
tramp to the mountain sanctuary (Earth) of an unnamed male saint to pray for
his intercession in attaining the grace of fecundity. After drinking holy water
(Water), the women process barefooted, feet in direct contact with the soil
(Earth), through the night with the solemnity of candles (Fire) and chants that
pervade the air (Air). Each woman brings an offering to the male saint.

Both the trappings of Christianity and the married state of the women are
mocked immediately upon the start of the scene in an off-stage song which sets
the tone and defines the real purpose of the "Romería":

> I couldn't be with you
> when you were a maid,
> but now that you're wed
> I'll take you to bed.
> And naked I'll make you,
> you pilgrim and wife,
> when out of that darkness
> the bell tolls midnight. (86)

The lecherous cynicism of the song is reinforced by La Vieja's cutting remarks
to the solemn women: "You come to ask the Saint for children and every year
more men come alone on this pilgrimage; just what is going on?" (87) Her
laughter punctuates the rhetorical question which, unanswerable, establishes the

hypocrisy of the women. The offerings by the women to the male saint will be less efficacious than those to be made to the numerous males present. Another female bystander amplifies the count of males at the "Romería" and in the process reestablishes the symbolic association of men and Water: "A river of single men comes down from those hills." (88) It is this river of men coming down the mountain slopes (Earth) that will fertilize the women, not the grace of God sought through the saint's intercession, for as La Vieja said of God earlier: "When are you going to realize that he doesn't exist?" (30) For the miracle of fecundity to take place, the women must give themselves to that river of men, as do the sierras to the water that runs down their slopes. Yerma had the opportunity to do just that with Victor, but realizing that she would not act dishonorably, he has left the village. Under the circumstances, not to take the natural course towards fulfillment — sexual relations outside of the non-productive marriage — is to court even greater frustration. Such is the case of the woman who "Has been coming for eight years without result." (87) For those who only pray, the *Romería* bears no results and only serves to demonstrate the inefficacy of Christian prayer. Thus, Yerma and her fellow supplicants must help themselves if they are to satisfy their maternal need. The *Romería* provides both the setting and the means for that activity which must precede the fecundity they seek.

The revels of the modern pagan feast are remnants of the Dionysian worship that spread through the Mediterranean world in antiquity. Dionysus was a nature deity and as such was associated with many of its manifestations, including the products of the earth, grapes and corn among them; one particularly important affiliation was with the fig tree and its fruit, symbolic of the female. Besides his relationship to flora, Dionysus was also manifested in the form of various fauna, notably the goat and the bull, animals which symbolized his status as a god born with horns.[16] What's more, Dionysus personified the male principle in Nature, entering the female (the Earth Goddess) by dying after the harvest, making her fecund again in the spring with his resurrection. Dionysus, therefore, was a fertility deity whose cyclical death and resurrection brought together the male and female principles in a natural bond. The copulation that marked his worship imitated the sacred union and was, therefore, an act of sympathetic magic that sought to ensure the fertility and continuity of all life, even in the face of death.

It is this ancient tradition that permeates the Romería scene in *Yerma*. After the staid, funereal Christian procession of the barren women at the opening, the inner scene of the Dionysian love feast bursts upon the senses. Nubile girls enter running, gracefully twirling ribbons symbolic of pregnancy. Their entrance is announced by the ringing of many different animal bells, themselves symbolic of the procreative energy of the fauna. All this commotion is in preparation for the appearance of two masked figures.

(The noise increases and two traditional masked figures appear.
One is male and the other female. They were large masks. El
Macho has the horn of the bull clenched in one hand. Rather than

> grotesque, they are of great beauty and possess a quality of pure
> earthiness. La Hembra shakes a neckpiece of large bells.) (90)

The children, with typical Christian ignorance of pagan tradition, misidentify the
masks as the Devil and his wife.[17] But El Macho and La Hembra are popular
representations of the age-old symbols of fertility associated with Dionysus and
his consort, the Earth Goddess; thus, Lorca identifies them as being "de pura
tierra."

In this powerful dance scene with dialogue, the Elements are finally brought
together towards actualization in the women who will follow the pagan way. As
La Hembra sings first of the barren wife, her words show that all the Elements
are indeed at hand:

> In the river of the mountain
> the mournful wife would bathe.
> Over her body, the spirals
> of water would ascend.
> The sand of the shores
> and the air of morning
> brought fire to her laugh
> and a shiver to her back.
> Oh, how naked was the maiden
> who bathed in the water! (91)

Like Yerma, the woman in the ballad has all the Elements within her reach and
needs only the natural inclination to cojoin them in a procreative way within
herself. It is during the Dionysian Romería, which celebrates that most fundamental of human encounters — mating, that the time is propitious for such action: as La Hembra proclaims: "When the night of the revels comes round / I
will shred the ruffles of my petticoat." (91) Only by tearing apart her own
undergarments (a rending akin to that in the Dionysian rites and, here, symbolic
of Yerma's need to shred her oppressive Christian mores) will the woman be
able to find the fruition that she seeks. Thus, El Macho sings of her as he
moves the phallic horn suggestively: "Poppy and carnation she'll then become /
when El Macho spreads his cape on the ground." (92) Just as nature flowers in
spring through the rebirth of Dionysus, so will the married woman who gives
herself freely to a virile man. Then El Macho, approaching La Hembra with the
patent sensuality of the gypsy tablao flamenco and the overt sexuality of the
Dionysian bacchanale, sings of how the orgiastic spirit must resolve itself into
the sexual union of one man and one woman:

> Go by yourself behind the walls
> where the fig trees are densest
> and there bear my earthen body
> till the white whimper of dawn. (92)

The encounter will take place where the fig trees are densest, the fig being symbolic of the vagina ("cerradas" could also be taken literally as closed, thus the closed vagina is to be opened in the sexual union). In that Dionysian setting, El Macho's earthiness ("cuerpo de tierra" could be earthy body, body made of earth, or body that belongs on or to the earth, as with that of the dying-resurrected Dionysus) will transform the barren wife into a mother. Once again, Fire is the Element that will serve as the agent of the transformation. As she undergoes the Dionysian initiation, the woman will respond with the same fiery passion that La Hembra shows in her sexual dance: "Oh, how she glows! / Oh, how she glows, / oh how the married woman quakes!" (92) The verb *cimbrear (cimbrar)* means to shake, sway, bend, vibrate, tremble, or quiver. *Cimbre* means subterranean passage or gallery. Used with the verb *relumbrar* (to be aglow, to shine brilliantly, to be afire with passion), "cimbrea" has an obvious sexual meaning, that of passionate quivering in the woman's innermost recesses during coitus. The power of Dionysus is manifested in the physical union of El Macho, the horn, and La Hembra, the fig.

The act of love simulated in the erotic dance is narrated by El Macho as a numerical extravaganza worthy of the Bacchanale's orgiastic ends:

> Seven times she cried out,
> nine she was aroused,
> fifteen times they united
> jasmines with oranges. (93)

The numbers themselves are symbolic of sexuality and fertility. Seven, the most mysterious of numbers to many ancient civilizations and to mystics, in this context is related to the menstrual cycle of women (the lunar month on which a woman's period is based consists of four phases of seven days each): it is the cycle on which all human life depends. And the woman's moaning ("gemía") represents both her sexual pleasure and the pain attendant on her menstruation. Nine is the marker of the transition between simple and compound numbers and is, consequently, the number of initiation (the sexual act is itself initiatory when first performed, as well as integral to entrance in many mystery religions of antiquity): it is also the number of the months of gestation of the human fetus (Lorca emphasizes pregnancy with "levantaba," a word descriptive of the pregnant woman's abdomen). Fifteen is a number of marked erotic symbolism and is, therefore, Dionysiac; from it is derived sic (15=1+5=6), the number of harmony (as in the union of "jazmines con naranjas," with its echo of the earlier "cuando tu carne huela a jazmín"). Lastly, fifteen also stands for woman in the role of mother, a state dependent upon her union with man in the sexual act.[18]

All these numbers are odd, which in Numerology represents the male; thus, the seven, nine and fifteen here are male-dominant integers. In the society that Lorca depicts in *Yerma*, it is the male who instigates the copulative union through his forcefulness and animal lust. El Macho exemplifies this when he states:

> In this pilgrimage
> the male always commands.
> Husbands are bulls.
> The male always commands. (93)

The male principle always rules in a Dionysian rite of fertility. It is "el varón" (he of the rod) who represents both virility and authority, as El Macho with his symbolic horn. Thus, the sexual reward is for the man who takes the initiative: "And the pilgrim flowers / belong to the one who earns them." (93) The lesson for Juan, who is present at the "Romería" but not participating, is obvious: he must act like a lusty man and arouse Yerma's sensuality. But Juan chooses to remain a bystander while the other males — from the child to the older men — are caught up in the frenzy of the torrid dance, shouting lasciviously to El Macho: "Get her now with the horn!" ... "Get her now with the air!" ... "Get her now with the branch!" (93) And El Macho replies:

> Come and behold the fire
> of the woman who bathed! (93)
> . . . .
>
> Let burn both the dance
> and the glimmering body
> of the chaste married woman. (94)

The woman who had bathed alone in the cold water of the stream is now portrayed as being afire, purged of her earlier reluctance by the fire of passion. The Elements, which had been close at hand but inactive, have now been brought together and activated in the crucible of shared passion. It is fitting then that the fertility ritual end with words which herald the procreativity of the woman:

> Heaven has its gardens
> with rosebushes of joy,
> between one bush and another
> is the rose of marvels. (94)

This fruition of nature is symbolic of that achieved by the barren wife who has given herself wholly to the Dionysian spirit. The "rose of marvels" represents the child, the flower that turns a woman into a mother.[19] Such is the reward of those women who follow the pagan way.

What remains is for Yerma to emulate those women. And yet, despite the exhilarating rite of passage that she has witnessed, Yerma refuses La Vieja's offer of her virile son as lover. The approaching tragic consequences of her obstinacy are underscored in the ensuing dialogue by the negative use of the Elements as applied to her; Yerma's references to Water are exemplary: "poisoned pond." ... "Water cannot turn back." ... "I am like a dry field. " ... "What you offer me is a small glass of well water." ... and "Marchita!" (95–97) This last word, more negative than her own name, denotes a condition without hope of reversal. In her own eyes, Yerma has withered; lacking the wherewithal for life herself, she sees no possibility of ever giving life to the child she has so ardently desired. Thus, her husband has no further purpose in her life and, when he belatedly tries to make love to her in the sexual spirit of the "Romería," she rebels against his impassioned embrace. Uttering a primal scream, she strangles him with frenzied force until his body lies inert on the ground, as ironic and useless in death as it was to her in life.

Juan's demise is the culmination of a series of rejections. Besides turning his back selfishly on Yerma's maternal hope, Juan has also rejected a natural principle. Like Pentheus in Euripides' *The Bacchae,* who went to the Dionysian feast to mock the god and his rites, Juan attended the Romería with cynical disdain. Both Pentheus and Juan failed to give Dionysus his due and, as a consequence, each forfeited his life as a sacrificial victim. The death of each represents not only the deletion of the individual in life but, especially, the termination of his line: an irreversible sterilization. Just as Pentheus will be incapable of continuing the male line of his noble family, so Juan can no longer be the potential sire of a child. In contrast to the Dionysian symbolism of the god's death and resurrection, the execution of these males who failed to honor the god will not result in even a symbolic rebirth.

Yerma, of course, has been the most obvious rejector of Dionysus. In her youth, she accepted as her husband a man she did not love, never revealing that Victor was the one for whom she cared. Consequently, she never wanted Juan as lover, only as the man who could legitimately give her the child she craved. Yet, when he failed her, she neither sought out Victor nor La Vieja's son to satisfy her need. Even facing the revels of the god, Yerma stood steadfast against the Dionysian spirit.

In her refusal to cojoin the male and female Elements through the Dionysiac, Yerma becomes her own victim. She has built a series of rejections throughout the play that culminate in this denial. Incapable of loving Juan as a man, she has victimized herself by not allowing him to love her as a woman, thus eschewing the fullness of the marital state. Yerma's rejection of Juan's embrace in the final moments of the play mirrors his rejection of hers earlier; her impulsiveness in that previous encounter, together with her avowed desire to be a "montaña de fuego," can be seen through hindsight as precursory of the deadly "embrace" of the finale. Juan's consumption in the fire of Yerma's manic frustration is more than the victimization of her husband by the wife; in killing Juan, Yerma has committed the ultimate act against herself: she has exterminated the possibility of ever having a child. With the approaching chorus of the Romería as a blatant counterpoint, Yerma rises from the ground and utters the terrible words that denote the end of hope: "... I have killed my son; I myself have killed my son!" (101)

Unlike a recognition scene in classical tragedy, Yerma's cognizance of her action does not contain the promise of redemption and renewal. Rather, her words close the play with a finality that indicates a rending of her being akin to the physical dismemberment in the Dionysian rites of antiquity.

This rending, as for Agave — who killed her son Pentheus during the bloody feast of the Maenads in *The Bacchae* — is one of the spirit, each woman having to live out her life in the knowledge that she has killed her own son. Such is the punishment meted out by Dionysus to those who have failed to accommodate the libidinal imperative in their lives. Pentheus and Juan may have suffered a physical death for mocking the god, but the punishment of Agave and Yerma for their crime against human nature is that of a living death.

The lesson is clear in both Euripides' and Lorca's tragedies: in the confrontation between the Apollonian and the Dionysiac, each must be given its due if the human condition is to attain purity. The lesson from psychoanalysis, derived from clinical experience, is the same: repression of the libido is dangerous to the psyche, for it will force it to recoil upon that which is abnormal in the individual. Therefore, it is fundamental to the well-being of the person that the ego be allowed to function as mediator between the primitive drives of the id and the social and moral demands of the milieu in which that individual lives.

In the symbolism of *Yerma,* the protagonist must cojoin the four cardinal Elements in order to realize her potential as mother, thus attaining that harmonious state of being which results from the integration of the Apollonian and the Dionysiac. But Yerma's excessive adherence to the Christian ethos blocked her pursuit of that end through licit or illicit means. That she recognized the impossibility of her pursuit of that fusion long before the finale was made evident when she exclaimed to Victor: "What a terrible loss not to be able to feel the teachings of the ancients!"[20]

NOTES

1. Federico García Lorca,*Yerma*. Buenos Aires: Editorial Losada — Biblioteca Clásica Contemporánea, 1967, p. 69. All subsequent textual references are to this edition; pagination will appear in parentheses after each quote.

2. For a study of *Yerma* from this perspective, see: Robert Lima, *The Theater of García Lorca*. New York: Las Américas Publishing Co., 1963, pp. 217–240.

3. In *The Birth of Tragedy from the Spirit of Music* (1872), Friedrich Nietzsche differentiates two modes of human behavior, the Apollonian and the Dionysiac. For the purposes of this essay, these dual factors that create the tension of living will function as exemplary of the struggle between Christian principles and pagan tradition.

4. Yerma's father has chosen Juan, a farmer, over Victor, a shepherd as husband for his daughter. The choice demonstrates an ancient prejudice among settled peoples in favor of the homesteader. The reason may be that in being tied to his land, the farmer is more reliable that the wandering shepherd, at least in the eyes of the community. However, in quite a different context, it is the shepherd who wins favor. The story of Cain and Abel is, on one level, a tale of the contention between the homesteader and the shepherd. When Cain kills Abel, the given reason for the homicide is that the farmer resents the rejection of his offering and the acceptance of the shepherd's by God. The Old Testament God had a marked preference for blood sacrifices and an ironic enjoyment in having his "chosen people" live as nomads. It was, at best, a mixed blessing being a shepherd. Perhaps the rejection of Victor as a suitable mate for Yerma stems from a subconscious racial memory of such origins.

5. In Euripides' *The Bacchae,* the conflict is between those who deny Dionysus his rightful place in the pantheon of the gods and those who acknowledge his divinity through worship. Dire consequences accrue to those who deny Dionysus his proper place in the scheme of things. Just as the Dionysia or Bacchanale gave rise to tragedy in ancient Greece (most notably in Attica), so too the tragic manifests itself in *Yerma's* modern Dionysian revels, the "Romería" scene at play's end. The parallels will be discussed in that context.

6. See: Joseph Campbell, *The Masks of God: Primitive Mythology*. New York: Viking Press, 1959, p. 458. Also see: Jack Lindsay, *The Origins of Astrology*. New York: Barnes and Noble, Inc., 1971, pp. 20–21.

7. See: Herodotus. *The Histories*. New York: Appleton and Co., 1899, p. 226. Also see: Tacitus, *Complete Works*. New York: Modern Library, 1942, p. 728. For the Henry Cary (tr.) association of Earth with masculinity, see footnote 13.

8. See: René Guenon, *Man and His Becoming According to the Vedanta*. London: 1945; passim.

9. See: Eithne Wilkins, *The Rose-Garden Game*. London: Victor Gollancz, Ltd., 1969 pp. 102, 113-114, 124. Also see the Old Testament's Song of Solomon, 5:2.

10. Although not normally used in Spain to refer to the sexual act in a vulgar way, *coger* is widely employed in that way throughout Latin America, most notably in Argentina, Uruguay and Cuba, countries that Lorca visited and where he may have come across the taboo usage.

11. In: Henry Cornelius Agrippa, *The Philosophy of Natural Magic*. Secaucus, New Jersey: University Books, 1974, pp. 43, 49.

12. The collective title of those esoteric writings centered on Hermes Trismegistus, the syncretic Mediterranean deity who ruled the four Elements.

13. Adamic Man is the protagonist of the familiar creation story in Genesis 2:7 — "Then the Lord God formed man out of the dust of the ground and breathed into his nostrils the breath of life, and man became a living being" — and in Genesis 2:21–22 — "The Lord God cast the man into a deep sleep and, while he slept, took one of his ribs and closed up its place with flesh. And the rib which the Lord God took from the man, He made into a woman, and brought her to him." However, there is a *previous* creation, that of Primal Man, recounted in Genesis 1:26–28 — "God said, 'Let us make mankind in our image and likeness,' ... God created man in His image. In the image of God He created him. Male and female He created them. Then God blessed them and said to them, 'Be fruitful and multiply.'" This *first* creature, so-called Primal Man, was not made of the earth but in the "image and likeness" of God and was a simultaneous creation of "male and female," possibly an androgynous creature representative of God's duality. The story of Primal Man ends abruptly, replaced by that of Adamic Man, a creature made of the earth.

14. Nietzsche, *op cit.*

15. The God of the Hebrews manifested himself as Fire on various occasions, most notably on Mt. Sinai when he gave Moses the Tablets of the Law and again in the "burning bush" episode. He could not be seen because he emitted a searing light.

16. Horns are among the oldest symbols of male sexuality and are attributes of numerous gods in antiquity, among them: the Semitic El; the Greek Actaeon, Pan and Zeus; the Egyptian Amon; and the Persian Mithras. These and other deities bore the horns of goats, rams, bulls or stags, animals whose energy and sexual prowess made them fitting symbols of their fertility gods. In Tantra, the yoga of sex, horns are the emanations of male vitality which, kept from sexual ejaculation, mounts upwards through the spine to the head in the form of mystic energy and accumulates as the outgrowths.

17. Misidentification of the Horned God as Satan is typical of Christianity, which saw all pagan traditions of fertility as inspired by that personification of evil which the religion called the Devil. The concept of the Devil's wife stated here may stem from the Jewish folkloric personage named Lilith, said to have

been Adam's first mate until she rebelled against God's authority and became an evil creature: the idea may also be based on those Mediterranean goddesses associated with fertility, likewise condemned by the Church. See: Henry Ansgar Kelly, *The Devil, Demonology and Witchcraft*, Garden City, N.Y.: Doubleday and Co., 1968; Margaret Murray, *The Witch Cult in Western Europe*, London: Oxford University Press, 1921 and *The God of the Witches*, London: 1933.

18. See: "Numerology," In: Richard Cavendish, (Ed.), *Encyclopedia of the Unexplained*. New York: McGraw-Hill Book Co., 1974, pp. 158–167. See also: "Numbers," in: Cirlot, J.E. *A Dictionary of Symbols*. New York: Philosophical Library, 1962, pp. 220–227.

19. The rose as a symbol of the female has a complex history. See Wilkins, *op. cit.*, among many others.

20. See note 1, above.

BETTINA L. KNAPP
Hunter College

García Lorca's *Yerma:* A Woman's Mystery

García Lorca's *Yerma* (1934) is a modern reworking of an ancient mystery which might have been enacted at Eleusis, Samothrace, Venusberg, or any other sacred shrine. It involves the dramatization of secret doctrines and initiation rituals, of verbal and gestural symbols.

In that *Yerma*, a three act tragedy, deals with a woman's barrenness, the numinous happenings focus on fertility. Originally part of agrarian family cults, fertility rituals, and this is implicit in *Yerma*, include protective or entombing ceremonies (I, i; II, ii), purification rituals (II, i), and a lysis (III, i, ii): sacred sequences when the mystai thrashes out the religious experience directly. Because such exteriorizations of primordial encounters have lived in the cultures and psyches of peoples throught history, they can be said to be of mythic proportions. *Yerma* is no exception.

Because *Yerma* is a myth (from the word *muthos,* meaning "fable" and *logos,* "discourse" or "reason"), the happenings in *Yerma* transcend linear time; they live in a kind of eternity. Nor are the events dramatized to be considered necessarily personal; they are also collective; not something invented for the sake of entertainment, though it may be also that, but rather a living and burning reality that exists in the Spanish culture and psyche as a whole and in Lorca's own vision. *Yerma*, then, is to be approached as both an individual and collective happening, with emphasis focused on woman, on Mariolatry in particular and its inherent polarities (saint/sinner); and on the victimization of son/husband by a would-be Mother.

In that *Yerma* is a mystery and mythic in quality, its protagonists are not to be looked upon as flesh and blood human beings, but rather as archetypes. The collective and eternal powers peopling Lorca's stage, live on the most primitive of levels and act in keeping with their own inherited and biological patterns of behavior. Yerma, the protagonist of Lorca's tragedy, makes us privy to the agony of the barren woman: she has been married for two years when the play begins and seven years pass between Act I and II, and still she remains sterile. The archetype of the infertile woman is not unique, as attested to in the Bible. Not only did some women long after the child-bearing age give birth to children, but several of them were even visited by angels before the birth: Sarah had Isaac; Rebecca, twins, Esau and Jacob; Hannah, Samuel; Manoah's wife bore Samson after the event was announced to her by an angel; the same was true for Elisabeth, John's mother, for Anne who conceived Mary immaculately, and for Mary who was told that she was "highly favored" and "blessed" among women before giving birth to Jesus.[1] Nor are such births requiring the help of divine intervention unknown in ancient times: Isis bore Horus through the intercession of the Holy Spirit, Kamutef.[2]

That Yerma's desire for a child is her sole raison d'être is understandable. Though it is intimated that Victor, the shepherd, had been the object of her desire, as an obedient daughter she agreed to a loveless marriage to Juan. Nor does her wanting to become a mother violate the dictates of her culture. On the contrary, it would have enhanced her stature in the community: she would have been exactly like the others and not differed from them. Her inability to become pregnant sets her apart, and she suffers the excoriating torments of one who is not like the others — a pariah of sorts. Yerma's personality also distinguishes her from the typical young, jovial, loveable and natural girl. She is a woman corroded with religious and sexual problems: she is psychologically empty. Her attitude toward her husband is cold, distant, perfunctory. He is there to fertilize her: to function as a stud. Such a relationship can yield no fruit since no *feeling* of *fire* exists between them. Because the dichotomy between the two is unbreachable, Yerma's fantasy world takes over. It alone, at least at the outset, allows her a modicum of happiness.

That the play opens with a dream vision — or a *visitation* — is not surprising in that we are dealing here with a mystery. It is spring: early in the morning and she and her husband are asleep. The stage is bathed in a strange light, that of atemporal happenings. "A Shepherd enters on tiptoe looking fixedly at Yerma. He leads by the hand a Child dressed in white." Not only do the dream figures reveal a compensatory image for the void Yerma experiences in her life, byt they also lend an eerie and *irrational* quality to the proceedings.

Who is this Shepherd about whom Yerma is dreaming? Certainly a reference to the strong and powerful Victor, the keeper of the flock; the Abel of Lorca's mythic proceedings. While Juan, thin and pale, is, like Cain, a tiller of the soil. He works so hard inseminating the earth, that he has not time to do the same for Yerma: or if he does, he does so ineffectively. That Victor leads a Child dressed in white, suggests the arrival of the "Son of Man": the pure, resplendent hope of her future — that element that gives her life purpose and love. If the child archetype is considered as a conjunction of opposites, it indicates a fluid relationship between the unconscious and consciousness: a condition able to pave the way for a spiritual and psychological change in the individual dreaming about such an image.

The shock of reality intrudes when Yerma awakens. The disparity between her dream (an unconscious compensatory urge) and the actual situation takes effect and arouses anger. She projects her trauma onto her husband and castigates him for his wanness and feebleness. Still hopeful of remedying the situation, she offers him a glass of milk. It will make him more robust: "Your body is not strong enough for it," referring to the sexual act.

That she offers him milk is in keeping with her desire to strengthen him: it is also associated with the mystery revolving around the Virgin Mary. Lactation was the only biological function she was allowed outside of the asexual act of weeping.[3] Yerma's gift of milk to Juan, then, is to be identified with the joy of a nursing mother in general: it is she who passes on her nourishing power to her newborn. Images such as Mary nursing Christ or Hera, her son Hercules, or Isis, Horus, are all implicit in fertility rituals.

Yerma's emphasis on Juan's frailty is her way of castigating (castrating) him. He is to blame, then, for her failure to conceive. Jealous of his attention to Mother Earth and of his continuous insemination of this unquenchable collective power, little energy is left to perform the sexual act. Even more important is the fact that Juan has no understanding of his wife's anguish; not having any progeny seems not to bother him. His concern centers upon his crops and the money these will yield; and the maintaining of his honor. What others say and think about him and his wife dominate his thoughts. Since Juan's world is centered *outside of the home* and not within it, he is uninvolved in what is brewing in this inner sphere. The opposite is true of Yerma.

Yerma's only means of assuaging the void within her — her sexual and spiritual emptiness — is to make Juan her scapegoat: her *shadow* figure. The shadow is defined as that part of the unconscious that contains aspects of a personality of which "the individual is unaware, may contain inferior characteristics and weaknesses which the ego's self-esteem will not permit it to recognize."[4] Let us mention the fact that in ancient times, the collective shadow viewed as the evils of a community, was projected or heaped onto a goat by a priest; the animal was then sent out into the wilderness and the clan was purged of its sins: the evil of the community supposedly disappeared along with the animal. By blaming Juan for a failure that might have been hers — or of both parties, Yerma is not facing her problem authentically. By avoiding it, she is unable to come to terms with it and so rectify it.

What increases her turmoil is Juan's insistence that she remain within her home. "You know well enough I don't like you to be going out," Juan told her. "I never go out," she responds. The home, viewed psychologically, encourages a condition of introversion; it fosters dream and reverie — the irrational sphere. It may also be looked upon as a uterus, feeding and nurturing the creative factor within an individual — those aspects that develop one's potential. When mystery religions flourished in Egypt, at the time of Imhotep (2980–2950 B.C.) and in Greece when Aesculepius was worshipped (c. 600 B.C.) the ill would enter temples and sanctuaries, and were hoisted feet first into deep, dark, and narrow grottos inhabited by snakes and venomous creatures, there to remain until such time as a healing dream came to them. After they explained their dream to the priest, it was interpreted, and if considered positive, the patient was declared to be in good health and was released.

Unlike such incubation dreams, however, Yerma's periods of withdrawal into her home, yielded not healing, but rather entombment: incarceration. The forced seclusion foisted upon her by Juan — in keeping with the customs of the day and, therefore, crucial to the maintenance of his honor, encouraged periods of deep introversion on her part. More and more she felt cut off from the world outside and from herself. She could not share her pain and sorrow with the others: her solitude mushroomed, as did her fantasy world. A concomitant split between reality and compensatory imaginary conditions deepened.

A woman who concentrates only on the home and her husband's welfare rarely, if ever, experiences a sense of identity outside of the home: as an individual in her own right. Wedded to the family, particularly in rural areas and in Lorca's time, the feminine principle never evolved, never experienced a sense of personal purpose in life. She was a funnel, a servant, a mediatrix: she served as a procreative force in society, seeing to the physical and moral welfare of others and in so doing, of herself.

Remaining enclosed within four walls, Yerma could not express her problems with the hope of solving them: but rather compounded them. Her thoughts revolved exclusively around the *child archetype*. This archetype, like any severe complex, is endowed with what one may call a type of electric current composed of affective charges and feeling tones. The affects given off by complexes are sometimes so great as to be capable of acting physically upon the person experiencing the complex. Rather than surrendering to this energetic force inhabiting her unconscious and thereby working with it openly, Yerma is shattered by it. Her ego (the center of her conscious personality) is dominated by this single image which generates in its wake continuous frustrations, perpetual obstacles preventing her from reaching her goal. The greater her imprisonment in her house (her unconscious), the more powerful is the domination of her *idée fixe*. Chaos inhabits her subliminal realm; rigidity, her conscious sphere. Like a hermetically sealed jar, Yerma's inner pulsations grow increasingly cataclysmic. The situation becomes explosive.

As Yerma's shadow figure, Juan represents all that is negative, impotent, and uncreative in her life. As an aspect of the patriarchal collective sphere, he stands for systematization, morality, and feminine incarceration. A fixed, unyielding, unbending, and sterile force, then, has proclaimed dominion over her. She, who must remain obedient and subservient to him, is in no way emotionally involved. Since she is cut off from her feelings, no growth, no evolution, no warmth can be hoped for in her arid and sterile world. Increasing resentment on her part paves the way for a heightening of her aggressive, threatening, and desperate ways. Only *destruction* or *dismemberment* can come to pass, leading perhaps to a *renovation*, or at least to an end of the repressive status quo she is compelled to endure.

Other factors are also present. Yerma's barrenness may be seen symbolically, as a sign of the time. Not only as a paradigm of the disharmony between husband and wife, but as a basic antagonism existing in the very foundations of Spanish culture and its dominant religion, Roman Catholicism. Under the patriarchal system of the time, the feminine principle was not only demeaned, but violated. A woman was a man's appendage; she served one function: to bear children. In keeping with the practice of Mariolatry, she was either a saint and, therefore, to be worshipped, or a sinner, to be reviled. In either case, she was an *object*. Because she was nothing in her own right, if she differed in any way from either of these extremes, she became an outcast and stagnated or regressed to an insalubrious world. In that Yerma was thus far unable to fulfill the "saintly" task of motherhood, she lived alienated from her fellow beings and from herself. Yet, she keeps trying to rectify her condition.

Once Juan leaves to fulfill the daily chores in the fields, Yerma begins sewing, then "passes her hand over her belly, lifts her arms in a beautiful sigh," as if cradling, nursing, loving and warming her newborn, sings out her lyrical verses about the baby she hopes to have. That Lorca chose song — music — to express the wonderment of motherhood, allows him to convey the tenderness of the mood: Yerma's words caress the ear; their smooth intonations touch, as if gently stroking the velvety smoothness of an infant's skin. She is *Mother* now, bathing in the beatific and passionate love of one so dependent upon her. The stillness of the home, no longer an entombment, has been *transfigured*. A *temenos,* a sacred space, exists for her, filled with the beauty and power of the archetypal image representing mother and child.

Sewing, like weaving, also replicates the mystery of creation. As Yerma commands her thread, her colors, her network of designs, she is organizing her destiny visually: fashioning and building a way of life for herself. Let us recall that the Greek Fates were women, that they made, wove, and cut the thread of life. So, too, does Yerma hope to be the artificer of her future.

Maria, married only four months, walks into Yerma's home carrying material, laces, tassels, and ribbons. She tells Yerma that when her husband learned she had become pregnant, he gave her money to buy these things and she did not even have to ask him for it. How did it all happen? Yerma asks. How does it feel to be with child? Her husband pressed his mouth against her cheek, Maria answers, and "it seems to me my child is a *dove* of fire he made slip through my ear."

Such symbols are implicit in the mystery of the annunciation. The Holy Ghost, it is said, flew down in the form of a Dove, fecundating the Virgin Mary through the Ear. That the Ear was the area chosen for the conception, indicates her obedience to the divine Word. By having heard and accepted the announcement, she freely conceived of Jesus.[5] Let us recall that the dove was also Aphrodite's bird: a paradigm of love, beauty, and grace — factors present in Maria's relationship with her husband. The *Ear* which hears the *Word,* is not only a symbol for comprehension; it is also a sexual image, along with *Fire,* referring to the energy needed for the insemination process. Mother Earth and Father Heaven, then, are necessary for the flame of insemination to fecundate woman. In Maria's statement, we not only learn that she experiences passion, as attested to by the use of the word fire, but spiritual and emotional contentment and involvement are also factors in the Dove and Ear images.

Yerma cannot even begin to understand the meaning of the mystery of passion in lovemaking. She feels no flame for her husband, either sexual or spiritual. He is an inseminator, a procreating agent, a rain maker; while she is the funnel, the bridge to the future. Although she longs to open herself up to the mystery of life — the process of pregnancy she seeks to have enacted in her body — she cannot. She has no sense of her flesh or of her sexuality, so bound is she by her *idée fixe,* by the child archetype which saps her instinct, her vitality, and drains her ego. She also knows that if she does not conceive, her blood will turn to *poison:* love will turn to hate, health to sickness, peace to war.

A driven woman who is incapable of relating to her husband sexually or in any other way, tries — as initiates have since ancient times — to enact rituals that she thinks might help her achieve her goal. At night, for example, she walks on the ground outside of her home or does so when bringing her husband his food in the fields. As she puts her feet down and touches Mother Earth, she hopes to be secretly impregnated by the contact with this nurturing force: a power her husband is forever inseminating symbolically each time he breaks ground to plant his seeds , and also when he waters them, making the area moist and receptive to the germinating process — rituals he carries out with love and care.

When Victor, on his way home from work, stops at Yerma's home and learns that she is still not pregnant, he encourages her to have Juan "try harder" (II,i). After he leaves, Yerma walks toward the place Victor had stood and "breathes deeply" as if she were inhaling sheer joy, strength, rapture — the very essence of life denied her by her restrictive and regressive husband. Victor, the Shepherd, could have been her inseminator; she could have procreated carnally with him. With Juan, she knows only frigidity.

That Yerma is frigid toward her husband is made evident in her reactions to an Old Woman (I,ii) she meets when carrying a basket of food to her husband in the fields. The Old Woman who has had fourteen children and two husbands, lives "with her skirts to the wind" and that is why "children came like water." Yerma wants to learn her secret: "Why am I childless?" she questions. The Old Woman tells her she has always looked upon her body as something beautiful; not like the Christians who consider it sinful. Nor does she believe in God: in fact, she despises him. Feelings of guilt, sin and asceticism do not concern her at all. Passionate and sensual, she has a lust for life. Unlike St. Theresa of Avila who forever sought to do penance, or the Flagellants, who indulged in a collective *imitatio Christi,* scourging themselves until they drew blood, the Old Woman enjoys the beauty of Nature in all of its forms.[6] "Don't you feel something like a dream when he brings his lips close to yours?" she asks Yerma. "No," is the response. Yet, as she thinks back to Victor, there could have been such a time. Now, however, pleasure has been banished from her world.

Two Girls appear on the scene: one has left her baby at home and is in a hurry to return; the other is married, has no children and does not want any. She hates to cook and to wash. Her parents insisted she marry. For what? she wonders. "We did the same things as sweethearts that we do now. It's all just the old folks' silly ideas." Unwilling to conform to what she considers unpleasant, she is determined to tend to her needs and desires as much as possible and not remain "stuck" inside a house doing what she does not like to do. Her life will be a bed of roses; not a veil of tears.

Yerma, making her way home, hears Victor's jubilant, earthy, and physical voice singing out in the distance: "Why, shepherd, sleep alone?" They meet and she comments on the vibrancy of his voice. "It's like a stream of water that fills your mouth." Like Abel, he is a man at peace with himself; he knows — he feels he is loved, and as such, happiness overflows. As the two look at each other fixedly, Juan intrudes. Fearful of what neighbors might say if they see Victor and his wife talking together, he orders her to go home. He will not return; he must water the trees.

Alone and entombed in her coffin/home, Yerma's suffering turns into a virtual martyrdom, a paradigm of the negative and destructive side of Christianity. Like the Penitentials who suffered atonement, who prayed, sacrificed, repented, humiliated themselves in all ways to earn salvation, Yerma is plunged into the agony of helplessness.

That Act II (i) opens on a purification ritual is in keeping with the ceremonies enacted in the ancient mystery religions as well as in contemporary ones. The village girls are washing their clothes in a flowing mountain stream, singing out their loves, their pleasures at life's rewards. "Joy, joy, joy" is chanted by one whose swollen womb is visible beneath her dress. Gossiping is also the rule of the day. Yerma is their focal point; they are convinced that Victor is her lover because "she carries his picture — in her eyes." As a sinner, therefore, she cannot bear a child.

The scene shifts from this highly active, entertaining, and happy one to Yerma's home at twilight (II, ii). Juan, so intent upon saving his honor, has asked his two maiden sisters to move into his home so that they can supervise his wife. Like elements of a Greek Chorus, they are there, present or behind the scenes, following her every move, even divining her inner thoughts. Once an area that had served Yerma as a refuge for her dream world, is now transformed into a prison, her home has become a destructive domain — where rage and pain alone prevail.

Returning from the fountain with the two pitchers of water for the home, Yerma is severely reprimanded by her husband. A sense of shame is instilled in her, as are feelings of guilt. She goes out too much: "The sheep in the fold and women at home." Yerma knows only too well that she must adhere to the status quo. "I'll learn to bear my cross as best I can ... If I could suddenly turn into an old woman and have a mouth like a withered flower, I could smile and share my life with you. But now — now you leave me alone with my thorns." If only she could be divested of her youth.

Increasingly outspoken, Yerma looks straight at Juan, fixedly, deliberately — with passion. Not the passion of love, rather of hate. She speaks of her feelings of entombment, of incarceration — "tied tight in my coffin." He has no understanding of her pain, her needs. Men have many activities that take up their attention: cattle, trees, conversations. Women have only children. Angrily, he responds: "You persist in running your head against a stone." The stone image describes his feelings most exactly, hard, inert, yet a living power. Stones also represent sacred forces: the Kaaba for the Muslim, the Omphalos for the ancient Greek, the Beith-El for the Hebrew, the Philosophers' Stone for the alchemist, Christ, the cornerstone of the church; the refined angular stone of the Mason. Neither sacred nor enduring forces interest Yerma who counters Juan's statement by suggesting that he should speak of a "basket of flowers and sweet scents," thereby invoking more feminine, beautiful and gentler images.

Increasingly ill at ease as Yerma's anger festers, Juan tries to run away from his obligations rather than face them. Like a cornered animal, he speaks about his work in the fields, his inability to remain with her: "you're not a real woman," he blurts out. Her psychological and sexual ambiguity becomes most overt as she confesses, "I don't know what I am." No identity; faceless, alienated from her own deepest feminine nature, Yerma has grown increasingly onesided, stunting her emotional development further. Neither male nor female, she has become an unworkable appendage of the phallic Mother.

Act III (i) which takes place in the house of the sorceress, Dolores, is also in keeping with mystery rituals. Viewed by a patriarchate as the primitive aspect of the feminine, Dolores, a prognosticator of future events, participates secretly in Nature and as such, is a redoubtable and threatening power. Considered by the ancient Egyptians, Greeks and Romans as part of the life process, priestesses or sibyls were approached with awe and trepidation — not as Evil forces. The Christians, on the contrary, looked upon them with dread, as somber and fearful powers, to be destroyed. As representatives of hidden desires, of unregenerate instincts, priestesses and sorceresses took on the countenance of terrifying energies, incompatible with the prevailing collective ego. As such, they are most frequently represented as ugly, diabolical, manifestations of the irrational, instinctual, undisciplined, and undomesticated world; the antithesis of the idealized, ordered, peaceful woman as viewed in Mariolatry. But she who is spiritual, sinless, beautiful is an abstraction and, therefore, unrealizable.

That Yerma came to consult Dolores indicates the power of her pain; the pathos of her condition. She is not afraid of partaking in the mysteries relating to Mother Earth as represented by Dolores. Two other old women are also present; one advises Yerma to find refuge in her husband's love while she waits "for God's grace." He is a good man, she tells her. No, Yerma feels nothing for Juan. "He goes out with his sheep over his trails, and counts his money at night." And when he is near her, "I feel a waist cold as a corpse's," she confesses. She has changed, she realizes. She who had always despised passionate women wishes she could become "a mountain of fire." This, she understands, is her only salvation.

That Dolores tells her she must recite the "laurel prayer," twice and St. Anne's prayer as well, links Christian and "pagan" mysteries and ideologies together. Laurel, for example, was chewed or burned by the Delphic Oracle before she announced her prognostications; when a favorable answer was forthcoming, she returned with a crown of laurel leaves on top of her head. This same plant, consecrated to Apollo, brought wisdom and victory. Because it remained green in winter, the Romans associated it with immortality, fecundity, and vegetation. As for St. Anne's prayer, it absolved a believer from sin, allowing the penitent to experience the numinosum — opening him or her to divinity through the feminine principle.

Before Yerma departs from this sacred precinct, Juan and his two sisters enter Dolores' hut. Although he deprecates his wife for sullying his honor, Yerma seems to have been strengthened by her exposure to the realm of the Great Mother, as incarnated in Dolores and the other women present. Through them, she has touched her own deepest feminine roots, that inner force which heightens a woman's might and insight. The added energy enables her to respond in kind to her husband's vilifications, unwilling now to accept the guilt for which she is innocent. "I too would shout, if I could, so that even the dead would rise and see the innocence that covers me." It is Yerma who realizes that she must protect her own honor from being sullied by her husband; and so rectify a wrong. The more certain she becomes of her *way,* the more overt are her actions and demeanor; and the more fearful a force — *a vagina dentata* — she becomes in her husband's eyes. Juan is unconsciously terrified of this archetypal figure over which he now knows he has no control. She now appears to him as a deceiver, a corruptor, a demonic potentate. "I'm no match for your cleverness," he says. Yerma's eyes, meanwhile, are like two piercing forces, "two needles" ready to pounce upon her husband. She is Evil; she is Death for Juan, ready to dissolve the status quo. Accusing him of sterility, of impotence, of nonfunctioning sexually, a transfiguration seems to be taking place, preparing for the play's *lysis.* Releasing affective charges and feeling tones as she speaks out her powerful lines, Yerma virtually bombards — better still, slaughters — rational attitudes and thought processes. Two archetypal powers are warring on stage, not merely husband and wife, each pointing to the other as the guilty party — but collective forces each vying for supremacy.

Yerma, nevertheless, also has her other side. In a deeply moving sequence, she speaks of her need of Juan, of her love for him, and as she moves forward to embrace him, he commands her to "Get away." Alone again, and as always, she feels like "the moon searching for herself in the sky" and cries out her pain; her martyrdom, and emptiness. Silence, he commands. The neighbors might hear. But Yerma no longer cares about saving face; nor about life. Freedom is what she needs and not constriction, incarceration — entombment. "At least let my voice go free, now that I'm entering the darkest part of the pit." For the first time her body has given birth — to song, to poetry, to rapture, *to the beauty of the Word!* Like the Virgin Mary who conceived through the Ear, so she, too, has become a procreative power — be it spiritual or abstract — giving lyrical expression of her innermost soul state. As Juan has suggested, she lives in her head and not in her physical being. "Cursed be the body!" she cries out, victimized as she is by the asceticism which her culture has forced upon her — cutting off soul from flesh.

That the concluding scene (III,ii) should take place at night in a hermitage high in the mountains is in keeping with the numinosity of the happenings. Some mountains — Faust's Walpurgisnacht, Tannhauser's Venusberg, Bacchants' Mt. Cithaeron — are believed to contain the throne of the Great Goddess or the Mountain Woman.[7] It is on the mountain, a sacred area, that men and women allow their pent up emotions to be unleashed, their repressed instincts buried deep within their collective unconscious, to be acted out. Unchanneled impulses, however, sometimes spell destruction and may lead to a dissociation of the personality. When they have free range, they sometimes overwhelm the ego, thereby obliterating any kind of real relationship with the outside world.

As pagan and Christian rituals fuse in this mountain scene, fertility celebrations are encouraged on one side of the stage, and on the other, Catholic chapel ceremonies. Revellers and a chorus of dancers carrying bells, leap about in wild abandon, voice their erotic needs, accompanying these with songs observing the joys of natural life. As reality is increasingly obliterated the energy released paves the way for the most obscure primal forces to come into being.

Juxtaposed to the scene of frenzy is Yerma, who accompanied by six women, comes to pray in the chapel. Barefoot, she carries decorated candles to honor her patron saint, to beg for his intercession in worldly matters.

It is not surprising that a male and female personification of the devil, with all of the paraphernalia including masks, dances, songs, gesture their way on stage, miming the act of sexual intercourse and conception. The Christian prejudice against the world of instincts and earth forces equated with sinful and Satanic powers, compelled the faithful to long for its opposite: the inhuman divine/ideal sphere. Extreme asceticism elicits its opposite. Attempts to repress the spontaneous impulses of an inner spirit by an overly conscious control of the ego only serves to accentuate the imbalance within individuals, leading more urgently to a need for redemption.

The Devil, symbolizing all forces that trouble, weaken, and dispossess a person of grace is for this same reason, a Lucifer — a Light Bringer: illuminating what has been buried in darkness, in chaos. Through the concretization of these repressed forces, individuals better understand what inhabits them. In keeping with this idea, Lorca wrote in his stage directions: "The beauty of this scene must be overt." As the Devils cavort about, they "are not in any fashion grotesque, but of great beauty and with a feeling of pure earth."

A complex of opposites is lived out on stage: Earth and Heaven, Body and Spirit, Good and Evil, God and the Devil make their presences known. Two ways of life which until now had been antipodal one to the other, will merge. An Old Woman tells Yerma, "Women come here to know new men. And the saint performs the miracle." She understands what troubles Yerma and so invites her to live in her house with her children; to pay no attention to what people will say, to overcome the repressive forces dominating her world. Yerma, however, cannot divest herself of her honor, of her inheritated mode of psychic functioning. Caught up in her own masochistic, repressive world, she sums up her psychic condition perfectly. "I'm like a dry field where a thousand pairs of oxen plow, and you offer me a little glass of well water. Mine is a sorrow already beyond the flesh."

Juan, who has been hiding behind a cart, has heard the entire conversation. Unaffected by his wife's sorrow, nor caring whether he has children or not, he is caught up in the atmosphere of instinctuality and is dazzled by its power and beauty. He wants to take his wife, sexually, powerfully — formidably and only for the pleasure it will yield him. "Kiss me ... like this," he sings to her triumphantly.

Yerma's rage knows no bounds. Unable to express her feelings of excoriating hurt and divestiture in any other way, she suddenly shrieks out the *Word* for the *Ear* to hear, seizes Juan by the throat and chokes him to death.

> Barren, barren, but sure. Now I really know it for sure. And alone
> ... Now I'll sleep without startling myself awake, anxious to see if
> I feel in my blood another new blood. My body dry forever! What
> do you want? Don't come near me, because I've killed my son. I
> myself have killed my son!

The entire lysis, is reminiscent of Euripedes' *Bacchants,* in its harrowing viscerality, the priestesses of Dionysus, those "wild women" who also danced their release from a patriarchal repressive environment, dismembering their prey in the process, so Yerma, symbolically *devoured the future genitor!*

The symbolic *dismemberment* disrupted previous orientations and values. Confusion reigns; chaos has broken loose. Nothing is clear; nor are values distinct. Yerma is the one who gave *birth* to a new *life* force. She emerges victorious from Lorca's tragedy; for it was she who unseated and toppled *what was,* adhering to Nietzsche's premonitory dictum: "We must liberate ourselves from morality in order to be able to live morally."[8]

NOTES

1. Marion Woodman, *The Pregnant Virgin*. Toronto: Inner City Book, 1985, p. 81.

2. Marie Louise von Franz, *Apuleius' Golden Ass*. New York: Spring Publications, 1970, 2, xi.

3. Marina Werner, *Alone of all her Sex*. New York: L. Alfred A. Knopf, 1976, p. 251.

4. Edward Edinger, "An Outline of Analytical Psychology," unpublished, p. 9.

5. C.G. Jung, *Complete Works*. New York: Pantheon, 1956, p. 101.

6. Lyn Cowan, *Masochism. A Jungian View*. Thalwil, Switzerland: Spring Publications, 1982, p. 24.

7. Erich Neumann, *The Great Mother*. New York: Pantheon Books, 1955, p. 99.

8. Liliane Frey-Rohn, "Evil from the Psychological Point of View," *Evil*. Evanston: Northwestern University Press, 1967, p. 156.

BIBLIOGRAPHICAL SOURCES

García Lorca, *Tragedies*. New York: A New Directions Book. Translated by James Graham-Luján and Richard L. O'Connell.

Rupert C. Allen, *Psyche and Symbol in the Theater of Federico García Lorca*. Austin, Texas: University of Texas Press, 1974.

Lorca. A Collection of Critical Essays. Edited by Manuel Duran. Englewood Cliffs: Prentice Hall, Inc. 1962.

Felicia Hardison Londre, *Federico García Lorca*. New York: Frederic Ungar Pub. Co., 1984.

ARTURO JIMÉNEZ-VERA
San Diego State University

The Role of Spanish Society in *Yerma*

Almost all of the studies that have been done on *Yerma* focus upon the protagonist, Yerma, and rightly so. Even the title of the drama, for example, emphasizes her role as the central figure. The play starts and finishes with Yerma. As the action begins, she introduces the main theme, the tragedy of a married woman who desires but has been unable to have children. In her, the theme is brought to life, for the driving force behind her actions is her concern about her childless state. An analysis of the dialogue reveals that in the majority of the conversations she is either the speaker or the subject of the discussion. She not only receives the most exposure or any character in the drama but also is the best developed. Nevertheless, perhaps in a more subtle manner and to an extent that is more difficult to discern, we also get a sense of the tragedy of Juan, her husband.[1] The very fact that the drama reaches its climax with his death at the hands of Yerma makes him a tragic figure. Can we separate the lives of Yerma and Juan? They are husband and wife, and the threads of their lives are interwoven because what affects one will have repercussions on the other. For this reason, when the tragedy of *Yerma* is analyzed only from the point of view of one of the spouses, its meaning and impact is diminished. John W. Falconieri goes as far as to say:

> ... on experiencing *Yerma,* not only through a reading but most particularly through viewing a performance, one senses a frustration which sets him searching for the causes of this frustration. The excellent poetic elements, the richness of imagery, the symbolism, though all well-wrought and conceived, come to naught if the tragedy is unconvincing, unsatisfying.[2]

Having had a similar reaction to that of Falconieri and in an effort to find a more satisfying interpretation of the play, I propose to analyze it not from the point of Yerma or of Juan, but rather from both their perspectives; that is, as a married couple facing a serious problem, and to ascertain the extent of society's responsibility for their tragedy.

In its most basic form, *Yerma* presents us with the story of a young couple. When the play unfolds, they have been married for two years. In the course of the drama another three years pass. This couple has a problem: they do not have children. At the beginning they attempt to establish a dialogue by bringing their concern to the surface. There even seems to be a hope that a child will come. When Juan exclaims, "We've got to wait!" Yerma responds, "Yes; loving each other."[3] Unfortunately, their efforts to understand each other fail for one sees the situation from a completely different perspective than the other. Of the two, Yerma takes the stronger position and to the very end insists on the rightness of her stance. She is convinced — and this may be due to her lack of knowledge of how children are conceived — that the husband is the dominant factor in a woman having or not having a child. It never occurs to her that the cause of her barrenness may lie within her. Yerma's position seems to be based more on hearsay than evidence. She admits her ignorance of the facts of life in her conversation with the First Old Woman:

> Girls like me who grow up in the country have all doors closed to them. Everything becomes half-words, gestures, because all these things, they say, must not be talked about. And you, too; you, too, stop talking and go off with the air of a doctor — knowing everything, but keeping it from who dies of thirst. (114)

In order to discover the cause of their differences, we must return to the period before their marriage. Although this occurs before the play begins, we are provided with sufficient information to define the problem. Its underlying causes are clearly identified. Yerma and Juan had different expectations of marriage.

Yerma admits, "My father gave him to me, and I took him" (113). For her, then, this was not her choice but rather an arranged marriage, and as such, she — and quite possibly her family — stood to gain from it economically and perhaps with higher social status in the rural area in which they live. She clearly admits that she does not love Juan:

> FIRST OLD WOMAN. I mean — do you really love him? Do you long to be with him?
>
> YERMA. I don't know.
>
> FIRST OLD WOMAN. Don't you tremble when he comes near you? Don't you feel something like a dream when he brings his lips close to yours? Tell me.
>
> YERMA. No. I've never noticed it.
>
> FIRST OLD WOMAN. Never? Not even when you've danced?
>
> YERMA, remembering. Perhaps ... one time ... with Victor ... (112)

Victor is the only man to whom Yerma has been attracted. He, however, is poor and might not have been acceptable to her family.

Juan is presented as a hard-working young man who owns land and animals; he is trying to get ahead and to increase his wealth. Yerma's family must have taken this into consideration in pushing her into this union with him. We can imagine also that they may have had to argue persuasively, stressing her suitor's positive qualities and the benefits that this matrimony would bring to them all. Furthermore, besides these socio-economical benefits, Yerma stands to gain in status by marrying because the society in which she lives accords the married woman a much higher level of respect than it does the single one. As Mary Salas points out, "The single Spanish woman endures being treated as an inferior: in the family where in general she is not respected and in society where she has no place."[4] Therefore, it is not surprising that Yerma acquiesces to the urging of her family. Moreover, in Spanish rural society, the parents have the final say about whom their daughter is to marry. As Julian A. Pitt-Rivers tells us, "Girls whose first engagement is broken off tend to marry less easily subsequently."[5] A man prefers to be the first suitor rather than to follow in the footsteps of another. To do so would result in a certain blow to his pride. Beauty or the possibility of an inheritance might make such a sacrifice justifiable. Although Yerma is presented directly and indirectly through what others say of her as being extremely attractive, she may have worried about the risk she would be taking if she were to break off with Juan. After all, he might be followed by a *novio* of less promise, or by no one at all. In accepting him as her husband even though she does not love him, she acts in accordance with social realities. However, Juan's situation differs completely. As a man, he is permitted to make his own decisions about whom he will marry. We can assume that he decides to marry Yerma because he has fallen in love with her and wants to, and that no one has pushed him into it. In fact, at the end of the play, he speaks of his love for her and of his desire for her as a woman.

As mentioned above, Yerma marries Juan not because she loves him, but in obedience to her family while he marries her because he so desires. Therefore, each has a completely different reason for entering into this marriage. This information proves helpful to us in comprehending the conflict that is developing between this young couple. There is neither a sound basis for their marriage nor a mutual caring between the two. However, in fairness to Yerma, we must keep in mind that in entering into their marriage she only does what society expects of her.

Yerma soon finds a solution to her problem of marrying someone whom she does not love by concentrating upon her future role as a mother. Her fixation upon motherhood is presented in a dream scene at the beginning of the play. A strange light envelops the scene as she dreams of a child and a shepherd. The child is the baby she yearns for and the unidentified shepherd, the means of having it. The dream centers upon the child, not the man, and shows us the extent to which she is obsessed both consciously and subconsciously with the idea of becoming a mother. Yerma's tragedy of barrenness begins with her dream and slowly develops and increases in magnitude. She has created a psychological expectation that motherhood will be her means of finding happiness. She may not love Juan, but as her husband he will give her children; and this will make her happy. From then on, she regards him not so much as her husband but as the means for her to have children. She confesses to the First Old Woman, "I gave myself to my husband for his sake, and I go on giving to see if he'll be born — but never just for pleasure" (113). Hence, we see that considered solely as her husband Juan is not acceptable to her, but as the man who legally can give her the children she wants, he is. Yerma's point of view is understandable. She attempts to deal in the best way that she can with an unhappy situation not of her making. So far, she has satisfied social demands successfully by accepting her parents' choice of a husband and by marrying. Now she must become a mother. In doing so, she will fulfill the social code and regain the happiness that she has lost by marrying without love. Gwynne Edwards sums up Yerma's situation and predicts what is to come:

> As a consequence of and a compensation for the emptiness of her life, her need for a child becomes more desperate and more hopeless. And it is not so much that she or Juan are responsible for the situation as that the situation, initially imposed upon them, makes demands with which, given their characters and aims, they cannot cope. They are caught in the vicious circle of their own incompatibility, brought together by custom and tradition, and bound by the inflexible demands of honour.[6]

Although she has no feeling for or attraction to Juan, he does for her. He looks upon her as the woman he loves and only secondarily as the future mother of his children. In fact, he insists that he is not concerned about having children and after five years of childless marriage, he advises Yerma to accept the situation as it is: "Resign yourself!" (152). Yerma is the woman he loves and with whom he wants to share his life, and whether or not they have children does not seem of great importance.

As a result, we realize that not only does the basis upon which Juan and Yerma entered their marriage differ considerably but also their outlook on their relationship and their problem. Inevitably, when children fail to come, these differences create a steadily widening gap. They must resolve them before they become completely separated. There is not a single instance in the play when we see the two working together to find a mutually acceptable solution that would cement their matrimony. Nor does either one seem to understand fully the feelings or the position of the other.

To make matters worse, the people of the rural society in which Yerma and Juan live are of a mentality that finds it difficult, if not impossible, to accept anything that does not fall within their social norms and "where fathering children is regarded as proof of manhood and bearing them proof of womanhood."[7] The failure of Yerma and Juan to have children makes them vulnerable to the gossip of these people. Of the two, Yerma seems to be the more affected. Although she has managed to conceal her lack of love for Juan, she cannot hide the fact that she does not have children. As a result, not only does she suffer the misery of not conceiving a child, but she is also divested of her dignity before a society that thinks a "farm woman who bears no children is useless — and even bad" (132. This increasing social pressure makes her situation even worse.

The question that people ask is why she has no babies. Although we never learn the answer, we can imagine that their conjectures hurt Yerma terribly, in addition to staining her honor as a woman. She reflects upon this, saying that she is "filling up with hate" (113), and she will do so even more as the tension continues to mount. Yerma confesses that she is "hurt and humiliated beyond endurance" (132), for she cannot escape the reality of her barrenness. She feels so desperate and sorry for herself that she never thinks of Juan as a person and of how he may feel. She never sees that he too is the victim of her tragedy.

On the surface, Juan does not seem overly concerned with the situation and on one occasion, as we have said, he even advises Yerma to accept it. Nevertheless, we cannot help but wonder whether his lack of concern about having a family and his ready acceptance of the situation really are psychological attempts to resolve for himself as well as for others any questions about his manliness. For as we have said, the rural society in which Yerma and Juan live praises the married woman who becomes a mother and judges the masculinity of the married man in direct proportion to the number of children that he has fathered. It is quite possible that as the years pass and no babies come he may feel his honor increasingly threatened before society. We know too that despite his seeming indifference about having children it is not completely true that he does not want any because in the course of the drama he proposes to adopt a baby from Yerma's brother. Admittedly, his feelings about having them are not as strong as Yerma's, but that should not be construed to mean that he is totally opposed. Furthermore, even if he does feel his manhood threatened, it would not be within the decorum of his society to lament this; rather, as a man, he must remain strong and silent. Thus, Juan's seeming indifference about having children and his easy acceptance of his situation are his means of coming to terms with a problem that is getting out of his control in a way that is acceptable to the social code that rules his life. It may be too that his love for Yerma has blinded him to the depth of her suffering since for him, she suffices, but for her, he does not.

Nonetheless, Juan is more fortunate that Yerma simply because as a man he has his work and in addition to that the freedom to occupy himself with other interests outside the home. In contrast, the role of a wife is to stay in the home. Her work consists of caring for the needs of her husband and having and raising their children. As a wife, Yerma has no other choices available, and since Juan is outside most of the time, her desire for and need of children to occupy her time is understandable. Without them, she has little to do. With them, she will be busy and find happiness. As a married woman in this type of society, she can find fulfillment only by having a large family. Yerma shows a painful awareness of this when she tells Juan, "Men get other things out of life; their cattle, trees, conversations, but women have only their children and the care of their children" (129).

One must ask why Yerma wanted to be a mother. Was she moved by a feeling of love for children, the wish to fill her empty life by raising them, or the need to satisfy the expectations of society? Perhaps the answer to our question is a composite of these three needs. We see, for example, that when she tells María, who is expecting a baby, "Don't walk very much, and when you breathe, breathe as softly as if you had a rose between your teeth" (107), she expresses herself with such tenderness and in such a delicate way that her warmth comes across to us. Beyond a doubt, she believes that with children to fill her house it will become a happy home. On the other hand, when Juan suggests that since a child has not been born to them they should adopt one, she becomes indignant and replies, "I don't want to take care of somebody else's children. I think my arms would freeze from holding them" (129). Granted that adoption would leave her honor stained in the eyes of society since she would not have born the child herself, but she at least would have it to love, thus fulfilling to some extent her wishes to be a mother. Again, perhaps the answer is mixed, or perhaps the approval of society is becoming of greater importance to her as her barrenness makes her more and more a target of its disapproval.

Yerma, not Juan, is the one who initiates action, and behind her words and deeds the image of the child she wants is ever present. As the play begins, she seems to express loving concern for the health of Juan:

YERMA. Won't you have a glass of milk?

JUAN. What for?

YERMA. You work a lot and your body's not strong enough for it. (103)

However, the truth is that beneath her demeanor of love her real concern lies hidden: She wants to make strong the man who can father her child. Especially in the early years of their marriage she succeeds in masking her goal of motherhood by treating Juan with seeming love. As the years pass, she abandons this approach and continuously dwells upon her desire to have a baby. She complains so often that finally Juan reacts, saying that he hears "Always the same thing" (129). He has had to listen to this too many times before. We also see that he begins to spend a great deal of time outside working in the field. He is there from dawn until dusk and even passes some of the night outside the home. Although he is presented as an ambitious young man and a hard worker, this behavior is so extreme that it lacks credibility. One could easily surmise that Juan stays outside the house so much because he does not want to listen to the laments of his wife. He is trying to avoid Yerma because he feel oppressed and persecuted by her continuous complaints. Moreover, he simply does not know how to placate his wife.

One more question remains: Which of the two is responsible for their failure to have children?[8] We are not provided with a physiological reason. Yerma blames Juan for not giving her children. At the same time, she clearly states that he has relations with her and complains, saying that she finds his "waist cold as a corpse's, and I, who've always hated passionate women, would like to be at that instant a mountain of fire" (140). However, this does not answer our question. Yerma also argues that Juan does not want children, but we know that if that were true, he would not have offered to adopt a child. The play provides no answer to the question of responsibility. The possibility certainly exists Yerma could be the source of sterility. C.B. Morris surmises:

> The difference between barrenness and infertility clarified by enlightened medical investigation makes it essential for the reader or spectator of *Yerma* to distinguish between women who cannot conceive through some physical or pathological malfunction and women who do not conceive through psychological or emotional stresses. Yerma belongs to the second category, and out of her mental and emotional disturbances Lorca has extracted great tragic force. Yerma's nervous condition is circular, self-perpetuating: she does not conceive because she is tense, and she becomes more tense because she does not conceive. Intuitively Lorca has captured the mental disturbances that medical research has proved to be a cause of infertility ...[9]

Throughout the play we get the impression that Yerma is an exceptionally tense and dramatic person who cannot free herself of her obsession to bear a child. However, this is only a possibility. As stated above, we have no answer. All we can do is wonder.

In the play, Yerma accuses Juan of being responsible for her childless state. With this thought in mind, she resorts to other means of achieving motherhood. She and the people in this rural area are uneducated. Their beliefs are a curious mixture of superstition and religion. Consulting a sorceress for help is acceptable in her society, and this is Yerma's first step. Through witchcraft — the repetition of certain prayers in the local cemetery, she hopes to conceive a child. However, doing this requires her to leave her house without her husband at night, an unacceptable action in her society because it implies a lack of marital unity on the part of a couple. People begin to gossip, and what they say stains honor. Juan expresses his concern clearly when he tells her, "The sheep in the fold and the women at home. You go out too much. Haven't you always heard me saying that?" (128). Moreover, by seeking the help of a sorceress as a means of becoming pregnant, Yerma advertises to all that her husband is not man enough to father her child. This wounds Juan's sense of manliness and perturbs him greatly. As a result, for the first time in the drama, he initiates action, bringing to the house his two spinster sisters to keep Yerma under watch at all times. At this point the rumors and gossip have gone so far as to hint that Yerma is seeing Victor again; even the possibility of adultery is mentioned. Although Juan appears to believe that Yerma is faithful to him, he does not like his name and hers being made the target of common gossip. His honor as well as hers is in question.

Yerma's final attempt to find a solution takes her on a personal pilgrimage to the hermitage of a so-called *santo* where she hopes to obtain a miracle and become pregnant. Other women with no children have come to him and some have become pregnant. However, this has not resulted from a miracle but rather from their having been taken advantage of by the many men who hang around the cave for this very purpose. Yerma would not consider any such involvement for, although she would have been happy with a miracle that would enable her to conceive alone, she cannot accept love from a man other than her husband as that too would stain her honor. By that criterion, even Victor is unacceptable. Only Juan can father her children. With this realization on her part, the final resolution of the drama is set. In the final scene, at last, their conflicting points of view openly clash. In the moonlight Juan comes to her. Yerma is beautiful, and he wants to love her without her making any demands. He regards her as the woman he loves and tells her that she is enough, that he does not want children. Her reaction to Juan's avowal of love is desperate rage. Driven to insanity by her obsession with motherhood, Yerma kills Juan and thereby resolves her problem. She thus vindicates herself before those who have criticized her. How could this be otherwise? Even for the many literary critics who have studied Yerma, "her actions and statements are accepted with sympathy while the accusations levelled at Juan are proclaimed just and his murder justified."[10]

Beneath the surface of the play and expressed in a very subtle manner, García Lorca presents a strong criticism of society. He does not attempt to provide a solution, but rather to bring to the surface the powerful role that the social code of conduct plays in the life of people — here represented by Yerma and Juan. Although the action centers specifically on the characters of Yerma and Juan, a generalization is made at the end of the third act in the scene in which the pilgrimage to the hermitage of the *santo* takes place. This is an annual ritual and many women participate in the hope of receiving the miracle of fertility. The implication here is that other women besides Yerma have been unable to bear children and are desperately looking for a solution. Seen from this perspective, the tragic situation of Juan and Yerma is not unique but one shared with other couples, also victims of a strict and rather cruel social code. One may generalize even further and say that the rules of social conduct that play such a decisive role in the life of Yerma may also do so, to a lesser or greater degree, in the rest of Spain. Robert G. Sánchez suggests the idea when he states:

> Lorca scorned surface realism. His last plays are dramatic synthe-
> ses of a mentality that dominates men and women in Spain in their
> relationships in terms of honor and sexuality. He exposed roots;
> and Spain's roots are deep and cling tenaciously.[11]

The society that García Lorca shows us in this play is one in which the parents have the final word about the future of their daughter, in which the feelings and wishes of a girl who is about to marry are not fully considered, and in which love is relegated to second place behind socioeconomic considerations. Furthermore, no alternative is provided to marriage that would permit a single woman to lead a rewarding life. Nor does this society offer an alternative to the couple without children that would enable it to retain respect. On the contrary, the wife suffers degradation and the husband's manliness comes into question. However, women suffer the most. Both at home and in the eyes of society they becomes souls in pain, souls without hope. Only by studying this play with the role of society in mind can the tragedy of Yerma take on its fullest and deepest meaning for us.

NOTES

1. Many critics do not concern themselves with the tragedy of Juan. For example, in *García Lorca,* London: Jonathan Cape, 1969, p. 163, Edwin Honig states that "the whole tragic burden in *Yerma* is borne by a single woman, and is measured by the deepening of her struggle with the problem of frustrated motherhood."

2. John V. Falconieri, "Tragic Hero in Search of a Role: Yerma's Juan" *Revista de Estudios Hispánicos.* I (1967): 17.

3. James Graham Luján and Richard O'Connell (trs.) *The Tragedies of Federico García Lorca.* New York: New Directions, 1955, p. 105. Subsequent references will be given parenthetically.

4. Mary Salas, "La mujer soltera en España," *Cuadernos para el Diálogo* (Número extraordinario), II (1965): 26. The translation is my own.

5. Julian A. Pitt-Rivers. *The People of the Sierra,* Chicago: The University of Chicago Press, 1971, p. 96. In: *South from Granada,* London: Readers Union, 1958, p. 251, Gerald Brenan echoes this: "a girl who was known to have danced with a man or to have had a *novio* on even the most distant terms had put herself out of the running."

6. Gwynne Edwards. *Lorca: The Theatre Beneath the Sand.* London: Marion Boyards, 1980, p. 179.

7. C.B. Morris. "Lorca's Yerma: Wife without an Anchor." *Neophilologus.* LVI (1972): 286.

8. In: *Psyche and Symbol in the Theater of Federico García Lorca.* Austin: University of Texas Press, 1974, p. 125, Rupert C. Allen states:

> The problem is to see how critics have answered the question of why the marriage of Yerma and Juan is barren. Of the forty-two critical commentaries consulted, five are non-committal, and three involve analyses of the situation that transcend considerations of efficient causes. Of the thirty-four remaining critical interpretations, then, ten clearly "blame" the wife, and twenty-four clearly "blame" the husband.

9. C.B. Morris, op. cit. p. 293.

10. John V. Falconieri, op. cit., p. 19.

11. Robert G. Sánchez, "Lorca, the Post-War Theater and the Conflict of Generations." *Kentucky Romance Quarterly.* XIX (1972): 26.

III. Lorca's Enduring Impact

DIONISIO CAÑAS
Baruch College, CUNY

The Poet and the City: Lorca in New York

1. The Poet and the City

There was a time when malignant spirits inhabited nature, woods dark forests. In those places human fears transformed themselves into realities. With the ancient city a new space emerges and displaces nature without replacing it, and although it is in the remote parts of the country and in the mountains, in deep forest, and in wide deserts or in the mountain's altitudes, where evil inhabits, these malignant spirits also live in the city. In this way, sharing the mystery, the menacing nocturnal, with the natural world, grow the Medieval, Renaissance, and Baroque cities. With the beginning of the 18th century industrial city, a new order is established in society: capitalist speculation, organized exploitation and the marketing of pleasure are the sign of the new era. This new scientific period also brought an end to superstition and the exile of the spirits of evil from woods and from dark and mysterious forests. But science also made human beings slaves of machines and of progress. On the other hand, poets elected to stay on the side of freedom, mystery and imagination.

As a city grows, an historical awareness evolves among its inhabitants. It is not by chance that Sigmund Freud, in *Civilization and its Discontents,* discusses Rome, its historical past and its present, nor that he transforms the city of Rome into a metaphor of birth and formation.

It is in the 18th century that reason explains everything, classifies and organizes religions and remote beliefs. The mind that catalogues gods and myths, produces interminable lists of birds and flowers, insects and trees in alphabetical order. It is this mind that presents itself as a founding model of a world where everything has its explanation, its cipher, its place. Yet, this 18th century position, is not subordinate to any god, faith or religion, and recognizes reason as the sole divinity.

In the heart of the industrial city grows the cancer of alienated men and women, of masses without an identity. The old bucolic theme which contrasted country and city is revitalized by the romantic imagination. Heir to the emotional and mysterious burden inbred in nature since ancestral times, the poet appears as someone who does not know how to adapt to the new scientific reality. The city and the bourgeois system repel the poet, with his telluric attitudes, his romantic gaze oriented toward the dark roots of earth, toward the invisible immensity of the universe.[1]

The break between city and poet is resolved, in part, when there appears an ironic attitude like that of the French poet Jules Laforgue. The hostile position of poets toward the city and its inhabitants does not diminish in the 19th century, but the city no longer connotes the Christian image of a place of perversion, where heaven and hell are one. Secularized, the evil city is transformed into the place where men and women are exploited by capital: one devil replaces the other. This is the vision that Federico García Lorca has of New York City.

2. Poet in New York

The time that Federico García Lorca spent in New York, from June 1929 to April 1930, was transcendental for his work as well as for all contemporary Spanish poetry. The poems that Lorca wrote in this city constitute part of a poetic mythology that characterizes Manhattan. His tragic vision of the city, pointing to the plight of alienated men and women, underlining the violence of the big city, has prevailed until the present. Lorca had intended to write a volume of prose under the title of *The City,* but his project never came to fruition. In its place, he left an unpublished manuscript, an extraordinary book of poems: *Poet in New York.*

It has been said that the style of *Poet in New York* is surrealistic, but I find its language eminently expressionist. There is no single poem that is not the product of an experience in Lorca's life, and every poem has a clear intention. It is also obvious that most of the poems are poems of social protest, that they constitute an apocalyptic vision of the capitalist world and modern society, precisely what Lorca perceived in New York. Lorca's image of the metropolis is the product of his subjectivity. He uses the big city and its inhabitants to project his own tragedy. In this manner, Manhattan becomes a great stage on which the poet plays the most important role and the skyscrapers form his grand scenography. In the poem "Landscape of the Vomiting Multitudes",[2] the author presents the figure of the poet with these words:

> The gaze that preserves me
> must issue on waves where dawn never ventures:
> I, poet and armless, adrift
> in the vomiting multitudes,
> lacking even the spirit of horses to crop
> the rank moss of my temples.

Lorca shares a belief in the basic goodness of the human race, a goodness that he does not find in the city, which extends to a firm belief in the need to protect the spirit of the blacks from machines, science and a mercenary society. Even his free verse is not surrealistic but rather close to that of Walt Whitman's free and open style, a style very well-known among expressionists in Europe. The social consciousness present throughout *Poet in New York,* so clearly expressed in "New York, Office and Denunciation", distances Lorca's book from the self-absorption and dream style of Surrealists' so-called automatic writing. *Poet in New York* is a totally different matter. It is a violent vomit of denunciation, a nightmare with open eyes. It is not an escape from reality. Rather it is an immersion in a painful reality, expressed from the subjectivity of an Andalusian, an Andalusian who sees the world with his heart, his senses, and his emotions.

In the same way that Alfred Döblin's novel *Berlin-Alexanderplatz* (1929) became the expressionist epic of the big city, *Poet in New York* is an epic canto of Manhattan, but an epic in the Spanish manner, an "esperpentic" epic, a twisted one, in which heroes are reflected in concave mirrors, as are the heroes in Valle-Inclán's plays. It happens that expressionist language and style reaches its most powerful heights in contact with the images of the city. The poetic image that Lorca introduces with *Poet in New York* is of a man in the throes of a fantasmal nightmare, yet, unlike a dreamer, he remains eminently aware. Everything he encounters wounds his sensibility. In his writing on the city, Lorca superposes the syncopated rhythm of North American jazz upon the expressiveness of African art, and the vision of the city as an architectonic functional iceberg.

3. Lorca's Prose on His Poetic New York Experience

I will not examine here Lorca's poems written in New York, for all have been extensively studied. It is his experience of New York as a platform for his writing in general that concerns me. I shall examine a lecture in which he commented on the poems produced in New York, and on his experience of the city, contrasting the content of this lecture with that of a letter which he wrote from New York City.[3]

In opposition to the terrible impression of the metropolis that we find in *Poet in New York,* we have his experience of the city in a letter written to his friend Carlos Morla Lynch:

> I'm living at Columbia University, in the heart of New York, in a splendid place near the Hudson River. I have five classes and spend the days greatly amused as if in a dream. I spent the summer in Canada with some friends and I'm now in New York, which is a city of unexpected happiness. I've written a lot. I have almost two books of poems and a theatrical piece. I'm relaxed and happy.

That "city of unexpected happiness" emerges occasionally in *Poet in New York,* but it is surprising when juxtaposed with the tearing tone of most of Lorca's poems. We can only surmise that this is the result of a split personality in conflict with society, typical of Lorca's characters and of his own personality. The most tragic manifestation of this dual personality appears in his insistence on hiding his homosexuality. This presents us with one of the most interesting aspects of *Poet in New York.* In this city Lorca seems to have taken the firm decision to proclaim his homosexuality through his writing. It is also in New York that Lorca's work begins to consider the topic of the social repression of passion and desire. Only in his post-New York days does he openly discuss homosexuality in plays like *The Public* and the unfinished *The Destruction of Sodom.*

At the close of his lecture Lorca says something surprising: "I was leaving New York with feeling and with deep admiration. I was leaving many friends there, and I had received the most useful experience of my life." It is between the *unexpected happiness* of his letter to his friend and this last *deep admiration* for the city, that Lorca had written the sorrowful verses of *Poet in New York*. Epistolary interchange does not necessarily give a real view of facts.

It is hard to believe that the poet of Lorca's book and the Andalusian poet are the same individual. Nonetheless it would be an error to think that what Lorca wrote in *Poet in New York* has nothing to do with the life of the poet. We have no other option than to think that the figure of the haunted poet, through which Lorca makes a myth of Manhattan, is a projection of his tormented mind, that in secret he suffered in New York City irrespective of what he write to Morla Lynch and what his poems reflect.

This internal torture makes more acute Lorca's sensitivity to the most negative elements in metropolitan life. Let us read his first impression:

> The two elements the traveler first captures in the big city are extrahuman architecture and furious rhythm. Geometry and anguish. At first glance, the rhythm can seem to be gaiety, but when you look more closely at the mechanism of social life and the painful slavery of both men and machines you understand it as a typical, empty anguish that makes even crime and banditry forgivable means of evasion.

From the beginning Lorca announces this duality of gaiety and pain. This reality creates in the poet a feeling of exile and alienation that emanates from the city, as well as a deep feeling of loneliness resulting from the fact that he comes from a rural town in Granada. That Lorca justifies crime and banditry as an answer to machines and to a society organized around capital and its profit obviates his romantic attitude. There is an implicit criticism in *Poet in New York* of modernism in its architectural expression (Lorca says "extrahuman architecture"). This aspect of Lorca's book is both crucial and visionary. Indeed, decades after the writing of *Poet in New York,* we find, among architects of the so-called "post-modern" school, a reiteration of that critical attitude toward rational, purely functional architecture, which Lorca sets forth with such vehemence in his text.

The basic contradiction of big cities in relation to their founding principle is that originally, the creation of the metropolis was joined to the idea of establishing a community in which life would be more pleasurable, a community bound by common values. However, a very different reality resulted from this effort, and cities became a place of egoist individualism and indifferent crowds. Lorca depicts this alienated city in his poem "Landscape of the Vomiting Crowd":

> On its way home from the fair, the crowd sings and vomits in groups of hundreds over the railings of the boardwalk. In groups of

a thousand it urinates on the corners, on abandoned boats, or on the
monument to Garibaldi or the unknown soldier.

You cannot imagine the loneliness a Spaniard feels there, especially an Andalusian. If you fall they will trample you, and if you
fall into the water, they will bury you under their lunch wrappers.

The impression of the crowd arouses in the citizen and in this poet a painful
feeling that he lives in a desert or in an aquatic space. The famous line of Co-
leridge "Water, water, everywhere, / nor any drop to drink" has now become a
brutal reality. The fundamental anonymity that is the basis of modern cities
makes possible a masked individual who perpetrates his fantasies without involving himself in relationships with another individual, or with the community
at large. The anonymous fantasy affords the only way to express the impulses
of the libido without clashing with social obedience and with the demands of a
highly organized democracy, in which work, family and religion are the supreme
values.
    In his lecture, Lorca alludes to two very important poetic presences central to
Poet in New York:

And the crowd! No one can imagine just what a New York
crowd is like, except perhaps Walt Whitman, who searched it for
solitude, and T.S. Eliot, who squeezes the crowd like a lemon in
his poem, extracting rats, wounds, wet shades, and fluvial shades.

Although in truth Whitman sought loneliness among the crowd, he also talked
about "the certainty of others." This certainty gave sense to the poetic voice of
Whitman the man; this essential otherness Lorca finds in his Spanish gypsies
and in the Negros of New York. It is also very tempting to compare T.S.
Eliot's *Waste Land* with *Poet in New York* [4] Lorca writes:

The sky has conquered the skyscrapers, and from a distance New
York's architecture seems prodigious and, no matter what they intended, it moves one as much as a natural spectacle, a mountain or
desert.

The impression of desert given by New York architecture, and the indifference of
its crowd, exacerbates Lorca's anxiety.
    Another striking aspect of the life and works of the Andalusian poet is his
sense of theatricality. It is a positive theatricality, by means of which Lorca
transforms every room, house or city into a stage on which the poet and men in
general can become an actor. In this manner, Manhattan was the grand stage on
which Lorca becomes the main character in the great tragedy of modern civilization. If we visualize the figure of the poet as a tragic young man, placed in the
middle of a "prodigious" architectural cityscape that looks like "a mountain or

desert", we can realize what the poet felt, looking at the big city: a perception of the sublime. Anguish and pleasure form part of the feeling of the sublime. It is from the vision of something magnificent, something that cannot be apprehended by the human mind or eye, that this sensation emanates. In a modern context, the sublime acquires a new meaning, a meaning far removed from the sense of timelessness that motivates the romantic observers. In the modern city, the sublime becomes an extraordinary fact that takes place in the here and now, giving us a sense of temporality of the instantaneous.[5] This is what I think Lorca felt in his visual experience of Manhattan.

In Lorca's poetic vision, the sublime becomes a negative element. He sees the city as a desert because he feels it has no roots, that is to say, history. Everything appears to him new, recently constructed, pure imitation. For Lorca, as a poet close to a strong poetic tradition, born in a country of tradition and historical continuity, the only thing that could be done was to break with his traditions when he had to face such a disturbing city as New York. At the end of his lecture he insists: "My first impression, that the world has no roots, remains with me ..." Therefore, his tendency to use the fragmented imagery observed in *Poet in New York* is not surprising. Perhaps with this in mind, Lorca wrote the following lines in his "Play and Theory of the Duende":

> But there are neither maps nor disciplines to help us find the duende. We only know that he burns the blood like a poultice of broken glass, that he exhausts, that he rejects all the sweet geometry we have learned, that he smashes styles ...

Lorca sees a rootless world in New York City. He could have conceived only of a subversive solution for big city corruption: violence. This violence is twofold: violence against the ruling class, and at the same time the poet's self sacrifice to redeem the white race. This attitude is clearly related to a secularization of the Christian myth of salvation.

The "sleepy boy", as waiters who knew him in New York called Lorca, was in an urbanscape which he saw as a compound of "form and anguish." In this sort of city Lorca searched for something spiritual, and he found a world in which spirituality was related to success, money and profit. This Philistine idea had given shape to the colonization of the country, leaving no room for pleasure, fancy, or esoteric spiritual activities — the puritan concept of hard work and religious worship as the price to be paid for the production and accumulation of riches. Thus were built the cities of the United States.

Lorca will find a spiritual side of America among the most creative and poorest group in New York City — the blacks. For Lorca, Wall Street symbolized the most anti-spiritual aspect of American society. On the other hand, Harlem became for him the metaphor of the only spiritual values not buried beneath America's Philistine puritanism.

The antagonism between Wall Street and Harlem is fundamental to the dynamics of *Poet in New York*. These places are symbolical of the most productive encounter of two cultures, the Western and the African. The symbiotic art that resulted from these two cultures lies at the very heart of modern aesthetics. It seems, however, that Lorca misinterpreted the violent social circumstances of New York. He thought the antagonistic situation between the white and black cultures was also reflected in an antagonism between "white" and "black" art. When in fact white culture was tremendously influenced by black culture, and vice versa. Let us examine, first, his vision of Wall Street:

> The terrible, cold, cruel part is Wall Street. Rivers of gold flow there from all over the earth, and death comes with it. There as nowhere else you feel a total absence of the spirit.
> (...)
> I was lucky enough to see with my own eyes the recent crash, where they lost various billions of dollars, a rubble of dead money that slid off into the sea, and never as then, amid suicides, hysteria, and groups of fainters, have I felt the sensation of real death, death without hope, death that is nothing but rottenness, for the spectacle was terrifying by devoid of greatness.

If we compare this vision of death in America with is description of death as a positive element in Spanish culture, we will realize how negative his approach to Wall Street as a symbol of the most destructive element of American society is. In "Play and Theory of the Duende" he says:

> Everywhere else, death is an end. Death comes, they draw the curtains. Not in Spain. In Spain they open them. Many Spaniards live indoors until the day they die and are taken out into the sunlight. A dead man in Spain is more alive as a dead man than any place else in the world.

And he will add: "Spain is the only country where death is a national spectacle."[6]

But what Lorca describes in *Poet in New York* is an epic of the negative, an "esperpentic" epic, and he uses the 1929 Depression in the United States as a background upon which to project his negative view of white culture in the city.

It is in Harlem, among the blacks, the García Lorca meets with what he considers the spiritual element of American society. He discovers that they possess an atavistic nobility, an origin and a history full of mystery — precisely those elements that he misses in the white ruling class. He writes in his lecture:

> Every race in the world turns up in New York, but the Chinese, Armenians, Russians, and Germans keep on being foreigners. Everyone except the blacks. There is no doubt that the blacks exercise great influence in North America, and, I don't care what anyone says, they are the most delicate and spiritual element of the

world. Because they believe, because they hope and they sing, and because they have an exquisite religious purity that saves from all their dangerous present-day troubles.

All that the Andalusian Lorca sees in the blacks, he finds passionate. He sees freedom expressed in their dance, their songs and music. Lorca discovers in the black race a "yearning to be a nation", and "spiritual depths that are unbribable." For this reason he denounces the fact that these "creatures of paradise" have submitted to white rules and ways of living. He expresses his protest in his poem "New York, Office and Denunciation." He transforms the black into a monarch without dominion, a black king without an African forest, trapped in urban life:

I protested to see so much flesh robbed from paradise ... and I protested the saddest thing of all, that the blacks do not want to be black, that they invent pomades to take away the delicious curl of their hair and powders that turn their faces gray and syrups that fill out their waists and wither the succulent persimmon of their lips.

Lorca sees in the blacks a possible salvation for the United States, this nation dispossessed of spirit. Consequently, he denounces everything that separates blacks from their genuine natural life. This romantic neoprimitivism in Lorca's works, is present in *Poet in New York* in many ways. He gives greater importance to nature and to animals.[7] He always appreciates the natural attitude of human beings but disdains their urbanity. In his "Ode to Walt Whitman" he attacks the affected homosexuals of cities, because he sees in them the worst expression of city perversion. In Walt Whitman, a man who compares bodies with rivers, he sees the perfect natural homosexual. Love in the big cities is bad, and "life is not noble, or wholesome, or holy", he says in this ode.[8]

Lorca sees his own contradictions, fears and desires reflected in the multi-faceted mirror that is, for him, the city of New York. In some way, the real self discovery of Lorca as a poet and as an individual takes place in New York. As we noted earlier, the city becomes a grand stage for the playing out of Lorca's own tragedy. During his stay in New York a sort of catharsis takes place in his life. The author's true identity is revealed to him. The result of this revelation is *Poet in New York*.[9]

4. Conclusions

In order for this catharsis to take place, there had to be in the poet's heart, a certain feeling of guilt. For Lorca, as for many, the big city represented heaven and hell, desire and fear, temptation and the threat of a final punishment. Lorca's hero in his "esperpentic" epic of the great city, was one who walked in a ghostly, though crowded city, where everything looked devilish, and death was without greatness.

Lorca felt that Wall Street was hell, and a symbol of the modern and capitalist society that he naturally rejected. On the other hand, Harlem was the place where "creatures of paradise" lived, with their music, their dance, their flamboyant flesh. At the same time, he was living in limbo — Columbia University — among friends and scholars, and the brightest and richest young men of America. It should not surprise us that he wrote a violent book, for he was in a uniquely violent city, the city that was going to become a symbol: of modernity, and later of the postmodern attitude. With this book, Lorca is one of the first witnesses to the accumulation of contradictions in Western culture, contradictions that were the seeds of an uneasiness we feel today in art and in politics.

The conflict between poet and city was partially resolved in the 19th century, in a negative way, with the self-absorption of the poet in his work. The figure of the poet in ancient history was that of a man rejected by society. Later he became a vagabond, and in the Renaissance he turned into a universal man totally immersed in the city. Finally, his poetry became permeable to urban language. Octavio Paz has pointed out in several articles, that what distinguishes the poetry written in the last forty years from that written before 1940 is the incorporation of city language into the poetic discourse. *Poet in New York* is a transition between a self-centered poetry with romantic tones and the incorporation of the city as poetic language.

We do not know exactly why Lorca left Spain. Neither do we know what he sought in New York. But we do know that he did not find in the modern metropolis an ideal human being who could challenge the alienation of modern life. That is why Lorca turned to a precultural myth of the natural man which he found in some ways in the American blacks. The result of his New York ordeal is one of the most astonishing books of modern poetry. In it he combines social denunciation, personal self-exploration, aesthetic findings, and a unique portrait of the most sublime and most sinister aspects of our modern civilization.

NOTES

1. I would like to express my gratitude to my friends Dominique Malaquais and David M. Caskey for the careful reading of the manuscript.

2. Essential to the elaboration of this article has been Burton Pike's book *The Image of the City in Modern Literature*. Princeton: Princeton University Press, 1981. Thanks to Prof. Franco Zangrilli, I read some chapters related with my topic of a book by Italo Calvino, *Collezione di Sabbia*. Milano: Garzani Editore, 1984.

3. García Lorca, Federico. *Poet in New York*. (Complete Spanish Translation by Ben Belitt). New York: Grove Press, 1955, 1983. All of my quotations are taken from the new edition.

For the textual problems of *Poet in New York*. See: Eisenberg, Daniel. *The Textual Tradition of "Poeta en Nueva York"* published in Spanish as *Poeta en Nueva York: historia y problemas de un texto de Lorca*. (traducción de Carlos Pujol) Barcelona: Ariel, 1976. There is an interesting article partially dedicated to this book by Jenaro Talens, "El discurso poético lorquiano: medievalismo y teatralidad". Granada: Universidad de Granada, 1983.

4. García Lorca, Federico. "A Poet in New York". In Maurer, Christopher (ed. and tr.). *Deep Song and Other Prose*, New York: New Directions, 1980. All of my quotations of Lorca's conference as well as quotations from "Play and Theory of the Duende" are from this translation.

The letter to Carlos Morla Lynch is found in: Gershator, David (ed. and tr.) *Federico García Lorca. Selected Letters*. New York: New Directions, 1983. There are other letters to different people where Lorca's contradictory feelings toward New York appear. He writes to Philip Cumming: "I hope you'll answer me and won't forget this poet from the South now lost in this Babylonic, cruel and violent city, filled on the other hand, with a great modern beauty." He writes to Melchor Fernández Almagro: "I'm not going to do descriptions of New York for you. It's immense, but it is made for man, the human proportion adjusts to things that from far away seem gigantic and disordered." (From *Federico García Lorca. Selected letters*).

An interesting book based on conversations, comments and interviews with Lorca's family, friends and critics, is the book by Mildred Adams, *García Lorca: Playwright and Poet*. New York: George Braziller, 1977. Lorca's experience in New York is discussed in Chapters 6, 7 and 8.

5. See Durán, Manuel. "Introduction" In: *Lorca. A Collection of Critical Essays* Englewood Cliffs: Prentice-Hall, 1962. pp. 8–10. Also del Río, Angel, "Introduction" to Ben Belitt's translation of *Poet in New York*. pp. XXX–XXXII.

6. For this new conception of the sublime see: Lyotard, Jean-Francois. "The Sublime and the Avant-Garde". *Art Forum* (April 1984): 36–43.

7. Philippe Ariès in his book *Western Attitudes toward Death: From the Middle Ages to the Present*, translated by Patricia M. Ranum, (Baltimore: The Johns Hopkins University Press, 1974), writes: "It seems that the modern attitude toward death, that is to say the interdiction of death in order to preserve happiness, was born in the United States around the beginning of the twentieth century" (p. 94). If we compare this quotation with Lorca's statement we can see the tremendous difference between American and Spanish culture in this respect.

See also "Death Denied" in the book by the same author *The Hour of Our Death*, translated by Helen Weaver (New York: Vintage Books, 1982).

8. See: Higginbotham, Virginia. "Reflejos de Lautréamont en *Poeta en Nueva York*." In: Gil, Ildefonso-Manuel (ed.) *Federico García Lorca*. Madrid: Taurus, 1973.

9. I think that Lorca's attitude against affected homosexuals of cities is related to his comparison of Walt Whitman's homosexuality and than of Hart Crane, whom Lorca met in New York. Mildred Adams writes: "The meeting with the young Hart Crane was less fruitful [than his visit to Wall Street]. The friend who took Federico to Brooklyn to meet the American described it with some hesitation. Crane, whose homosexual tendencies were hardly secret, was at the time surrounded with young sailors. Illegal beer ran freely. All of them were drunk. It was not an ideal moment for an American poet and a Spanish poet to forge a friendship. There was even doubt that the American had comprehended who the Spaniard was." (*García Lorca: Playwright and Poet*, p. 122).

10. In an excellent essay on this book Richard Saez writes: "The true agony of *Poet in New York* is in the *narrative* of Lorca's search for meaning and identity in the concrete jungle: a search which at times takes the shape of a quest for love, at times a quest for the poet's proper self, which he has lost in his inhuman and unidentifiable surroundings, and finally, a search which has as its central expression the attempt to establish a meaningful and ordered sacrifice that will give back to the quester as well as to the city their identity, virility, and place in the cosmic order." See: "The Ritual Sacrifice in Lorca's *Poet in New York*." In: Durán, Manuel, *Lorca. A Collection of Critical Essays* Englewood Cliffs: Prentice Hall, 1962. pp. 109–110.

ELENA GASCÓN VERA
Wellesley College

Stories of Madness: The Feminine in *Poet in New York*

> Anything that breaks away, that breaks with the established order, has to do with homosexuality, or with metamorphosis, or with becoming a woman.
>
> Felix Guattari
>
> To Lori Roses

When García Lorca arrived in New York at the end of June, 1929, he carried with him a mixture of feelings and desires that culminated in an excruciating need to remove himself from Spain and to distract himself from what he called his "penumbra sentimental."[1] This "shadow" was born of a deep depression which had lasted several years and against which he had struggled the preceding months; it stemmed from tensions caused by his relationship and break with a lover, Emilio Aladrén Perojo.[2] He also saw in this trip the opportunity of discovering, for the first time, an environment different from his own, distant from and opposed to the personal and professional acceptance that he enjoyed among family and friends in Spain. The idea of living in New York seemed aversive and therefore, in a personal and poetic sense, stimulating.[3]

We can reconstruct, with reasonable accuracy, Lorca's sentiments before departure and also what he experienced in that great city during the scant year that he spent there: through his own declarations, his letters, and the multitude of literary portraits and biographies that have been written about him.[4] Nonetheless, the most profound and revealing key must be sought in the poems he wrote during those months, that is, in the posthumous book, *Poet in New York*.[5]

Though the poet himself often repeated that his stay in New York had changed his poetry, a number of critics have pointed out, accurately so, that *Poet in New York* reveals themes and a style similar to his earlier poetry, which also aspired to the daring, the new, and a merging of personal experiences with poetic inspiration.[6] Still, the hermeticism and the imaginative freedom of this book reveal a greater liberation of the unconscious, a deepening of self-analysis and expression lacking in his previous poems.

It is true that Lorca and his critics have repeatedly denied the surrealistic dimension of his poetry to the extent that Surrealism can be defined by automatic and irrational writing,[7] but it is indubitable that the poems written in the United States seem to be a response to the harsh words that Salvador Dalí wrote to Lorca after the resounding success of the *Romancero gitano* in September of 1928.[8]

Dalí, at that time, was at the peak of surrealistic fervor and attempting to unite conscious and unconscious experience in the same plane of thought. He wanted the real world to appear expressed along with fantasy and dream in an absolute reality, that is, a surreality. Therefore, it is no surprise that he disliked the poetry in a popular vein that Lorca was writing in the *Romancero gitano*. In his letter he tells Lorca:

> Your current poetry falls into the category of traditional; in it I note the weightiest poetic substance that has yet existed: but linked in no way to ancient poetry, incapable of moving us nor of satisfying our present desires. Your poetry is tied hand and foot to old poetry. Perhaps you will think these images too bold or will find enough irrationality in your writing, but I can tell you that your poetry belongs to the "illustration" of the most stereotyped and conformist clichés.

Further on, the painter adds:

> The day you lose your fear, spit on the Salinas, abandon rhyme, in sum, art as it is practiced among swine — you will do entertaining things, convulsed things, poetic as no other poet has done.

In other parts of the same letter, Dalí makes reference to more personal things and relates the infantile thumb, almost prenatal, of the poet, to his penis, telling him that he sees him imprisoned by his own arms as in a straight jacket, introducing the image of the armless trunk that Lorca would use as a phallic symbol in *Poet in New York*. At the end, Dalí commits the slip of writing "invierto" for "invierno" and encourages Lorca to jump into the void: "This inversion [sic] I invite you to jump into the void. I have already been in it for several days, never have I felt so secure."

This "void," which in its variations of "hole" and "cavity" and "nakedness" appears many times in *Poet in New York*.

> Do not ask me. I have seen things
> which end in void while searching their course
> There is pain of cavities in the air without people
> and upon my eyes appear creatures dressed without nakedness.
> 1910 Intermission

> No preguntarme nada. He visto que las cosas
> cuando buscan su curso encuentran su vacío.
> Hay un dolor de huecos por el aire sin gente
> y en mis ojos criaturas vestidas sin desnudo!
> 1910 Intermedio

Throughout Dalí's letter there is a clear intent to incite Lorca to liberate his amorous, sexual and poetic desires, to fully accept his true self and to express it in his poetry. Buñuel, too, disliked the *Romancero gitano,* as he said to a mutual friend, Pepín Bello:

> I saw Federico in Madrid, and once more we were close; my opinion will seem more sincere to you if I tell you that his book of ballads *El Romancero gitano* ... strikes me as bad. It is a poetry fine enough and approximately modern enough to please the Andrenios, the Baezas and the gay Cernudian poets of Seville. But from that to the truly exquisite and great poets of today there is an abyss.[9]

This rejection of his surrealistic friends toward the folkloric, Andalusian and gypsy poetry that Lorca was writing before 1928, must have influenced him a great deal because he immediately commented to his friend Sebastián Gasch on his book:

"It has died in my arms in the most touching way. My poetry takes a different, even more acute, flight. A more personal one, I think."[10]

It is this personal element that permeates all the poems in *Poet in New York* and which, in many ways, seems to carry Lorca to extremes of mad desolation and abandonment. It is this aspect that interests me in relation to the theme of the feminine which I attempt to develop in this essay.

Before outlining a possible reading of this theme in Lorca, I wish to comment on the first poem of the Séneca edition, "Vuelta de paseo"[11].

Home from a walk

Assassinated by the sky
between the forms that are moving toward the serpent,
and the forms that are moving toward the crystal.
I'll let my hair fall down,
with the tree of amputated limbs that does not sing,
and the boy with the white face of an egg,
with all the tiny animals who have broken heads
and the ragged water that walks on its dry feet.
With all the things that have deaf and dumb fatigue
and the butterfly drowned in the ink pot.
Stumbling over my face that changes everyday,
Assassinated by the sky!

This poem, though there is nothing in the text to justify it, has always been analyzed by critics as the impressions collected by the poet upon his return to

his home from a walk through the streets of New York. The cause of this interpretation lies in the fact that Lorca presented it thus in his lecture and recital of
Poet in New York in Madrid in March of 1932. Lorca said at that time:

> I, wandering alone, exhausted by the rhythm of the immense neon
> lights of Times Square, fled in this brief poem from the immense
> army of windows from which not one person has the time to gaze
> at a cloud or converse with one of those delicate breezes that the sea
> stubbornly sends us without ever receiving a response.[12]

It is quite possible that Lorca was taking refuge in "Vuelta de paseo" from a
feeling of loneliness in the big city, but the real meaning of this poem has little
to do with New York. We all know that poets are not completely sincere in
their recitals and less so a Lorca who was endeavoring to maintain his homosexual preferences as hidden as possible from the public. Thus, beneath the text of
the Dalí letter which I have just mentioned, and bering in mind the context of
the entire work, one must see this poem as an *Ars Poetica*. With it the author
announces thathe is about to being a new poetry, in which he accepts his homosexuality. "Home from a walk" must be read along with the "Poemas from Lake
Eden Mills", "Your childhood in Menton", "Little boy Stanton", "Little Vien-
nese Waltz", "Unsleeping City", "Brooklyn Bridge Nocturne", "Ode to Walt
Whitman", all of which contain unequivocal homosexual references.[13] To comment briefly on "Vuelta de paseo," in the first verses Lorca begins accepting the
sexual ambiguity which torments him. He feels: "Assasinated by the sky / between the forms that are moving toward the serpent [phallus] / and the forms that
are moving toward the crystal [chastity]" [vv. 1–3].

He feels "assassinated by the heavens" that have marked him since birth with
an inversion that tends toward masculine forms": "serpent" which signified the
temptation of the phallus, transgression, and sin; at the same time he is torn between his desire for purity and sexual normality represented by the word
"crystal". Later on he takes up the images that Dalí insinuated in his letter and
with which he urged Lorca towards liberation: "I'll let my hair fall down" [let
one's hair down] /"With the tree of amputated limbs that does not sing" [phallus
/ repressed voice] [vv.1–2]

With the phrase: "and the boy with the white face of an egg", he alludes to
the Spanish expression: "Child, clean the egg off your face!" which means ignorance, innocence, immaturity. In "with all the tiny animals who have broken
heads," he alludes to the tattered stuffed animals that remain when childhood is
over, and also expresses an allusion to a possible castration; and in "and the
ragged water that walks on its dry feet", he uses the customary symbols of water
as opposed to dryness, to connote repressed desire.

In verses 9 to 11 he indicates how he has felt until now because he tried to
conceal in his poetry his true homosexual nature: "With all the things that have
deaf and dumb fatigue / and the butterfly drowned in the ink pot / Stumbling
over my face that changes everyday" (vv. 9–11).

In "deaf and dumb fatigue", he returns to the idea of the unexpressed voice and the desire to begin to free it. With "butterfly drowned in the ink pot" he refers, with another characteristic metaphor, to his homosexual poetry, until now repressed. In "Stumbling over my face that changes everyday", he accepts his ambiguity, his doubts, and his fears.

The last verse, which is identical to the first: "Assassinated by the sky!" (V. 12), now changes its meaning and no longer means marked by birth, but the acceptance and the fear that his liberated poetry will represent, perhaps, rejection and exclusion from society and religion.

Despite this commentary which, as I have said before, is indispensable before turning to *Poet in New York,* I do not intend to perfomr a classical Freudian psychoanalysis, because it has already been attempted, with greater or lesser fortune, by some critics.[14] I wish to see this work in the context of the cultural and political theories expressed in the modern concepts of desire, homosexuality, and femaleness, to adjust them, in certain instances, to the modernity of *Poet in New York.* Of course this theme is so broad that it will only be possible, in the space allotted here, to allude to a possible reading from these points of view, and to determine the critical possibilities that lie therein.

In the first place, I begin by considering *Poet in New York* as an autobiography, that is, as an attempt at personal expression that, in my opinion, coordinates with a wish of self-definition that is typically female. That is, in his poems there is fragmentation, chaos, doubt, constant reference to voids and faults, to pain and fears — themes and attitudes that modern feminist criticism inscribes within typically female literary allusions.[15]

I am fully aware of the perils and the risk involved in considering a book of posthumous poems, edited by friends years after the assassination of the author and the tragedy of the Civil War, as an autobiography. Nonetheless, no one can dismiss a re-grouping and re-structuring of the poems. Lorca's poetic self is in constant dialogue with certain places and concrete times in a specific external and internal world in the face of which he, in favor or against, is defining and expressing himself.

Poet in New York is in the same tradition as the autobiographical experiments of Yeats, T.S. Eliot, William Carlos Williams, and Robert Lowell and also the *Memorial de Isla Negra* of Neruda, since in all those texts the poetic self of the author is the principal and primary subject and object of the verbal action. Yet, what draws me to Lorca's text is the conjoining of the analytical and the auto-analyical, where there is a reluctance to delimit and complete the thematic and representative intention of his poems, creating a poetry that, without being surrealisitic, in the irrational sense, introduces a variety of indeterminate images that elude a purely rational explanation but achieve a union of author and reader in an intuitive interpretation. *Poet in New York* is clearly opposed to the conventional male autobiography, whether in prose or in verse, where the author tries to impose order on his life and the external world, to achieve a fullness of being and thereby acquire an exact and certain place in the world.

The autobiographical author, generally, seems to be certain of his purpose in life, and in his work he tries to reconstruct it with detail and control. On the contrary, the female autobiographies in prose or poetry such as, for example, *The Bell Jar,* by Sylvia Plath, depart in principle from the skepticism of their own interest, tend stylistically towards indefinite pronouns, fragmented phrases, and interruptions. In Lorca the force and the abstraction of the images and metaphors denote an indeterminacy and an aperture to interpretive intention, at the same time that they liberate the desire to create the most intimate poetry, unconstrained by the ideas of attaining power and control. There is nothing in *Poeta in New York* that does not relate to the revelation of the most personal, profound and intimate reality of Lorca, that is, the expression of his anguish upon a mature acceptance of his homosexuality. We can easily comprehend why, though he knew it was his best poetical work, he resisted publishing it.

From this point about intimacy I wish to extract the elements of femaleness from a poetry that, at first glance, presents a fullness of phallic and eminently masculine symbols. Nonetheless, it is in this homosexual masculinity referred to obliquely in many of the poems, where I intend to follow the definition of desire, homosexuality and femaleness of Gilles Deleuze and Félix Guattari, because they, seeking a definition of the anti-oepidal man and a program for an anti-fascist form of life, define elements that can well be applied to the poems of *Poet in New York.*[16]

Deleuze and Guattari consider human desire a flux that is latent in us, previous to birth. It is formed by whatever the world and its affections offer us outside of ourselves and in spite of ourselves, and flows from us in an involuntary and continuous form. To them, this flux is not an indifferentiated magma, but rather the human being, man or woman, is like a "desire machine" which regulates and connects the fluxes, but does not recognize distinctions between persons, organs, material flux or metaphoric and semiotic fluxes. This desire is located in the entire body, and can be equated with sexuality which, according to Deleuze and Guattari, can be expressed with words such as "interaction", "transform", "convert", "become", etc.[17]

Nonetheless, according to them, the body and sexuality are repressed by capitalism and the tendency of the Western world toward fascism. Since the female has traditionally been alienated from power, she is more likely to feel desire, because she, unlike the male, has not concentrated her sexuality in the genital zone, but has preserved it on the surface of her body. Thus, they believe that in the relation that the human being has with the body, there is an affinity among the sexually marginal, that is, among homosexuals, transvestites, and women.

Taking into account these ideas, we see that a comprehensive reading of *Poet in New York* will show an obsession with the female body, but projecting a disfigured and grotesque image of this body.

In "Landscape of the vomiting multitudes (Coney Island Dusk)", Lorca says:

The fat lady came on,
pulling up roots and wetting the drum-skins;

the fat lady
who turns up cuttlefish and leaves them to die, wrong side out.
The fat lady, hostile to moons,
raced through the streets and the tenantless levels,
leaving pigeon-skull trails in the corners,
kindling the furies of obsolete feasts,
calling the demon of bread from the slopes of swept sky
and sifting light's ardor into underground transits.
They are graveyards. I know it. They are graveyards, a sadness of
kitchen sunk deep under silt;
another times's pheasants and apples; those who tighten our
throats are the dead.
A muttering came from the forest of vomit:
woman's sterility, molten-wax children,
fermentation of trees, and unwearying waiters
serving platters of salt under harps of saliva.
No help for it! Vomit it up boy! No other way.
Not the vomit of hussars on the breasts of their harlots,
or the vomit of cats unmindfully gulping down frogs.
Those who scratch with the clay of their hands
on the doorways of flint and the rotting confections and clouds,
are the dead.

The fat lady came on
with the crowds from the boats and the bars and the gardens.
The fanfare was light on the drumheads of vomit
by the daughters of blood
who seek the protection of moons.
Welladay! Welladay! Welladay!
My gaze, that was one time my own, is no longer my own,
a gaze trembling naked in alcohol,
launching incredible navies
on quays of anemone.
The gaze that preserves me
must issue on waves where dawn never ventures:
I, poet and armless, adrift
In the vomiting multitudes,
lacking even the spirit of horses to crop
the rank moss of my temples.

But the fat lady came on, as before,
and the crowds called for drugstores
where the tropical bitters were waiting.
And not till the first dogs arrived, and they broke out the flags,
did the city swarm out the rails of the jetty, as one.

It is clear that in this poem Lorca indicts the dynamism of the woman, fat, overwhelming, implacable, and insatiable for power over all domestic and vital activity, blaming her for chaos and death. He contrasts her, negatively, with his own experience as a suffering poet, impotent, solitary, persecuted and abandoned, who seeks in drink the blurring of a reality that confronts him. Finally, he seems to find a palliative for his feelings of loneliness, for his desire for sexual and emotional contact, through the poetic word.

For Lorca his attitude toward the female implies a rejection of the essence of femininity and seems to function for the poet as an exorcism of female tendencies which, in his homosexuality, tormented him. A clear example of this ambiguity of acceptance and rejection of the female can be seen in the "Ode to Walt Whitman" when he speaks of the two types of homosexuals that, according to him, exist:

> That is why I do not raise my voice, aged Walt Whitman,
> against the little boy who writes
> a girl's name on his pillow,
> nor the boy who dresses himself in the bride's trousseau
> in the darkness of the wardrobe,
> nor the solitary men in clubs
> who drink the water of prostitution with nausea,
> nor the men with a green stare
> who love man and burn their lips in silence.

These he considers: "the perplexed, the pure, / the classicists, the noted, the supplicants." In contrast to them, he attacks another type of homosexual:

> But against you, yes, pansies of the cities,
> of tumescent flesh and unclean mind,
> mud of drains, harpies, unsleeping enemies
> of Love which distributes crowns of joy.
>
> Against you always, you who give boys
> drop of soiled death with bitter poison.
> Against you always,
> Fairies of North America,
> Pájaros of Havana,
> Jotos of Mexico,
> Sarasas of Cadiz,
> Apios of Seville,
> Cancos of Madrid,
> Floras of Alicante,
> Adelaidas of Portugal.

He looks down on them as:

Pansies of the world, murders of doves!
Women's slaves, bitches of their boudoirs,
opened with the fever of fans in public squares
or ambushed in frigid landscapes of hemlock.
Let there be no quarter! Death
flows from your eyes
and clusters grey flowers on the shores.
Let there be no quarter! Take heed!
let the perplexed, the pure,
the classicist, the noted, the supplicants,
close the gates of the Bacchanalia.

Thus, it is possible to see that for Lorca, homosexuals who imitate women openly and shamelessly are despicable and should be destroyed. It is obvious that in this stance there is an anti-female phobia that he also expressed in some interviews and that, at the same time, appears in all its ambiguity and terror in his poetry. As I said earlier, this phobia presents itself, at times, as an unconscious necessity to exorcise the female tendencies that were implicit in his homosexual preferences.

On the other hand, it is necessary to mention here that the personality and the physical appearance of Lorca must have been quite effeminate, because his biographer Gibson mentions that in the Instituto de Granada where he studied as a youth, his fellow students teasingly called him "Federica" and refused to play with him because they considered him a sissy.[18] Also, he had heard comments that as an adult, he himself, in the intimacy of his homosexual friends, liked to be called Federica. Moreover, we have the testimony of Phillip Cummings, a friend with whom Lorca spent some time in Vermont, in an interview done by Dionisio Cañas en *El Pais,* where Cummings mentions that Lorca complained of his brother Paco always warning him to watch his feminine mannerisms.[19]

The phobia of the female in certain homosexuals has its psychoanalytical basis in the Freudian explanation of the development of the oedipus complex of the child, when he begins to move away from the mother and identify with the father. This conflict, according to Freud, appears unresolved in homosexuals.[20] The paradox in Lorca is that he rejects the feminine implicit in certain social situations, in which the woman and the men who imitate her, appear as beings whose only role is to be a housewife or a sexual object for men. In a conversation with a friend, Lorca says:

The thing is, if it is true what you are telling me, you are as abnormal as I am. Which truly I am. Because I have only known men; and you know that the inverted man, the pansie, makes me laugh, it amuses me with his desire to be a woman, to wash clothes, to iron, to sow, to make up his face, to wear skirts, to speak with effeminated gestures and expressions.[21]

Thus it is evident that the latent negative force toward stereotypes of the female, in a patriarchal misogynist society, of the first half of the twentieth century, in which Lorca lived, caused him to reject everything that could be identified with the ordinary attributes of femaleness. While on the other hand, he considers homosexuality as a sexual and amorous choice superior to the heterosexual, because, he believes, only in homosexual love can one attain true romantic equality. Lorca goes on to say, in the interview,

> What is normal is limitless love. For love is more and better than the dictates of a dogma, than Catholic morality; no one can make me resign myself to the idea of simply having children. Both ideas are very clear in my mind. Each is as it must be. Without reversals. No one controls, no one must dominte, there must be no submission. There must be no assigning of roles. No substitutions or changes. There must be only abandonment and mutual pleasure. But a true revolution would be necessary. A new morality, a morality of complete liberation. What Walt Whitman called for.

Yet in his call for a homosexual revolution, Lorca seems to accept the feminine, as Deleuze and Guattari describe it in their anti-edipal theories, in which they explain that homosexuals and women, having been repressesd sexually for so many centuries, are superior to heterosexual men, because they have access to a desire in which the entire body participates erotically in a situation of equality. The heterosexual man also can participate in that revolution if he accedes to desire. To that end he needs to discover his body and through it his own sexuality. Because, they believe, man will only be able to have a heterosexual or for that matter any successful relationship, when he is transformed into a homosexual or a woman. That is, he must "devenir femme".[22]

This "becoming a woman" must not be seen as a social or textual change but a true metamorphosis. It does not mean imitation or adjustment to a paradigm, but entering into a changing flux — a topological and geological process, not a historical one. It means an osmosis with entities that have not become anthropomorphized, such as women, children, animals, the marginal, the insane. They are a minority, and united they must oppose the representation of Western man, capitalist and fascist as represented by the majority. This is the "man-adult-white-heterosexual- who lives in the city - and who speaks a European language", who can be considered the "standard," he who controls and manages power. The modern human being must try to become a minority to be able to invent new forces and new images. Of all the processes to enter the minority, the first is becoming a woman because she is the minority closest to men. She is synonym of the valid, the transparent, the innocent, the dynamic, which is opposed to masculinity, virility, gravity, and power, all of which are negative and must change.

With their ideas Deleuze and Guattari combat three adversaries: those who want to preserve order and the "status quo" and who take a sad, ascetic attitude to what they consider the truth. They also combat those who try to annul the multiplicity of desire to reduce it to law and a unified structure. But, above all, they combat every form of implantation of power by force, all forces of fascism, not only the historical, but the fascism which is inside of our very selves, our mind, our daily conduct, the fascism which leads us to want power and to desire the things that dominate and exploit us.

Applying these theoretical points of view to *Poet in New York,* one can see that in this work Lorca, too, is liberating to the maximum that multiple and at the same time ordered desire, in an abstract way, to express greater intimacy of his being that could be expressed in the three capital themes which make up his book: the hatred of oppression; the rebellion against the inevitability of death and pain; and a gradual intention to express homosexuality.

In his poems he liberates his anguish by penetrating and exploring madness. He goes from the paranoia that he showed in the *Romancero Gitano* toward the schizophrenic tension of *Poet in New York,* expressing sentiments of dementia, conflict, psychic pain, and crime. He cries out his condemnation of racism in "Norm and paradise of blacks" and in "The King of Harlem"; against the power of the Church in "Grito hacia Roma"; against the fascism of Mussolini en "Suplcro judío"; against the power of money and capitalism in "New York oficina y denuncia". He identifies with the marginal, children, blacks, animals, and despite his rejection of femaleness, also with women. For example, in "Landscape of the Urinating Multitudes (Battery Place Nocturne)".

> They kept to themselves, being men,
> and awaited the rush of the ultimate cyclist.
> They kept to themselves, being women,
> and awaited the death of a boy on a Japanese cutter.
> Men and women: they kept to themselves,
> dreaming the death of the birds, with mouths open like birds,
> priking with parasol points
> the toad lately gutted
> in a thousand-eared silence
> by the outlets of water
> in mountain passes that resist
> the raging assault of the moon.
> The boy in the cutter wept on, there was breaking of hearts,
> in the anguish that broods on the vigil and witness of things
> and in a heavenly maze of dark footfalls,
> dim names cry out spittle and nickel-plate radios.
> And what if the boy, when the last nail goes in, is quiet?
> And what if a breeze is concealed in the cotton's corolla?

We remain in a world of the dead, with definitive sailors
that peer from the arches and curdle your blood behind trees.
Useless to look for the bend
where night misses the way
or ambush a silence that wants
a rag of torn, clothing, a husk, or a cry;
for the spider's diminutive banquet suffices
to shatter the balance of heaven.
No help for the man from the Japanese cutter
or the secretive stumblers on street-corners.
The field bites its tail to assemble its roots in a place
and the raddle of yarn in the grass seeks a length of ungratified
ardor.
The moon! The police! Klaxons across the Atlantic!
False fronts of horsehair and smoke; rubber gloves and anemones.
All wrecked in the night,
legs sprawled on the terraces.
All wrecked in warm gutterpipes
and a terrible silence of fountains.
Good people! Soldiers and wantons!
The journey must lead through the idiot's eye,
cross-country, to the hiss of the dazed and the housebroken
cobras,
landscapes of graveyards that foster the ruddiest apples.
For light without limit must fall,
and the well-to-do looking through lenses
quake at the smell of a body whose gradient doubles the rat and
the lily;
where those who encircle a moan with a spilling of urine
or the crystals withholding the never-repetitive wave,
must be utterly given to flame.

In this poem, and throughout *Poet in New York,* Lorca confronts and con-
demns the logic, the rational thought that, through technology, is annihilating
the freedom of the human being. He proclaims himself in rebellion and revolution, permeating his entire body with a multiple and agonized desire that merges
his identity with that of all creation. The poet offers himself as a witness and as
a victim in solidarity with those who suffer because of their longing for flux and
their resistance to be penetrated by power and oppression.

In closing, I wish to allude to an article by my former professor, Manuel
Durán, which says: "Beginning with his return to New York, [Lorca's theater]
becomes polarized around a dominant theme: the suffering and the frustration of
the Spanish woman."[23] Yet, my interpretation of the causes of the obsession
with this theme are different from those of Durán, who sees this new interest of
Lorca's as springing from the comparison he was able to make between the

American woman, liberated, and the traditional Spanish woman of 1929. My hypothesis is that, because of the alienation and the personal solitude that he felt in his time in New York, Lorca could identify first with New York blacks, who lived and suffered the racism of the dominant white population, and who in this oppression developed a subculture full of force and energy that elevated them above the reality in which they lived. Upon his return to Spain, he transferred his discovery of the oppression of the weak and the marginal that he already treated in the gypsy theme, to the equivalent of the oppression of women in a society dominated by men, identifying himself then, not only with the Spanish woman, but with the female essence that he rejected in himself out of his fear of society, but which he understood very well because he felt it clearly in his homosexual preference.

These interpretations expounded in my essay suggest a re-reading and a challenge to the usual ways in which *Poet in New York* has been interpreted by the critics. García Lorca's homosexuality, whether codified or de-coded, is an essential component of his opus and I invite you to re-read the latter and unmask its female codes.

I want to thank Lori Roses for his excellent translation of my original article: "Historias de demencia: lo femenino en *Poeta en Nueva York.*"

1. José Luis Cano, *García Lorca* (Barcelona: Destino, 1974), p. 73.

2. Ian Gibson, *Federico García Lorca. 1 De Fuentevaqueros a Nueva York, 1898-1929* (Barcelona: Grijalbo, 1985), p. 530–617.

3. Lorca wrote to his friend Carlos Morla: "New York seems terrible to me, but for that same reason I am going there" Carlos Morla Lynch, *En España con Garcia Lorca,* (Madrid: Aguilar, 1958), p. 85.

4. Christopher Maurer, ed. *Epistolario* (Madrid: Alianza, 1983), 2 vols.; C. Maurer, Ed., "Federico García Lorca escribe a su familia desde Nueva York y la Habana, 1929–1930", *Poesia. Revista Ilustrada de Informacion poética,* nos. 23–24; Angel del Rio, *"Poeta en Nueva York:* pasados veinticinco años", *Estudios sobre literatura contemporánea* (Madrid: Gredos, 1966), 235–62; "Juan Ramón Jiménez y Federico García Lorca: does poetas andaluces en Estados Unidos", *Cuadernos Hispanoamericanos,* nos. 376–378 (1981), 875–885; John A. Crow, *Federico García Lorca* (Los Angeles, 1945); Rafael Martinez Nadal, *El publico: Amor, teatro y caballos en la obra de Federico García Lorca* (Oxford: The Dolphin Book, 1970).

5. Federico García Lorca, *Poeta en Nueva York. Tierra y Luna,* ed. Eutimio Martín (Barcelona: Ariel, 1983). Miguel García Posada, *Lorca: Interpretación de Poeta en Nueva York* (Madrid: Akal, 1981), 15–59. For the English translations I have used: *Lorca and Jiménez. Selected poems.* Chosen and translated by Robert Bly (Boston: Beacon Press, 1973); *The Selected Poems of Federico García Lorca.* Ed. by Francisco García Lorca and Donald M. Allen (New Directions Publishing Corporation, 1955); *Poet in New York by Federico García Lorca,* a new translation by Ben Bellit (New York: Grove Press, 1955).

6. Richard L. Predmore, *Los poemas neuyorquinos de Federico García Lorca* (Madrid: Taurus, 1985), 37–53.

7. R. L. Predmore, idem, 34.

8. Ian Gibson, ibidem, 568.

9. Ian Gibson, idem, 570.

10. Ian Gibson, idem, 569.

11. I do not agree with the interpretations of this poem done by R. Predmore, ibidem, 56–60; and C. Marcilly, *Ronde et fable de la solitude á Poeta en Nueva York* (Paris: Hispano-Americana, 1962), 10.

12. C. Maurer, *Federico Garcia Lorca escribe a su familia,* ibidem, 112–113.

13. References to the homosexuality of Lorca appear in, J.L. Schonberg, *Federico Garcia Lorca: El hombre y la obra* (México: Compañia General de Ediciones, 1959); *A la Recherche de Lorca* (Neufchatel: La Baconnière, 1966).

14. Schonberg, idem; Carlos Feal Deibe, *Eros y Lorca* (Barcelona, Edhasa, 1973); Moraima Semprún Donahue, "Cristo en Lorca", *Explicacion de Textos Literarios,* 4 (1975–76), 23–34.

15. Estelle C. Jelinek, *Women's Autobiography: Essays in Criticism* (Indiana: Indiana University Press, 1980); William C. Spengemann, *The Forms of Autobiography* (New Haven: Yale U. P., 1980).

16. G. Deleuze, F. Guattari, *Anti-Epidus. Capitalism and Schizophrenia* (New York: The Viking Press, 1977).

17. Félix Guattari, "A Liberation of Desire. An Interview by George Stambolian", *Homosexuality and French Literature* (Ithaca: Cornell U.P., 1979); G. Hocquenghem, *Homosexual Desire* (London: Allison and Busby, 1978).

18. Ian Gibson, ibidem, 95.

19. Dionisio Cañas, "El amigo no identificado de Lorca en América", *El País,* 22 de dic. 1985, "Lorca: Cummings. Una amistad más allá del bien y del mal" *El País,* 23 Oct. 1986.

20. Sigmund Freud, *The Dissolution of the Oedipus Complex,* vol. 19 std. ed. (London: Hogarth Press, 1961); Dorothy Dinnerstein, *The Mermaid and the Minotaur. Sexual Arrangements and Human Malaise,* (New York: Harper and Row, 1976), chs. 4–8.

21. Cipriano Rivas Cherif, "La muerte y la pasión de Federico García Lorca, *Excelsior* (Mexico), January, 6, 13, 2, 1955.

22. G. Deleuze and Claire Parnet, *Dialogues* (Paris: Flammarion, 1977); G. Deleuze and F. Guattari, *Mille Plateaux* (Paris: Edts. de Minuit); G. Deleuze, *Différence et répétition* (Paris: PUF, 1981); Alice A. Jardine, "Becoming a Body Without Organs: Gilles Deleuze and His Brothers", *Gynesis: Configurations of Women and Modernity* (Ithaca: Cornell U.P., 1985), 208–226.

23. Manuel Durán, "Federico García Lorca: Poeta entre dos mundos," *Federico Garcia Lorca,* ed. I. Manuel-Gil (Madrid: Taurus, 1985), 191–200.

GLORIA DURÁN
The University of Connecticut at Waterbury

Conversation with Tulio Ossa, Director of United Theatre of the Americas, on *La casa de Bernarda Alba*

G.D.   Tulio, you've just staged Lorca's *La casa de Bernarda Alba*. What made you select this play to be presented by the United Theatre of the Americas?

T.O.   What attracted me to *La casa* was the feminist theme of the play. Even though it was written in the thirties, it's still relevant today, especially in the Hispanic world.

G.D.   Do you think that at the time Lorca wrote it, the play was an accurate reflection of the position of women in Spain or an exaggeration?

T.O.   It was an exaggeration, but probably necessary for the public to appreciate the problem better.

G.D.   Yes. Of course, he was particularly aware of the plight of Spanish women after his trip to New York where he saw the relative liberty of American women. But all of his plays have women as leading characters. *La casa* is merely the logical conclusion, with *only* women in the play.

T.O.   Still, it's curious that Bernarda Alba comes across at times with male characerics; perhaps it's because of Lorca's sexual preferences.

G.D.   Well, she's the heavy in the play, the person we really shouldn't like. I often compare her to the mother in *Bodas de sangre* because both plays deal with a similar situation, a dominant woman in a family and a wedding that is not to take place. Both conclude with the tragic death of a child of the woman. However, in *Bodas de sangre* the mother's strength seems more positive. We admire and like her.

T.O.   Still, though we may not like Bernarda Alba very much as a person, there's something about her I very much like. Her husband is dead and rather than sit down and feel sorry for herself, she's able to stand up and keep on with the tradition, and continue to preserve the fortunes of the family. Though she takes matters to an extreme with a mourning of eight years and her oppression of her daughters, the mere fact that she's going to do everything by herself without bringing another man into her life is something to respect.

G.D.   Do you think this is part of Lorca's idea about the superior strength of women — that Bernarda Alba represents strength and tradition, while the daughters represent another stereotype of women? You see, as a feminist, I take issue with Lorca. Although I appreciate what he was trying to do, I feel that women in his plays are much too stereotyped.

T.O.   I understand that. They're almost caricatures of women. I don't fully understand his intention. I think it was just an overreaction to the situation in order to make people change.

G.D.   Yes, although the word usually has bad connotations, there's an element of propaganda in works like *Bernarda Alba*.

T.O.   Of course, his theatre was very didactic. He was dedicated to changing the social situation in Spain of his time. He was director of *La Barraca* and he used theatre as a tool to educate, to show his audience that the honor of a family should be determined by more than the chastity of its women.

G.D.   Quite so. But let's get back to your directing of *Bernarda Alba*. You say that you admire certain qualities in her, and this comes through in your presentation. It seems to me that when I read the play I didn't particularly admire her, but that I became more sympathetic after seeing your play. Now do you think this was the result of the interpretation of the actress portraying the role or of your direction?

T.O.   A combination of both. Between us we sort of give birth to that character at that moment for that particular production. We tried to understand Bernarda and to give her a history beyond what was in the play.

G.D.   So you had to supply details that Lorca doesn't. You had to make the work live, you had to flesh it out.

T.O.   Yes, we gave birth to a new Bernarda, a Bernarda twenty years before the date of the play, fifty years before, the whole woman. We tried to look at the play with fresh eyes, to understand it from the viewpoint of the actress who was going to create the role, to give life to it even though it came from her own inner strength. But she knew there was a very thin line between reality and fantasy. We went through a series of discussions and exercises with our two leading actresses, the ones who played the role in English and in Spanish, so that their total persona could be given to this character, so that they couldn't disassociate themselves from it.

G.D.   Is this something you do with any play you direct or only with Lorca?

T.O.   Well, Lorca's are the most difficult plays to direct. There's so much symbolism. The plays demand so much from actors and actresses. My personal objective is to create as much reality as possible in the plays without losing their magic. Sometimes I give something of myself to a character, but I never know when he — or she — is taking off on his own. One has to be very conscious about how he plays with a character.

G.D.   Do you think that Lorca is more demanding of the director than other playwrights, that others give you more guidance as to staging? I've noticed that the play is very sparse in its stage directions.

T.O.   *Bernarda Alba* requires a lot of energy and cooperation on the part of director and actresses. And it's demanding because of the complex relationships, the symbolism, the entanglements.

G.D.   I'm interested in your remark about symbolism and entanglements. Paco Lorca talks about the symbolism of the rope with which Adela hangs herself. This is highly appropriate because of the symbolical rope which

Bernarda Alba kept around all of her daughters. But my impression is that the rope is a forced symbol at the end because the lapse of time between the attempted shooting of Pepe el Romano and the suicide of Adela is much too short to permit anyone to hang herself. Because if the time lapse were realistic, she couldn't possibly have gone into her room and arranged the hanging in such a brief period. It would've made much more sense on a realistic level to have her grab the gun and rush out to shoot herself after first determining whether Pepe were indeed dead or not.

Of course, there's a sacrifice of reality to symbolism. Obviously, you, as director, were aware of this problem. How did you cope with it?

T.O. Well, of course, I discussed it with the actresses and as you said, we all came to the same conclusion that the end doesn't make much sense. It wasn't logical for this woman to go into her room and in just a minute or so hang herself. She would've had to have enough time to go look for rope, because she wasn't prepared to hang herself, find a spot where she could thread it and do the actual hanging. In the meantime, even though she was so much in love with him, I don't believe she would've had enough time to think the thing through. So we all came to the conclusion that we were dealing with magic and accepted the situation as it was intended by the author and stopped being so intellectual about it and creating ways to deal with it. We just said, "That's what we're given, so that's what we're going to play with." So we stopped trying to fight it. Of course, if I had the choice of changing the scene, I would've done it. But I would've felt also that I was insulting the memory of the playwright, that I wasn't being true to Lorca.

G.D. Then do you really feel that La casa de Bernarda Alba is, as his brother seems to imply, Lorca's best tragedy?

T.O. I tend to have mixed feelings about La casa. I'm just as attracted by Bodas de sangre. But I chose La casa because of the feminist message which I think is most important.

G.D. Have you gotten any feedback from the audience as to whether this message got through?

T.O. There were many people who were happy that this was happening, especially in the Spanish-speaking community.

G.D. Do you refer to men or women?

T.O. To both, but particularly women. They're still so far from being liberated because of both social and economic factors.

G.D. Yet the play doesn't paint a very hopeful picture for women's liberation. Adela, the only liberated woman, commits suicide.

T.O. If it were up to me, I wouldn't have had Adela go away with Pepe el Romano, because that would've been another kind of trap. But let's get back to Bernarda again. After all, the play's basically about her. Do you think that she ever wears a mask, that there are several Bernarda Albas?

G.D. My feeling was that she was convinced of the rectitude of her ways, that there was no mask, that Bernarda Alba is as she is portrayed.

T.O. Yet there are moments, especially with La Poncia where she almost breaks down, where she knows she can't show all the authority that she would like with her daughters. There's also a very interesting element there, because we don't know who La Poncia is, where she came from.

G.D. It seems to me we have the same mellowing relationship between the mistress and the servant that exists in *Bodas de sangre* where it's the servant who discovers the "novia" and Leonardo and acts as a self-appointed conscience to the family, a custodian of the family honor. I think that Lorca was very much attuned to the servants and their commanding role in many Spanish households. But I wonder how much people can understand this relationship today when servants, let alone super-servants, are practically an extinct species. In fact so many elements have changed since Lorca's time. Women, at least in the United States, are not *that* oppressed. Servants are gone. And the conception of family honor as dependent on the sexual purity of the female members of the household must be almost inconceivable for the young actresses playing the roles of the daughters.

T.O. Well, what society are you talking about, North American, Spanish, or Latin American?

G.D. Let's say the group or actors and actresses who perform for the United Theatre of the Americas, the Hispanic youth of the New Haven community.

T.O. Well, these people don't make a big issue out of honor. But in Latin America or Spain honor, in this classical sense, is still important.

G.D. Would this contribute to the continued importance of Lorca in Latin America even at a time when other Spanish playwrights of the twentieth century don't enjoy such popularity? I've read that Lorca is the only Spanish playwright of this century who has made a real impact on Spanish American writers.

T.O. Well, on the whole I don't think there's been a great recent influence on Spanish American theatre by playwrights working in a traditional style. What may be attractive about Lorca is that he shares a common objective with most of the Latin American playwrights, that is he uses theatre to change society. The conditions that he seeks to change may be different from the ones in Latin America, but in both cases the purpose isn't to entertain so much as to educate.

G.D. Do you think that they may be attracted to him because Lorca, as a homosexual, approaches society from the critical stance of the outsider and, as I've read, Latin Americans have also always felt that they're outsiders, people living on the periphery?

T.O. Of course, they see Lorca as a fellow revolutionary who's trying to change society, to make the average person think about what's behind time-honored traditions.

G.D. And he went directly to the people, just as you do with your United Theatre of the Americas.

T.O. Well, I'm not trying to duplicate Lorca. But I do want people to think, to leave the theatre and want to do something about improving society.

G.D. That sounds a little like Brecht. Do you find Brecht and Lorca similar?

T.O. In terms of settings or character or what?

G.D. In terms of theme, and intent of the playwright.

T.O. My personal opinion is that Lorca is clearer than Brecht. Of course, there's symbolism in Lorca but the people, the characters themselves, are much more conventional, much easier to understand.

G.D. Except for *Así que pasen cinco años,* which perhaps you could explain.

T.O. Well, it does make sense if you look back at the influences of that time, at Surrealism and the friendship that he had with Dalí.

G.D. But in a way he and Brecht were subject to the same influences, the surrealism and other movements that exalted the unconscious, which is never easy to understand. And this means that both playwrights were, in a way, working at cross purposes within themselves. They wanted to influence the public, to get up and work change in society but at the same time the very medium that they used at times tended to muddy the message.

T.O. I agree, but artists can't help but be influenced by the fashion of their times. And if the message isn't quite clear, that's also good because it forces you to think. Something that's very clear doesn't do that. I think the artist has to steer a midway course between creating something that's too difficult to understand and something that presents no challenge at all. You want to make the audience think, at least a little bit.

G.D. Of course, that's the difference between propaganda and art. And Lorca generally strikes that right balance between them. Well then, let's suppose that you're going to present *La casa de Bernarda Alba* again. What would you do this time that would be different from the last?

T.O. This time I'd prepare my actors better. We'd allow enough time to get thoroughly into the characters. We'd avoid an intellectual approach.

G.D. Do you think that Lorca distinguishes the character of each sister sufficiently? Adela's obviously different since she has the guts to go out and do what she wants. But what about Amelia and Magdalena and the others?

T.O. Well, they all feel oppressed. As individuals their reactions are all different just as you and I are different. But the thing that they have in common is their lack of courage. Really, they're very typical of many women who desire change but don't dare speak up, act.

G.D. That may be. But my point is that they seem portrayed in the play by their common denominator rather than by the distinctive qualities that make each an individual.

T.O. You mean to say that you don't distinguish between them as characters?

G.D. Well, yes and no. In reading the play, they all, at least Amelia and Magdalena, seemed pretty much alike. Lorca doesn't even describe them physically, except to say that one is hunchbacked and another speaks with a nasal quality. But when I saw them on the stage, they did come alive. I suppose that's the magic of the theatre. But I'm wondering if Lorca doesn't leave too much up to the director.

T.O. Again, this is what we were discussing before. We don't have enough background for each character. For example, we've always been curious about where la Poncia came from. We have even wondered if perhaps there wasn't a blood relationship between la Poncia and Bernarda and if that's why Bernarda at times reminds her of her past. We never know how la Poncia got to the house, why she decided to stay for so many years while taking so much abuse. But in a way I like this lack of background because it gives us enough flexibility to think our own scenes and add what we want to add to these characters. It's the job of both actors and director to create the live character.

G.D. But were you faithful all the time to the actual text of the play?

T.O. Of course. We didn't add anything or correct any of the expressions. The only thing we added to the play was our analysis of who those characters were and we tried to create a background and personality for them.

G.D. You know, of course, that Lorca's brother said that these were all real people as opposed to *Bodas de sangre* where Lorca got the plot from a newspaper article and invented the characters. Here he knew the characters, and invented the plot as the logical outcome of their personalities. So I suppose if you wanted to research it, you could find out who la Poncia was.

T.O. Sorry, that doesn't interest me so much as the main themes in Lorca, that is the repression of sexual desire on the one hand and *machismo* on the other. They're part of the double standard that we have to get rid of. And it's interesting that women themselves reinforce this. You remember the episode of Paca la Roseta, the woman whose husband was tied up and who was then taken to the mountains by a group of men. In commenting on the scandal neither la Poncia nor Bernarda blame the men, but they condemn the poor victim and suggest that she enjoyed the experience. It's what they always say about victims of rape. But what control did Paca la Roseta have over the men's actions? And yet the comments of la Poncia and Bernarda are typical of remarks often made by other women.

G.D. Well, perhaps it comes from a feeling of powerlessness. After all, men had all the power in society, and women didn't feel important or strong enough to judge or criticize their actions. But there was nothing to be lost in criticizing each other. Marianism is, after all, the other side of *machismo*. It allows women to take a superior attitude regarding men as weak in self control and therefore blameless for their sexual activities. But according to this rationalization, women are stronger and naturally purer than men and so doubly to be criticized if they give suspicion to the contrary.

T.O. Then it's up to women right now to change that perspective.

G.D. If you don't mind, I'd like to change our perspective for the moment. I'd like to ask you if you think Adela is the heroine of the play or if you even think the play has a heroine.

T.O. No, I don't think Adela is a heroine. Adela can't be a heroine for me, because she chooses the cheapest way out of a problem. Rather than coming to terms with her life and doing something about it, she just decides to end her life so that she doesn't have to face her problems anymore. If I had to choose a hero for the play, I'd say that it's the audience itself. Because now they're presented with this play that they have to deal with. That forces them to think; what is there in their own personal lives, what is there in society that they can change for the better? So now they have to choose whether to become those heroes or heroines who will create change in society to make a better world for themselves. And this will require courage, which is the characteristic of a hero.

G.D. In short, they can't choose the route of Adela. Nor can they choose the position of Bernarda Alba because she is antagonistic to most of the ideas that they hold, so they're given no role model.

T.O. No, but they're given a problem and expected to find a solution, and doing that will take courage. They have to confront what is wrong not only in society but also in their own lives and effect a change. That's a real risk-taking situation.

G.D. So you're using the word "hero" and "heroine" in an entirely new sense which is different from that ascribed to the heroes of classical Greek tragedy or of Shakespearean tragedy because in these cases Adela might have been considered the hero, or the heroine. After all, her suicide isn't basically different from Juliet's. She kills herself in the mistaken belief that her lover's dead. She has dared to oppose her destined role of becoming a spinster like her sisters and is punished for this in the taking of her own life. Isn't she pretty close to a real heroine?

T.O. Only if you insist on measuring plays with the old criteria. But what we want to do today is to produce living theatre that forces the audience to think, to participate and to leave the theatre prepared to act. Maybe that's Brecht; maybe it's Lorca. But it's what we want to do today.

VIRGINIA HIGGINBOTHAM
The University of Texas, Austin

Lorca's *Así que pasen cinco años:* A Literary Version of *Un chien andalou*

Luis Buñuel's *Un chien andalou* became a landmark in cinema history when it premiered in March, 1929, at the Studio Ursulines in Paris. Yet we are only now beginning to understand its impact on the work of Buñuel's close friend, García Lorca. Speculation about Lorca's reaction to the film has now been laid to rest with Buñuel's acknowledgment, in a 1980 interview, of Lorca's indignation at his best friends' first film: "Cuando, en los años treinta, estuve en Nueva York, Angel del Río me contó que Federico, que había estado también allí, le había dicho: 'Buñuel ha hecho una mierdesita así de pequeñita que se llama *Un perro andaluz* y el perro andaluz soy yo.'"[1]

Buñuel denied that there was any truth in Lorca's interpretation. He always insisted that the film is nothing more than a collection of dreams which he and Dalí put together, deliberately discarding anything logical. He explains that its title refers to a collection of poems that he had written and never published.[2] To Buñuel's biographer, however, Lorca's opinion of *Un chien andalou* is not far off target. J.F. Aranda theorizes that Buñuel changed the article in the title of his book of poems, "El perro andaluz," from definite to indefinite so as to refer collectively to the Andalusian members of the Generation of 1927 who experimented with vanguardist aesthetics, but whose works seemed to Buñuel and his collaborator, Dalí, to lag far behind the revolutionary spirit of avant-garde art.[3]

In part, Aranda's theory has been proven to be accurate. In his recent memoirs, *Mon dernier soupir,* Buñuel recalls meeting with Dalí to hear Lorca read a new play he had just completed, *Don Perlimplín.* After only a couple of words, Buñuel, reacting against what he considered a hopelessly outdated and refined vocabulary, blurts out, "Ya basta, Federico. Es una mierda."[4] The poet's much acclaimed book, *Romancero gitano,* evoked a similar response from Dalí, who wrote Lorca a lengthy letter in which he scolded his friend for relying upon picturesque themes and logical discourse, both odious to dedicated surrealists.[5] By 1928 Buñuel and Dalí had, however briefly, evolved aesthetic and ideological perceptions so closely in tune with each other that they could work together in complete harmony on *Un chien andalou,* a fact which depressed Lorca. After Lorca received a hostile letter from Dalí attacking his recent book and thereby terminating their relationship, Dalí and Buñuel met in Cadaqués to finish the script of *Un chien andalou.*

In spite of their aesthetic differences, however, Buñuel never lost his admiration for Lorca, nor his feeling of gratitude. In *Mon dernier soupir* he credits the poet with having opened up for him the world of poetry, thus allowing him to develop into the artist he became: "Me ha transformado ... Yo le debo más que yo podré decir" he confesses in his memoirs.[6] Nor did Buñuel's disgust for homosexuals color in any way his feeling for Lorca: "Era marica. ¡Qué le vamos a hacer! Nació así."[7] Would Buñuel, who valued friendship as few have, make a derisive film about a friend whose idiosyncrasies he forgave and to whom he owed his poetic awareness?

According to Aranda, *Un chien andalou* can be seen as a psychological portrait of the group of poets from the south, including Lorca, who reached maturity in the nineteen-twenties. If this is true, the film "portrait" might include some of the same characters as a play — *Así que pasen cinco años* — by a member of that generation — Lorca — whose protagonist is of the same age, not only of the protagonist of *Un chien andalou*, but also of Lorca and Buñuel when they were friends at the Residencia de Estudiantes in Madrid.

In an enlightening comparative analysis of these two works nine years ago, Professor Gwynne Edwards proposes that the "treatment of theme ... and its general technique" is proof of influence of Buñuel's film upon *Así que pasen cinco años*.[8] My point of departure is Buñuel's revelation that Lorca, while in New York and working on *Así que pasen cinco años* not only knew of *Un chien andalou*, but was irritated by it. Comparing the characters, narrative structure, metaphorical devices, and emotional tone of the film and play, I shall explore the possibility that, since Lorca felt himself to be the butt of his friends' harsh jokes, he wrote *Así que pasen cinco años* not merely influenced by the film. Parallels and differences between Lorca's play and his friends' film suggest that in *Así que pasen cinco años* he both acknowledges and partially rebutts their mockery which was being acclaimed by surrealists as the beginning of a new genre — surrealist film.

Aranda's conception of *Un chien andalou* as Buñuel's film portrait of the Andalusian poets of his generation suggests several basic similarities between it and *Así que pasen cinco años*. The protagonist of both works is a frustrated young man in search of his sexual identity. Buñuel's timid cyclist is outrageously attired in frilly collar and cuffs, while Lorca's confused El Joven is fastidious and dislikes dust, noise, and bad smells ("Me molesta que las cosas de la calle entren en mi casa. Juan, cierra la ventana").[9] The two pursue their objects of desire, but confront opposition at every turn. Both authors appear to conclude that establishing sexual identity is essential for survival, and that failure to do so is fatal. In both versions, the young man's search for identity ends in death.

Lorca and Buñuel clearly ascribe the reasons for their protagonists' failure to cultural conventions that repress spontaneity and discourage open expression of sexual desire. Buñuel's indictment of conventional morality is implied in the now-famous image of the young man pulling behind him a load of two priests (one for each parent?), two grand pianos, and two decaying donkey carcasses. Lorca's El Joven has learned, not spontaneity, but that life's rewards come out to those who wait. He postpones enjoyment of even small pleasures such as eating candy: "Guardaba los dulces para comerlos después" (1046).

His sense of social refinement and manners causes him to hesitate in his quest for love. His scrupulous respect for others leads him to excessive soul-searching, as he asks a friend, "¿Crees tú que yo puedo vencer las cosas materiales, los obstáculos que surgen y se aumentarán en el camino, sin causar dolor a los demás?" (1071). As Cedric Busette observes, Lorca's tormented hero "Sólo puede ejercer su iniciativa cuando deja de estar atado por el deber social."[10]

Surrealists condemned Christian morality for repressing eroticism. The upper-class, educated protagonists of *Así que pasen cinco años* and *Un chien andalou* appear harassed and hesitant in contrast with the cool indifference of their more successful rivals. The Rugby Player who wins the girl in *Así que pasen cinco años* is a caricature of the silent film hero who does not speak but merely swaggers, looking strong and smoking cigarettes. A virile suitor, who, in his tennis sweater, also appears to be a young athlete, walks arm in arm with the young man's girl in *Un chien andalou*. As he strolls, he kicks aside his rival's frilly cuffs and hat that have washed up, like remnants of a distant shipwreck, along the beach.

Before 1929, the year *Un chien andalou* appeared, Lorca had not experimented with fragmentation of dramatic character. To surrealists, the double, or multiple character was of key importance, as José de la Colina points out: "Uno de los temas ... que está presente como una obsesión en *Un perro andaluz* es el tema del doble, o más bien del Otro ... el surrealismo podría definirse como una aventura de exploración de la otredad del mundo y de nosotros mismos, como una busca del más escondido *otro yo*." [11]

Lorca could well have observed the double character in Buñuel's cyclist. The young man is confronted in his room by a stranger who strips him of his frills and angrily tosses them out the window. Suddenly schoolroom desks appear and the cyclist grabs two books atop one of them. The books turn into revolvers with which the cyclist shoots the stranger. As the stranger falls, we see his face for the first time. He is the cyclist's double, a figure Linda Williams identifies as corresponding with Freud's superego — "a censuring agent of self-observation that measures the self against a social ideal."[12]

The protagonist of *Así que pasen cinco años* is also a character of multiple dimensions, and most of the play's characters personify facets of his personality. The censuring agent is easily recognizable in El Viejo, dressed in white wig and gold-rimmed glasses. He encourages El Joven to restrain himself, to wait, to avoid living. His favorite word is "recuerdo": "Es una palabra verde, jugosa. Mana sin cesar hilitos de agua fría" (1046). That part of El Joven that lacks vigor prefers to remember his past and his upbringing, even though the effect of doing so is that of the "hilitos de agua fría" which chill the spirit by "throwing cold water" on direct and spontaneous action. El Viejo also increases the young man's torment by taunting him: "¿No se atreve Ud. a huir? ¿A volar?, a ensanchar su amor por todo el cielo?" (1049). When El Joven loses the Mecanógrafa, his last chance for love, the voice of El Viejo quietly gloats, "Bravo" (1129).

El Joven's two male friends, Amigos Primero and Segundo, represent his inner voices in conflict with each other. First Friend is a Don Juan who visits him and sneers, "¡Huuy! ¿Quién era ese viejo? ¿Un amigo tuyo?" First Friend is El Joven's voice of freedom and sexual desire. He points out El Viejo's stifling effect and inquires about El Joven's lovelife: "¿Y dónde están en esta casa los retratos de las muchachas con las que tú te acuestas? Mira ... yo te voy a pintar de colorete esas mejillas de cera ... (1056).

In contrast to First Friend, Second Friend is an effeminate sort whose costume – impeccable white wool suit, gloves and shoes, lace jacket and tie – recalls the cyclist's frill in *Un chien andalou*. Emphasizing Second Friend's androgynous sexuality, Lorca suggests that the role be enacted by a young male or a female (1072). This infantile character sings of death: "Quiero morirme siendo /ayer. Quiero morirme siendo amanecer" (1077).

Second Friend's uncertain sexuality and death wish correspond to the androgynous female who faces certain death in *Un chien andalou*. Dressed in male attire, she stands in a city street surrounded by curious onlookers who watch her poke a severed hand, emblem of mutilated virility, lying on the ground. As the cyclist watches from his window above the street, a policeman (figure of authority enforcing moral order) picks up the hand and puts it in the striped box that contains the young man's frills. Hugging the box, the androgyne stands motionless in heavy traffic fearing disaster. Sure enough, she is soon flattened by a car. Like El Joven's Second Friend, Buñuel's androgynous female personifies the fatal consequences of the protagonist's sexual confusion.

Again Linda Williams' insight into *Un chien andalou* applies as well to *Así que pasen cinco años*. She points out that Buñuel's cyclist is a "self that is constantly splitting and is the focus of an evolving series of oppositions between the sexual signs of male and female, love and death ..." (103). While Buñuel's focus remains on the cyclist throughout the film, Lorca shifts back and forth between the male protagonist to various female characters — la mecanógrafa, Máscara, and a female mannequin, el Maniquí — who represent female variations on the young man's frustration, inaction, and despair. These characters, in addition to elaborating the central theme of sexual paralysis, also serve Lorca's keen sense of spectacle, for they are visually arresting, in contrast to the rather dull costume of El Joven.

The first, in order of appearance, is the mannequin on whom hangs the wedding dress that El Joven's fiancée was planning to wear for their wedding. La novia, wiser than her counterpart in *Bodas de sangre,* knew long before the wedding that she was making a bad match, and breaks off with El Joven. She leaves him confused ("¿Dónde voy?" (1099)) and alone, with only the mannequin to talk to. But the mannequin is *haute-couture,* with high-fashion make-up and an acute sense of loss all her own: "¿Quién se pondrá mi traje? ¿Quién se lo pondrá? / Se lo pondrá la ría grande para casarse con el mar" (1099). She blames El Joven for his lack of sexual drive, for being a "dormida laguna, / con hojas secas y musgo / donde este traje se pudra" (1101). His torment is increased when she pulls a little pink suit from the sewing basket and holds it up to him, saying "Y es tu hijo" (1103). El Joven wants a son and vows with fresh energy to search for his love: "traeré temblando de amor / mi propia mujer desnuda" (1105). He pushes aside his ex-fiancée's father, who clings to him crying "¡Espera! ¡Espera!" The curtain falls rapidly on Act II as a horn honks in the street below, the maid begins running about, the mannequin faints on the sofa, and a distant voice from off-stage echoes the old man, "¡Esperaaaa ... !"

After an introductory scene between Harlequin and a sinister clown dressed in sequined suit and powdered white face, Act III begins with the arrival of the other two female personifications of El Joven's dilemma — la mecanógrafa (The Typist) and Máscara (Mask). They are an unlikely pair. The Typist wears a tennis dress with a bright beret and a long cape, while Máscara, laughing and talking with a slight Italian accent, is decked out in yellow silk gown, hat and wig, with a white mask.

Like El Joven and Buñuel's cyclist, Máscara is a member of the upper class, a victim of its outmoded notions of refinement and elegance that repress spontaneous desire. She recounts a sad tale of her lost Count Arturo and his child. The Typist asks her when Count Arturo will arrive, but Máscara seems to avoid the question, asking her in turn, "Y cuándo llega tu amigo?" (1116). The typist responds flatly, "Tardará", which Máscara takes as a model reply, and repeats, "También Arturo tardará" (1117).

The Typist is El Joven's last chance for love. She, too, is searching and goes home with El Joven. He is eager, she, more hesitant; but the past, personified by El Viejo, intrudes. The figure of a dead child passes across the stage within a stage where most of Act III takes place, and El Joven acknowledges, "Sí, mi hijo." The Typist seems to resent this intrusion, and reminds him, "No es tu hijo, soy yo" (1125). She promises to run away with him, but now on the condition that "¡Así que pasen cinco años!" (1129). The scene ends with the sound of Harlequin playing his two-stringed violin.

Both Lorca and Buñuel have eliminated remnants of realism, such as character development, from these two works. The characters of both *Un chien andalou* and *Así que pasen cinco años* appear and disappear quite freely in a narrative structure based on what surrealists called "automatic" progression, uninterrupted by logical order. Buñuel explained that his film's plot "results from conscious psychic automatism ... [it] doesn't try to tell a story, although it benefits from a [narrative] technique analogous to that of dreams."[13] Indeed, *Un chien andalou* is gleefully chaotic. Its first subtitle is the gentle opener of folk tales, "Once Upon a Time." The action then runs from "eight years later" to "sixteen years before", finally concluding "in the spring."[14] These abrupt time frames are easily juxtaposed on film and flow smoothly in dream-like incoherence.

Although he never accepted the principle of automatic writing, Lorca patterns the narrative structure in *Así que pasen cinco años* on dream-time. In Act I, a clock strikes six, and the characters make brief reference to the hour. In Act III, Harlequin equates the passage of dream-time with that of real time: "El sueño va sobre el tiempo / flotando como un velero. / Nadie puede abrir semillas / en el corazón del sueño" (1108). Then, inverting the first line, he seems to merge the past with the future:

> "El tiempo va sobre el sueño
> hundido hasta los cabellos

> Ayer y mañana comen
> Oscuras flores de duelo."
>
> (1108)

The verses concluding this introductory scene in Act III make clear that, at least for Harlequin, dream and reality have become indistinguishable:

> Y si el sueño finge muros
> en la llanura del tiempo,
> el tiempo le hace creer
> que nace en aquel momento.
>
> (1109)

By the time the clock strikes twelve in the final moments of the play, there is still no sense of elapsed time. Only the protagonist's anguish, increasing in the final scene, indicates that, whatever the hour, his time is up.

Similar characters moving in a narrative structure of dream-time are depicted with strikingly parallel imagery in *Un chien andalou* and *Así que pasen cinco años*. Gwynne Edwards has already brought attention to the use in both film and play of the empty suit laid out upon the bed (135). The cyclist's girl takes out his striped tie from a drawer and places it upon the suit collar "dans l'attitude d'une personne qui veille un mort," a stage direction which seems to confirm the underlying meaning of the motif as lack of fulfilling an expected role.[15] When Lorca's protagonist looks at his suit laid out on the bed, he isntructs his valet, Juan, to change the ribbons on his patent leather shoes. This empty-role motif is echoed in the tiny pink suit which the mannequin filched from the sewing basket and holds up to impress upon El Joven his absence from his expected function in life as husband and father.

One of the famous images from *Un chien andalou* is the close-up of the cyclist's hand which his girl has slammed in the door. The camera closes in on the palm to reveal a swarm of ants, an image which has been variously interpreted as a visual pun for the cliché "itching with desire" to a visual comment on the hero's fear of castration.[16] In paintings from his surrealist period, Dalí repeats the motif of ants swarming in unexpected places. Reference to an ant serves Lorca as an image of frustration as El Joven, seeing a dead child cross the stage within a stage, explains to the Typist that this is his son: "Sí, mi hijo. Corre por dentro de mí como una hormiga sola dentro de una caja cerrada" (1125). Although mention here is of one lone ant, it is a negative sign of desperation. This image parallels the insect imagery that runs throughout the poems of New York which Lorca was writing at the same time he was working on *Así que pasen cinco años*. In "Nocturno del hueco", the poet feels himself surrounded by curious spectators "que tienen hormigas en las palabras," and the Assyrian dog's howls leave "hormigas de espanto" on those who hear it.

Another curious parallel in the imagery of Lorca and Buñuel is that of books as a negative value. It is not by coincidence that the schoolbooks the cyclist grabs from the desk in *Un chien andalou* turn into revolvers with which he shoots his double, the agent of self-censorship who throws away his frilly collar and cuffs and backs the cyclist against a wall as if threatening him. This sequence visualizes the self-destruction of a young man who, according to surrealists, is paralyzed by the authoritarian, repressive education associated here with schoolbooks.

The image of books seems to carry the same negative connotation for Lorca, since El Joven dies in his library. In the context of the play, the library corresponds to the surrealists' notion of reason and education as stultifying and obstructing release of instinctual energy rather than the traditional sign of enlightenment. It is in the library, rather than in the forest, where the final scene of Act III occurs, that the protagonist meets his death.

Images of maiming and death recur throughout the play and film. The hand which the androgyne pokes in the street before she is hit by a car still shows a bloody stump where it was severed from its owner. The young woman who is the cyclist's object of desire spies a death's head moth on the wall shortly after his demise. The opening image of *Un chien andalou* — the slicing of an eyeball with a razor — is still unsurpassed for sheer horror.

Así que pasen cinco años, a much less flamboyant work, dramatizes loss and death in more discrete images. A vision of death is announced in an encounter between a boy and a blue cat. The child complains of hearing nails being hammered into his coffin, while the cat tells of being stoned to death by children. Overt cruelty in *Un chien andalou* is subdued in *Así que pasen cinco años* but is echoed in the reappearance from time to time of the dead child, and the sinister atmosphere of a cynical Harlequin and a white-faced clown.

Neither protagonist is successful in his search for identity. The cyclist, after shooting his double, falls. As he goes down, his hand touches the back of a nude woman sitting in a forest. The object of his desire, however, is just beyond his reach. The cyclist's girl walks arm-in-arm along the beach with the handsome young man in a tennis sweater. They seem content, yet they, too, meet a grisly fate. In a long shot that Lorca may have had in mind when he wrote "Luna y panorama de los insectos," subtitled "Poema de amor", Buñuel's lovers are buried chest-deep in sand. The lovers of *Un chien andalou* are seen being eaten by large insects, a scene Lorca seems to recall in his poem: "Ya cantan, gritan, gimen: Rostro, ¡Tu rostro! Rostro".

After his second fiancée asks him to wait five years for her, El Joven gives up and shows visible signs of despair and decline. His death occurs in a modernized version of the ancient fatal game, in which three card-players dressed in long white capes visit him, begin a card game, and force him to play his last card, his ace of hearts. He dies lamenting that "Lo he perdido todo" (1143), a line that Buñuel's cyclist might well have uttered as he falls grasping but never possessing the object of his desire.

Both Lorca and Buñuel were, in this play and film, looking for a new poetic idiom. Each turned to dreams for inspiration, adapting metamorphosis of images and the narrative structure of dream-time to dramatize very real problems and experience. Use of overt realism without special effects in *Un chien andalou* was a conscious effort by Buñuel to prove to film makers who considered themselves avant-garde that surrealism does not lie in camera tricks or visual innovation but in a jolting critique of traditional social and religious codes.

Lorca, weary of his renown as the "gypsy" poet, was desperately seeking fresh imagery and renewed lyrical discourse. Like Buñuel, he too was attracted by the imaginative possibilities of surrealism and of film. When he lived in New York he wrote a filmscript, *Un viaje a la luna,* while at the same time composing the nightmarish *Poeta en Nueva York.* The scene between the boy and the blue cat in *Así que pasen cinco años* is conceived as a cinematic flashback that recalls the past of the central character of *Así que pasen cinco años.*[17] Lorca was working toward a theater of profoundly shocking material, as is clear from the fragments of *El público* and *Comedia sin título.* *Así que pasen cinco años* is only a first step in a more aesthetically aggressive direction. And herein lie the essential differences between *Así que pasen cinco años* and *Un chien andalou.*

The emotional tone of Buñuel's film, from its first frames in which the young director himself slits what appears to be a woman's eye (it was actually a goat's) with a razor, to the brief pornographic shots of the hero enacting his erotic obsessions, and the final frames of death by gnawing insects, is iconoclastic and revolutionary, if not nauseating. As the cyclist approaches his object of desire, the sound track, added later, of an Argentine tango and the "Liebestod" of *Tristan und Isolde* mocks his frenzied passion, born of repression. Modern audiences continue to laugh at this exaggerated scene, indicating clear perception of its comedy.

In spite of its moments of whimsy and child-like humor, *Así que pasen cinco años* is essentially a story of pathos. While it shares the central theme of frustration, the central character of an unnamed, sexually uncertain, well-to-do young man, and even dramatizes his despair with some of the same images, Lorca, unlike Buñuel, is not amused at his protagonist's predicament. In *Así que pasen cinco años* he seems to be retelling the same tale of identity crisis but from the point of view of one who suffered more acutely the losses it implies. Lorca's protagonist grieves bitterly at not being able to father a son, a loss which never occurs to Buñuel's cyclist. Buñuel ridicules his protagonist by dressing him in effeminate frills and placing him on a bicycle like a character from the American silent film comedies that inspire *Un chien andalou.* Lorca, feeling abused by the film, devoted three acts of a full-length play to dramatizing the pain, sense of failure, and pathetic hopelessness of the same theme.

When screened by a select audience at the Cine Club in Madrid, *Un chien andalou* received a mixed response: wild applause amid vociferous protest. There were some, however, who felt a sense of recognition when they saw the film. "Algo verdaderamente nuestro" wrote young film critic Juan Piqueras. "Todo él huele a España." Citing Eugenio Montes, who had seen the film in Paris, Piqueras agrees that in it "Todo … habla de España indirectamente." Closing his review, Piqueras, like Lorca an early victim of the impending Civil War, notes the enormous interest *Un chien andalou* had aroused. "Y el film no nos dejó de-cepcionados."[18] These remarks make clear that others of Buñuel's Spanish con-temporaries besides Lorca understood references to their own culture in *Un chien andalou* that foreigners did not detect.

Perceptions by Spanish critics and spectators of references to Spain in *Un chien andalou* may indicate that those who saw the film at its première in Madrid might, like Aranda fifty years later, have sensed its burlesque of a certain group of sexually indeterminate young poets at the Residencia. Yet, no extra-textual commentary is needed to confirm the relationship between Lorca's play and Buñuel's film. Structural parallels and similar imagery, themes and conceptions of character rather than anecdotes and theories, reveal *Así que pasen cincos años* as a literary version of the theme of identity crisis that Buñuel filmed in *Un chien andalou*. These similarities, as well as their differences in emotional tone, suggest the very likely probability that they are both highly personal versions of the experience of coming of age in Spain's most important artistic generation of the twentieth century.

NOTES

1. Interview with José de la Colina and Tomás Pérez Turrent in *Contracampo*. 16 (October-November, 1980), p. 33. Cited by Agustín Sánchez Vidal, "Sobre un ángel exterminador (La obra literaria de Luis Buñuel)" in *El surrealismo*. Victor G. de la Concha (ed.), Madrid: Taurus, 1982: 128.

2. Agustín Sánchez Vidal, "Sobre un ángel exterminador (La obra literaria de Luis Buñuel." In: de la Concha, Victor G. (ed.) *El surrealismo*. Madrid: Taurus, 1982: 128.

3. "Surrealismo español en el cine," *Insula* 337 (Dec. 1974):19.

4. Luis Buñuel *Mon dernier soupir*, Paris: Ed. Robert Laffont, 1982, p. 122. (Translation mine.)

5. Antonina Rodrigo, *García Lorca en Cataluña*. Barcelona: Ed. Planeta, 1975, pp. 262–264.

6. Luis Buñuel, op. cit. p. 194.

7. Max Aub, *Conversaciones con Buñuel*. Madrid: Aguilar, 1984, p. 105.

8. Gwynne Edwards, "Lorca and Buñuel: *Así que pasen cinco años* and *Un chien andalou*. *GLR*, IX (Fall, 1981): 128–141.

9. Federico García Lorca, *Obras completas*. Madrid: Aguilar, 1963, p. 1049. Further citations from this edition appear in parentheses in the text.

10. Cedric Busette, *Obra dramática de García Lorca*. New York: Las Americas Publishing Co., 1971, p. 163.

11. José de la Colina, "El díptico surrealista de Luis Buñuel." In: Buñuel, Luis, *Un perro analuz, La edad de oro*. México: Cine Club Era, 1971, p.10.

12. Linda Williams, *Figures of Desire. A Theory and Analysis of Surrealist Films*. Urbana: U of Illinois Press, 1981, p. 92. Further citations from this volume appear in parentheses in the text.

13. Frank Stauffacher, *Art in Cinema*. San Francisco Museum of Art, 1947, p. 30.

14. Gwynne Edwards, op. cit., p. 135.

15. Although available in English and Spanish, the original filmscript of *Un chien andalou* was published in French. My citations are from the original version reprinted in *L'Avant-Scène* 27–28 (June-July, 1963): 13–22. Further citations from this volume are indicated by page numbers in the text.

16. Fernando C. Césarman, *El ojo de Buñuel: Psicoanálisis desde una butaca*. Barcelona: Ed. Anagrama, 1976, p. 75.

17. Virginina Higginbotham, "Lorca y el cine," *GLR*, VI (Spring 1978): 90.

18. *La gaceta literaria*, Dec. 15, 1929: 469.

SUZANNE W. BYRD

García Lorca's Legacy:
Live Theatre at the Battle Front

Federico García Lorca was keenly aware of the patriotic concept underlying the tradition of popular performances in the Peninsula, a tradition that originated in the early Middle Ages with the performances of the *juglares*,. those wandering minstrels who served as both propaganda and morale corps, accompanying the military forces into battle. And ever since that remote era, theatrical entertainment in the Peninsula has continued to serve as a symbol of national pride and unity. According to Leandro Fernández Moratín, the Spanish theater was, by the sixteenth century, a necessity for the people,[1] and for that reason, it has become a symbol of national ideals and culture.

It was with this idealistic and patriotic concept of the Spanish theater that García Lorca had organized his traveling theater, La Barraca, just as Spain's new Second Republic came into existence. Through La Barraca, cast in the mold of the old *farándula,* with its strolling players, the young poet-dramatist hoped to inspire an enthusiasm for unity in their new government by introducing Spain's unschooled masses to the wealth of their national heritage in the performing arts. With this patriotic objective, García Lorca had traveled with his youthful troupe through Spain for four years, presenting classic dramatic works from Spain's great Golden Age theater.

Although Federico García Lorca's aims for La Barraca were avowedly a-political, the same patriotic objective in using the theater to inspire morale and unity was immediately seized upon by the Republican forces at the outbreak of hostilities in the Spanish Civil War in midsummer of 1936. It is fitting tribute to García Lorca that, in the early days of the conflict, the Republican government quickly reactivated La Barraca to serve as force to boost the morale of their troops in the bitter struggle for survival. Still performing the classics of the repertory developed by Lorca, the student troupe took their portable stage and equipment to the battle front to present the *entremeses* of Cervantes — *La cueva de Salamanca, El retablo de las maravillas* and *Los dos habladores.* These three pieces formed the program that was presented August 27, 1937 on the battlefield at Viveros de Valencia. On that perilous mission the dedication of the students was clearly evinced, as noted in an excerpt from an article in *Hora de España:*

> The students of La Barraca quickly found out how to rally to that outcry that was seeking all efforts for the war. If before then they had traveled over Spain's roads as on a joyous outing, in order to awaken the imagination of our villagers, or they went into the cities with their delightful art and their clever repertory, casting a youthful challenge to the professional companies and to the audience in Sunday dress that applauded them, now their mission, like

everything that deals with our struggle, has taken on the characteristics of impetuosity. In September of '36 in Madrid, La Barraca
was already giving its first wartime performance for the
"Motorizada de Hierro". From that time forth, they performed in
the Fontalba, in the Español and in numerous hospitals. But La
Barraca has not frequented only rear-guard theaters and hospitals, for
the soldiers of the Republic have seen the stirring characters of
Cervantes come to their fighting fronts, with their striped flannel
underskirts, their ruffs, their clumsy smiths and their cuckolded
husbands, just as always. Within two days of our triumph over
Italian fascism, here is La Barraca on the victorious field at
Guadalajara bringing joy to the loyal soldiers.

And it is no less certain that for some time the enemy bullets
have gone whistling over that fragile little stage of the *entremeses*.[2]

It is significant that throughout the Civil War, from 1936 until 1939, the
embattled Spanish Republic maintained active commercial theaters in Valencia,
Madrid and Barcelona. In spite of steady gains by the Francoists, the theater in
the unoccupied Republican zone remained an important symbol of patriotism,
adhering to the presecpts of García Lorca, giving regular performances in the
major cities until the very last days of the war. Throughout the entire wartime
period, the commercial theaters served as centers for fund-raising with constant
"Benefit Performances" to generate money, clothing and supplies for the men at
the fighting fronts. In Madrid, constantly under siege and actually an active battle ground, the Republican organization, "Arte y Propaganda," directed by María
Teresa León and Rafael Alberti, maintained a vigorous theatrical campaign in the
Teatro de la Zarzuela until the fall of Madrid.

Also in Madrid the troupe formerly known as "Teatro de Guerra," directed by
Manuel González, became the troupe "García Lorca." In mid-February of 1937
this theater group was commissioned by the Municipal Authority of Madrid to
perform for one month in the Teatro Español, the first theater of the capital.
And subsequently, month by month, that commission was to be extended, giving *bona fide* evidence of the cultural and artistic achievements of that active
wartime troupe. In the spring of that year Manuel González presented his
"García Lorca" players in *Bodas de sangre,* opening to a sell-out audience that
enthusiastically demanded no less than five curtain calls. The warm reception
accorded the opening of Lorca's play assured its continued popularity and patronage during the entire spring theater season, even though Madrid was hard pressed
to withstand the repeated onslaught of Francoist attacks. And in addition to the
active theater seasons carred on at the Teatro de la Zarzuela and the Español, that
city continued to support the operation of sixteen other theaters in the spring of
1937.[3] In the fall of 1937, a new group entitled "Arte y Cultura," sponsored by
the Partido Socialista Obrero Español, announced the intention to present a series of Lorcan works, including the following: *Bodas de sangre, Yerma, La
zapatera prodigiosa,* and a tribute to Lorca, *Responso lírico a García Lorca* by

Rafael Alberti.[4] It is obvious that Spain's Republican citizens and soldiers looked upon Lorca as the patron of their theater heritage.

In both Valencia and Barcelona the theaters continued to carry on scheduled performances, and in some instances those performances did not stop even during air raids. In fact, the enthusiasm of the people for the theater seemed to increase with the rising tensions and threat of defeat. Of special interest in Valencia was the theater campaign that accompanied the meeting of the International Congress of Writers for the Defense of Culture in July of 1937. For this occasion, Manuel Altolaguirre presented at Valencia's Teatro Principal García Lorca's *Mariana Pineda*. The splendid spectacle was enhanced by the decorations and costumes designed by Victor Cortezo. A moving description of that presentation was set down in *Hora de España*, in the words of Ramón Gaya:

> One of the things that I wish to point out forcefully is that never has the name of García Lorca been uttered more authentically and more worthily than on this occasion. A complete homage to the smiling poet, now lost, for that homage was not only an exterior expression, but rather, it was living and moving in its innermost aspects, in the most hidden and minute details. So much so that beginning with the modiste who made the costumes — the seamstress also for *Yerma* and for many pieces performed in La Barraca — all, all were his very own people. It could be said that Federico's work, that Federico himself was in their midst among such close friends. And nevertheless, to judge by the scant and poor newspaper critique, the significance, for example, of the fact that a poet — and who knows if perhaps he may be the most outstanding living poet — performed the role of Don Pedro seems to have eluded most of us.[5]

For playing the role of Don Pedro was Luis Cernuda himself, a close friend and associate of García Lorca. Also taking part in the production were Carmen Antón, who played the role of Mariana Pineda, and María del Carmen Lasgoity, who had performed with La Barraca during the entire period prior to the outbreak of the war. And the director of this production of *Yerma* was none other than Manuel Altolaguirre, who had been one of the sponsors of La Barraca.[6]

Since Valencia had, shortly after the outbreak of hostilities, become the wartime capital of the Republic, there was constant emphasis there upon the protection of the treasures of Spanish art and culture. And it was in Valencia that the Republican leaders chose to store the content of the Prado, since Madrid was the victim of recurrent air raids. With the same goal of escaping those perils, the distinguished poet Antonio Machado arrived in Valencia in November of 1936, and shortly after his arrival there he made a lengthy address at the Casa de la Cultura, denouncing fascism as "the force of inculture." In elaborating upon the fascist objective of destroying all cultural works, he affirmed that "The intellectuals of foreign countries are with the Spanish people. There are already very valid proofs of it ... It is not possible to remain impassive before the destruction of "Las Meninas," just as one wouldn't remain impassive before the destruction of the "Sistine Chapel," of the British Museum or of the Louvre." And subsequently in his discourse he stated, "With Lorca the most stupid and despicable crime has been committed. García Lorca lived on the fringe of politics, but within the real soul of the people. This was his offense, which he has paid for with his life. Fascism's obvious enmity toward the soul has determined the shooting of Lorca, not a political enmity, which could justify it, more or less."[7]

This same emphasis upon cultural values is again reflected in the journal *Hora de España,* published in Valencia during the wartime period. *La Vanguardia,* Barcelona's leading newspaper, carried on its front page on April 27, 1937 an editorial by Paulino Massip entitled "Hora de España," paying homage to the patriotic inspiration represented in this publication. And this editorial continued the theme of Machado's address as it stated:

> All Spain's poets are with us. The old masters and the apprentices and the officials who follow a school and create it. Up with Juan Ramón and Don Antonio Machado ... If you take an anthology of contemporary Spanish poetry, you will have the complete list. There is not a single deserter. And for many reasons: first, Federico García Lorca — a black moon, hungry for the light that glowed in him, snatched him from us. We have so much to weep, that we have not yet wept the silencing of that magic creature. Time will come, friends.[8]

Not only in Valencia, however, was there emphasis upon Spain's great cultural heritage, but in Barcelona too the arts served as a symbolic manifestation of Republican fervor. In January of 1937 the *Cartelera de teatros* listed eleven active theaters, all offering at least two performances daily, *tarde* and *noche,* and many presenting an 11:00 a.m. performance on weekends and holidays. The Apolo advertised on January 3, 1937 a free matinée with poetry readings and songs, featuring a recital of the poetry of García Lorca.[9] Subsequently, on March 19 of the same year, 1937, the Tivoli offered a similar program for its regular afternoon and evening performances. On this occasion, the rhapsodist, Pura de Lara, presented a noteworthy rendition of Lorca's poetry, as described in this report:

> A delicate and genuinely youthful figure, a pleasant and expressive diction, a warm and moving voice, placed in the service of poetry. Is the rhapsodist also a poetess, as were her ancient ancestors, the troubadours of Provence or Lusitania? The verses on her lips, in her voice, in her gestures, recall the tragedy of Federico, the author of the ballad of "La casada infiel," for whom
>
> Gitanas desmelenadas,
> en las sierras lanzan gritos

y el eco, lejos, responde:
¡Federico! ¡Federico!

Federico García Lorca, finally, is the one whom the rhapsodist wants the stars
to search:

¡Salga la luna a buscarlo
por toditas las veredas,
que, en sus brazos de oro fino
me lo traigan las estreyas![10]

Only two weeks later, and also in the Tivoli, there was a brilliant festival in
homage to the Consular Corps. And again for this occasion, the poetry of Lorca
served as patriotic inspiration for the celebration. Barcelona's *Vanguardia* published the following account:

Last night a fervent and interesting act of homage to the Consular
Corps took place in the Tivoli Theater. In brief and deeply-felt
phrases, Jaume Miravitlles offered homage to the foreign digni-
taries ... who are living through this sorrowful and poignant time
with us ... The program was made up of a selection of modern
verse, stirringly recited by the rhapsodist Manolo Gómez, who
rekindled the emotion of the audience with his rendition of Antonio
Machado's "El crimen fue en Granada," and Lorca's "Preciosa y el
aire," "La casada infiel," and "El romance de la Guardia Civil
española." ... In other poems now classic in recitals of this kind,
the art of Manolo Gómez also attained a full and well-deserved triumph. Barcelona's Municipal Band played as a finale de Falla's
"Amor Brujo," which was warmly applauded by the audience that
entirely filled the large auditorium of the Tivoli.[11]

In June of 1938 the Tivoli was again the scene of a Sunday Matinée benefit
performance for the members of the Industria del Espéctaculo who were then
serving in the armed forces of the Republic. Announced as "Fiesta de la Danza,
de la Música y de la Poesía, a la Memoria de García Lorca," the Symphonic Orchestra, directed by Fernando J. Obradors, opened the program with Rimsky-
Korsakov's "Capricho Español." Subsequently this festive performance became
a very personal tribute to the Granadan poet, as this account points out:

For their initial public performance the maestro Obradors presented
successfully three of his own beautiful compositions, based upon
García Lorca's ballads: "Romance de los pelegrinitos," "Canción
del café de chinitas," and "La casada infiel," ... which the tenor
Emilio Vendrell sang masterfully. Obradors' three Lorcan compositions, full of feeling and enchantment, and written with so much

mastery of musical technique as well as a deep sense of the Lorcan spirit, were received with the greatest favor by the audience ... The third part of the program opened with warm and vibrant words of tribute to Lorca by Carlos M. Baena, whose words kindled the patriotic and antifascist enthusiasm of the audience gathered there. And suddenly the unexpected bursts forth. Apart from the announced program, the maestro Leopoldo Cardona, in memory of García Lorca and for the glory of Spain, regales us with an unpublished composition of his own, "El puerto de Palos," based upon popular motifs and displaying great expressive force, which the audience warmly applauded ... Finally, now at 1:00 a.m., so full was the program, the second act of *Bodas de sangre* was performed with excellent interpretation ... The audience, that completely filled the theater, enthusiastically applauded all the performers, and with great satisfaction, made their departure from the beautiful and spirited celebration. In one box we saw the Counselor of Culture of the Generalitat, Don Carlos Pi Suñer, and in another, the subsecretary of Public Education, Señor Puig Elías.[12]

Less than a month later, in Barcelona's Palau de la Música Catalana, a festival was celebrated to commemorate the second anniversary of Lorca's death. Again the rhapsodist Manolo Gómez presented a faithful interpretation of Lorca's poetry. The program was:

First Part. "Prendimiento de Antoñito El Camborio," "Muerte de Antoñito El Camborio," "La monja gitana," "La pena negra," "Preciosa y el aire," "Romance sonámbulo," by Federico García Lorca, y "A la muerte de Federico García Lorca," by Miguel Alonso Somera.
Second Part. Fragments: "Fusilamiento de Torrijos," "Arbolé, arbolé," "Romance de las Manolas," "Doña Juana la Loca," "Bajo el naranjo en flor," "Escena del Macho y la Hembra," "La sangre derramada," by Federico García Lorca; and "El crimen fue en Granada," by Antonio Machado ...
Margarita Xirgu, the great Catalan actress, who now travels triumphantly through Spanish America playing García Lorca's *Yerma* and *Bodas de sangre,* sent to the Commissary of Theaters of Catalonia an expressive cablegram, pledging her personal dedication to the homage.

Following the same newspaper article is the account of the celebration of a homage to Lorca by the school which bore his name, the Grupo Escolar "García Lorca", under the administration of the Generalitat of Catalonia. The program had been opened with an address by the director, paying fervent tribute to the poet. Subsequently the students were given an account of his childhood, his works and his death. A group of students gave a representation of Lorca's "Balada de la Placeta," with musical accompaniment, performed against a scenic backdrop painted by the students for this solemn occasion. The rhapsodist Pura de Lara also gave a rendition of Lorca's poetry for this special program. The choir of the school sang selected songs by the poet at the close of the festival. As an indication of public sentiment inspired by this celebration, it was noted that representatives from Laya Films were present to photograph many of the scenes at this event.[13]

From these accounts it can be seen that the theater continued to serve as a symbol of patriotism throughout the three years of the Spanish Civil War. The most startling aspect, however, of this symbolic patriotic inspiration associated with the theater is found in the activation of theater troupes which followed the example set by La Barraca in the early days of the war as the students took their meager, portable equipment into the battle zones to entertain the fighting forces. Significantly these volunteer troupes were known as "Teatro de guerrilla" and "Teatro de Urgencia." With true patriotic zeal these performers went into the front line areas of combat to entertain the outnumbered, poorly equipped soldiers of the Republic, and to transmit their message, through loudspeakers on the battlefield, to the fascist enemy. The heroic efforts of these performers did much to sustain the morale of the Repulbican forces during the three years of conflict, and it is said that their battlefield performances at times resulted in the desertion of Nationalist soldiers who elected to join the forces of the Republic.

The efficacy of this theater is well described in the article titled "El Teatro en Nuestro Ejército," published in *comisario* in December of 1938, only a few months before the collapse of the Republic. The author, Antonio Aparicio, states:

> The theater is not a simple pastime; the theater, on the contrary, is a weapon of indisputable walue. With the war has come forth a kind of new theater, at least in Spain: the so-called "theater of emergency." On the fronts, through practical application, the usefulness of this type of theater has been proven — a theater done with short works in which is staged a typical wartime scene, an instructive episode, serving as a watchword. When the invaders attacked violently in the East, intending to arrive at the gates of Valencia, in those moments of confusion and despondency, when our line seemed obliged to give way before the pressure of the foreign hordes, the Commander of the Armies of the Central Zone, Comrade Jesús Hernández, requested the assistance of the "Guerrillas del Teatro," who were performing on the front at Guadalajara. The "guerrilla" took a bus and in a few hours was performing its repertory on the outskirts of Nules. The soldiers of the people, who had gone through intense days of agonizing combat, overcome by sleep and exhaustion, gained renewed strength before that little stage, from which a group of young ac-

tors were telling them that it was necessary to keep on fighting without giving in. They were saying it wittily, in the form of a song:

> Soldado que vas al frente
> a defender nuestra tierra,
> yo quiero verte valiente
> para que ganes la guerra.

And they were saying the same thing in the emotion-filled conclusions of those little pieces, full of courage and of confidence in the future:

> ¡Las juventudes de España
> sabrán ganar la pelea!

Simultaneously with this "theater of emergency " of antifascist propaganda, is performed the great popular theater of our best classic authors. In it abound short pieces, *entremeses, jácaras, mojigangas,* etc... Here is, in one word, the inexhaustible treasury of our marvellous classic theater: Lope de Vega, Calderón, Cervantes, Torres Naharro, Lope de Rueda, Quiñones de León ... And right now, in our own time, the light pieces —full of true poetic grace — written by the great poet of the people whom fascism so cowardly assassinated: Federico García Lorca.[14]

This article and many other similar in content attest to the everpresent spirit of Federico García Lorca as an inspiration to the outnumbered and poorly equipped soldiers of the Republic. And in these tributes to Lorca must be recognized the fruition of his efforts and enthusiasm in popularizing the theater as a symbol of patriotic fervor and national ideals. Unfortunately, however, as the tides of war turned progressively against the Republic, there were neither physical nor financial resources to sustain the cultural endeavor of the "front line theaters." Conversely, the Nationalists were gaining in resources and were striving to develop the amenities of stability within their own ranks and conquered territories, in order to restore unity. This need prompted Don Luis Escobar to activate his itinerant wartime theater, La Tarumba, on behalf of the Nationalists.

In an interview in Madrid, Señor Escobar informed me that his La Tarumba was, in reality, merely a reactivation of García Lorca's La Barraca which had been activitated by the Republic in the early days of the war. Subsequently, Escobar reassembled as many as possible of the former students who previously had staffed La Barraca, in order to form a theater for the Nationlist forces. La Tarumba's first performance took place at Huelva during the first year of the war.

After June of 1938, La Tarumba gave way to El Teatro Nacional de la Falange Española, which gave its first performance at Segovia with an outdoor presentation of selected classical works. During the final months of the war, this troupe performed in theaters and cathedrals as well as in outdoor arenas, presenting its works in the style of Lorca's La Barraca. There was no financial remuneration for the young actors nor for the director, Escobar himself, who, for the most part, sustained this theater group through his own personal resources.

With the cessation of hostilities, the germinal Teatro Nacional de la Falange Española ultimately evolved into Spain's Teatro Nacional. The initial performance of the Teatro Nacional took place on April 7, 1940 as a celebration of the first anniversary of the end of the Civil War. Signficantly, the establishment of Spain's National Theater took the form of a patriotic celebration, extolling the victory of the Nationalist forces. It is ironic that this National Theater should have had its root in the La Barraca of García Lorca. But nonetheless, it is a fitting tribute to the theatrical genius of Federico García Lorca that he should have laid the foundation for Spain's National Theater. His own words best express the idealism of his concept of nationalization in the theater:

What Government, whatever might be its political orientation, is going to ignore the magnificent grandeur of the classic Spanish theater, our greatest seal of glory, and is not going to understand that it is the surest vehicle for the cultural elevation of all the towns and all the inhabitants of Spain?[15]

NOTES

1. Leandro Fernández de Moratín, *Tesoro del teatro español.* I París: Librería Europea de Beaudry, 1838 p. 15

2. Juan Gil Albert, "La Barraca," *Hora de España.* 10 (Oct. 1937): 76–77.

3. Robert Marrast, *El Teatre durant la guerra civil espanyola.* Barcelona: L'Institut del Teatre, 1978, pp. 35–38.

4. *Ibid.,* p. 54.

5. *Ibid.,* p. 196.

6. *Ibid.,* .p 196.

7. "El insigne poeta español dice:" *Vanguardia* (Barcelona) (Nov. 29, 1936): 1.

8. Paulino Masip, "Hora de España," *Vanguardia* (Barcelona) (March 27, 1937): 1.

9. "Cartelera de Teatros," *Vanguardia* (Jan. 3, 1937): 9.

10. "Cines y teatros," *Vanguardia* (March 19, 1937): 5.

11. "Teatro Tivoli," *Vanguardia* (April 3, 1937): 4.

12. "Fiesta de la Danza, de la Música y de la Poesía," *Vanguardia* June 28, 1938): 5.

13. "A la memoria de García Lorca," *Vanguardia* June 24, 1938: 5.

14. Antonio Aparicio, "El Teatro en Nuestro Ejército." *Comisario.* 4, 1, (Dec. 1938): 47–50.

15. Federico García Lorca, *Obras completas.* (Décimoquinta edición) Madrid: Aguilar, 1969 p. 1749.

Appendix

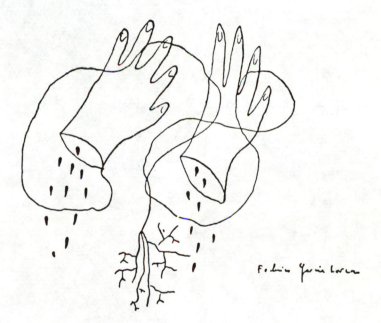

1. Manos cortadas.

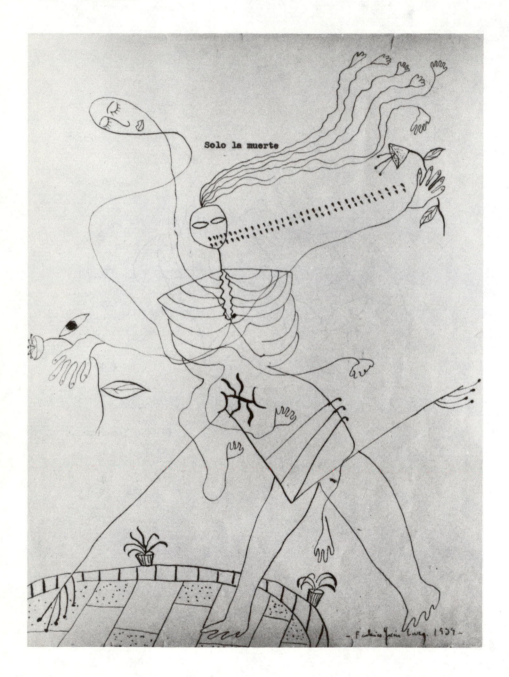

Solo la muerte

2. Muerte

3. The Angel.

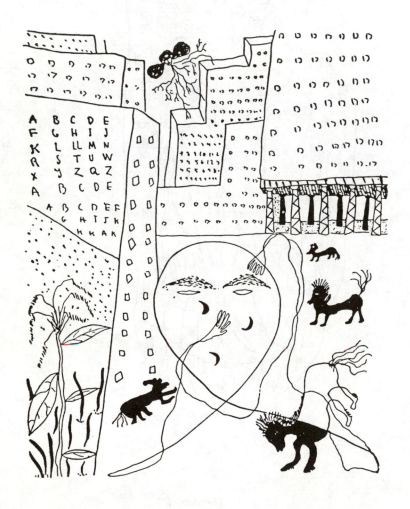

4. Perspectiva urbana con autorretrato

5. Columna y casa

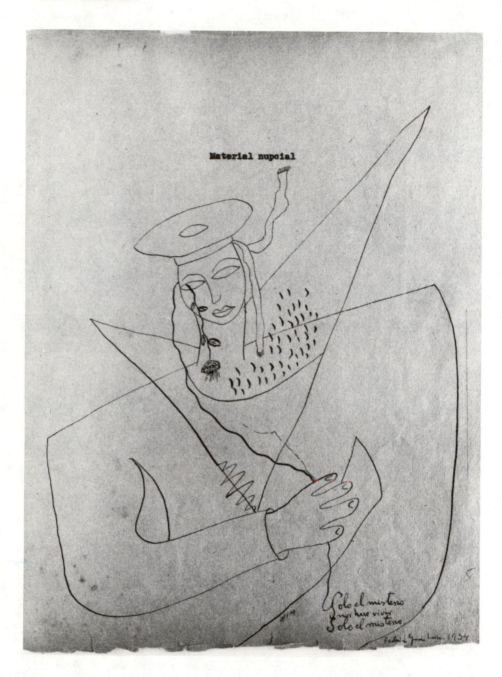

6. Sólo el misterio nos hacer vivir, sólo el misterio

7. Bandolero

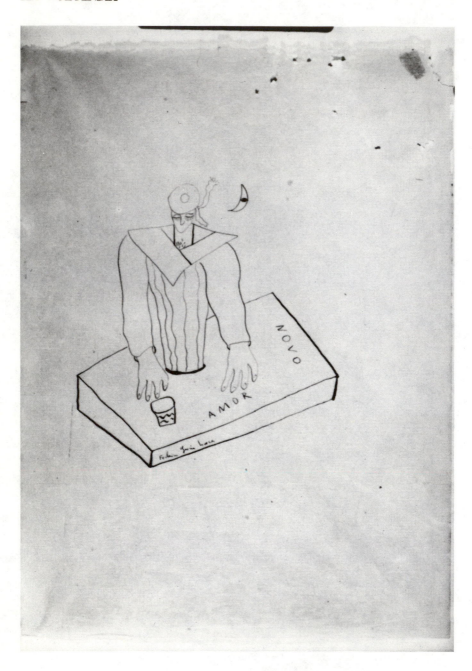

8. Amor novo

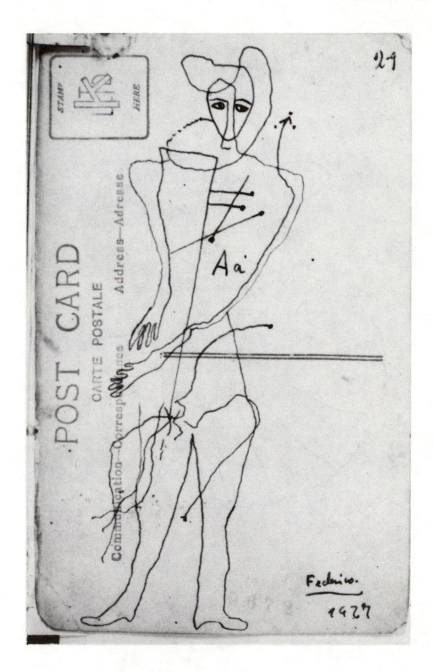

9. Figura

10. La careta que cae.

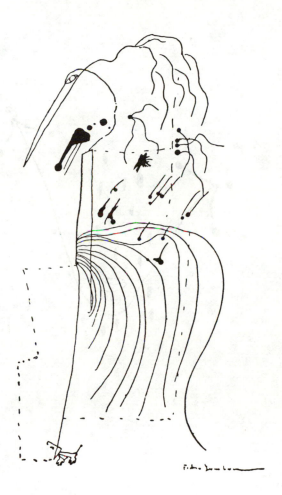

11. Pájaro y perro.

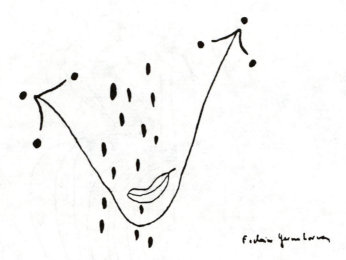

12.   *Rostro con flechas.*

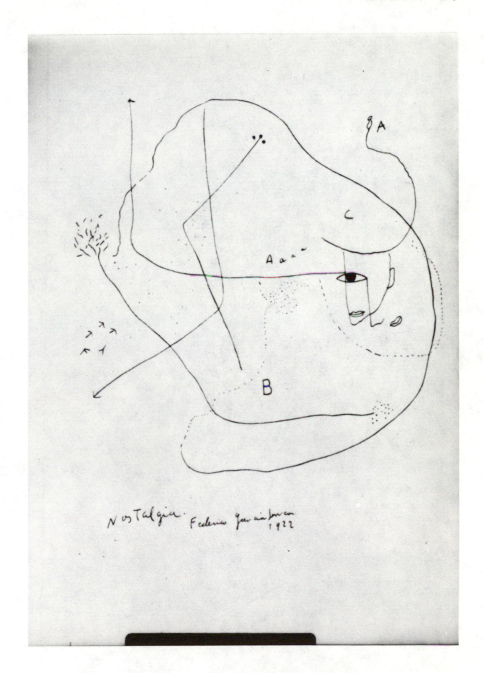

13. Nostalgia

DIBUJO
FEDERICO GARCIA LORCA

14. Amor

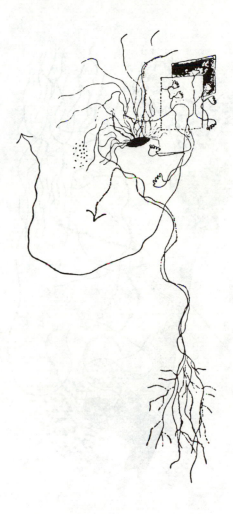

15. El ojo

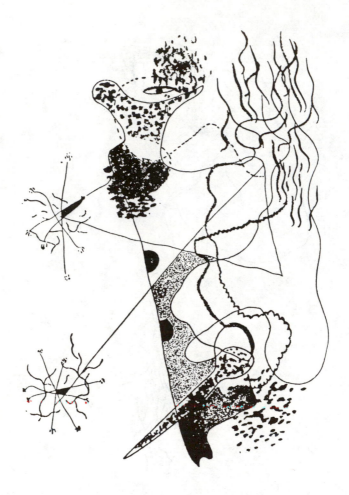

16. Ojo y vilanos

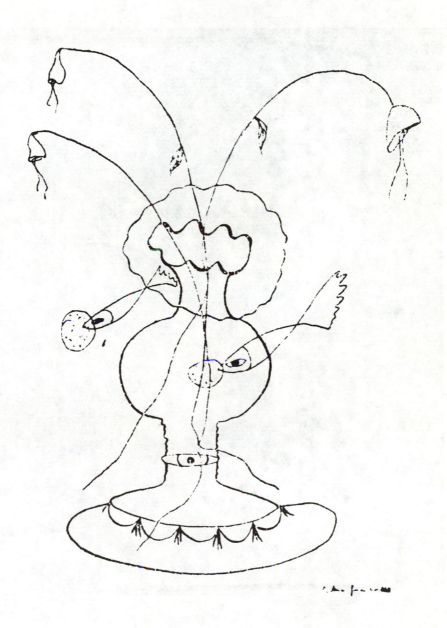

17. Viñeta

18. Naturaleza

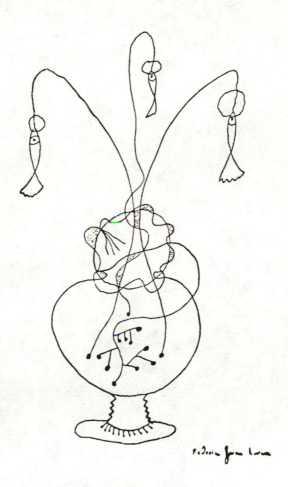

19. *Viñeta.*

20. Florero

21. Parque

22. *Parque*

FRANCESCA COLECCHIA
Duquesne University

Federico García Lorca: A Selectively Updated Bibliography

A cursory survey of studies, adaptations, translations, and editions of Lorca's work published in the past decade testifies to the undiminished interest in the Andalusian poet/dramatist. The items which appear below are not intended as a comprehensive listng of critical works about García Lorca that have appeared in recent years. Those materials found on these pages, which do not include republications of the author's opus, represent a selected sampling of Lorca scholarship published for the most part in this country and Spain.

Books

General

1. Bardi, Ubaldo and Ferruccio Masini (eds.). *Federico García Lorca: Materiali.* Naples: Libreria Tullio Pironti, 1979. xi, 354 pp.
2. Gibson, Ian. *Federico García Lorca, I: De Fuente Vaqueros a Nueva York (1898–1929).* Barcelona: Grijalbo, 1985. 721 pp.
3. Hernández, Mario and Laura de los Ríos de García Lorca (eds.), *Federico y su mundo.* Madrid: Alianza, 1981. 520 pp.
4. Higuera Rojas, Eulalia-Dolores de la. *Mujeres en la vida de García Lorca.* Granada: Nacional, Excma. Diputación Provincial de Granada, 1980, 215 pp.
5. Londré, Felicia Hardison. *Federico García Lorca.* New York: Frederick Ungar Publishing Co., 1984. 208 pp. Chronology ix-xii. Bibliog. 195–197. Index 199–208.
6. MacCurdy, G. Grant. *Federico García Lorca: Life, Work and Criticism.* n.p.: York Press, 1986. 40 pp.
7. Martínez Nadal, Rafael. *Cuatro lecciones sobre Federico García Lorca.* Madrid: Cátedra/Fundación Juan March, 1980. 111 pp.
8. Rodrigo, Antonina. *Lorca-Dalí: una amistad traicionada.* Barcelona: Planeta, 1981. 253 pp.
9. Zdenek, Joseph W., (ed.). *The World of Nature in the Works of Federico García Lorca.* (Winthrop Studies on Major Modern Writers). Rock Hill, S.C.: Winthrop College, 1980. 150 pp.

Poetry

10. Anon. *Darío, Lorca, Neruda: tres poemas inmortales.* Buenos Aires: Ediciones del Libertador, 1983. 84. pp. illus. (Limited edition of 500 copies.)

11. Arteaga, Domingo (ed.). *Tres poetas* (Miguel Hernández, Federico García Lorca, Pablo Neruda.) Mexico, D.F.: Editores Mexicanos Unidos, 1981. 167 pp.; illus.; 1983. 251 pp. illus.

12. Cobb, Carl W. *Lorca's Romancero gitano: a ballad translation and critical study.* Jackson, Miss.: University Press of Mississippi, 1983. xii, 116 pp. bibliog. 113–114.

13. García-Posada, Miguel. *F. García Lorca: Poesía.* n.p.: Akal, 1980–1982. 577+814 pp.

14. Lisboa, José Carlos. *Verde que te quiero verde: ensaio de interpretação del Romancero gitano de García Lorca.* Río de Janeiro: Zabar Editores (em convenio com o Instituto Nacional do Livro, Fundação Nacional Pro-Memória, 1983. 267 pp. (Includes text of Lorca's *Primer romancero gitano.)*

15. Martín, Eutimio. (ed.). *Poeta en Nueva York: Tierra y luna.* Barcelona: Ariel, 1981. 333 pp.

16. Predmore, Richard L. *Lorca's New York Poetry: Social injustice, dark love, lost faith.* Durham, N.C.: Duke University Press, 1980. xi, 111 pp. bibliog. 109–111.

17. Simões, Manuel. *García Lorca e Manuel de Fonseca: dois poetas em confronto.* Milan: Instituto Editoriale Cisalpino — la Goliardica, 1979. 144 pp.

Theater

18. Bauer, Carlos. (tr.). *The Public and Play Without a Title: Two Posthumous Plays.* New York: New Directions 1983. xx, 69 pp. introd. Carlos Bauer.

19. Byrd, Suzanne. *La Fuenteovejuna de Federico García Lorca.* Madrid: Editorial Pliegos, 1984. 137 pp., bibliog. 131–137. (Includes "Noticia sobre la barraca". Luis Sáenz de la Calzada, pp 113–130).

20. Edwards, Gwynne. *Lorca: The Theatre Beneath the Sands.* Boston: Boyars, 1980. 310 pp.

21. Feal, Carlos. *Lorca: tragedia y mito.* Ottawa: Dovehouse Editions, Inc., 1989. 157 pp.

22. Martín Recuerda, José. *Análisis de doña Rosita la soltera, o el lenguaje de las flores. [de Federico García Lorca]: tragedia sin sangre.* Salamanca: University of Salamanca, 1979. 67 pp.

23. Morris, C.B. *García Lorca, Bodas de sangre.* London: Tamesis, 1980. 93 pp.

24. Smoot, Jean J. *A Comparison of Plays by John Millington Synge and Federico García Lorca: The Poets and Time.* Madrid: José Porrúa Turranzas, 1978.

Other

25. Colecchia, Francesca, (ed.). *García Lorca: A Selectively Annotated Bibliography of Criticism*. New York: Garland Publishing Inc., 1979. xxvi, 313 pp.

26. Colecchia, Francesca, (ed.). *García Lorca: An Annotated Primary Bibliography*. Garland Publishing Inc., 1982. xxi, 281 pp.

27. Gershator, David, (ed.). *Federico García Lorca: Selected Letters*. New York: New Directions, 1983. xiv, 172 pp. introd. David Gershator.

28. Klibbe, Lawrence H. *Lorca's Impresiones y paisajes: The Young Artist*. Madrid: José Porrúa Turanzas, S.A., 1983. ix–xi, 165 pp., bibliog. 159–161.

29. García Lorca, Federico. *Viaje a la luna: guión cinematográfico*. Laffranque, Marie. (ed.). Loubressac (Spain): Broad Editores, 1980. 22 pp. introd. Marie Laffranque.

30. Tinnell, Roger D. *Federico García Lorca: Catálogo-discografía de las 'Canciones populares antiguas' y de música basada en textos lorquianos*. University of New Hampshire, 1986. ii +121 pp.

31. Utrera Macías, Rafael and Miguel García-Posada, (eds.) *García Lorca y el cinema*. Seville: Edisur, 1982. 133 pp.

Dissertations and Theses

Poetry

32. Britt, Linda Louise. "Swan Song: Late Trends in the Poetry of Federico García Lorca." *DAI* 48(1) 137A (University of Virginia, 1986).

33. Carrasco Galán, Alvaro. "Influencia de la poesía moderna española y sudamericana en la poesía contemporánea norteamericana: Influencia de Lorca y Neruda en Robert Bly." *DAI* 40:5071 A-72A (State University of New York at Buffalo, 1979).

34. Millán Jiménez, María C(lementa). "Interpretación de *Poeta en Nueva York* de Federico García Lorca, contexto y originalidad." *DAI* 45(8):2542A (Harvard University, 1984).

35. Newton, Candelas María. "*Libro de poemas* y los comienzos de la poesía de Federico García Lorca." *DAI* 41-2631A (University of Pittsburgh, 1980).

36. Poust, Alice Jan. "The Form and Function of Mythic Thought in Four Hispanic Poets: Federico García Lorca, Vicente Aleixandre, José Lezama Lima, Octavio Paz." *DAI* 43(7):2362A (University of Texas, Austin, 1982).

37. Quance, Roberta Ann. "Signs of the Past: Myth, Ritual, and the Poetry of Federico García Lorca." *DAI* 1982. 43(2):464A. (Cornell University, 1982).

38. Rapin, Ronald Francis. "Narrative Structure in Federico García Lorca's *Poeta en Nueva York*." *DAI* 47:3445A 1987. (University of Michigan, 1986).

39. Ruchames, Robert Mark. "A Wounded Pulse: A Translation of García Lorca's *Poet in New York* with a Critical Introduction." *DAI* 47:1721A 1986. (State University of New York, Binghampton, 1985).

40. Walker, Sandra Dianne. *"La tierra, la ciudad y la muerte en la poesía de Federico García Lorca."* *DAI* 41(1):278A. (Emory University, 1980).

Theater

41. Echeverría, Miriam Balboa. "La visión paralizante: El surrealismo en el teatro de Federico García Lorca." *DAI* 41(5):2139A. (University of Washington, 1980).

42. Kürtösi, K. "A XX. századi költoi dráma három tipusa: Szempontok T.S. Eliot, F. García Lorca és Brecht költoi drámáinak értelmezésésehez. *DAI* 192, 43(2):1571C.

43. Mains, Melinda Poole. "Staging Myth: Dramatic Techniques of Yeats and Lorca." *DAI* 41(5):2098A. (University of Washington, 1980).

44. Sturn, Suzanne. "Federico García Lorca and La Barraca: The Influence of Classical Spanish Theatrical Form and the Puppet on the Repertory of La Barraca and on Lorca's Approach to a Popular Stage." *DAI* 45(8):2307A. (University of Minnesota, 1984).

Other

45. Lee, Cecilia Castro. "El mundo crítico de Federico García Lorca." *DAI* 42(5):2157A (Emory University, 1980).

46. Poeta, Salvatore Joseph. "La elegía funeral y las elegías en memoria de Federico García Lorca." *DAI* 43(11):3618A (University of Pennsylvania 1982).

47. Rouse, Milton R. "George Crumb's 'Ancient Voices of Children' and the Function of Timbre." M.M. Thesis. Carbondale, Il: Southern Illinois University at Carbondale, 1980. bibliog. 111–113.

Chapters in Books, Articles in Journals

General

48. Aguilar, Helene J.F. de. "Warring with Time." *Parnassus* 9,1 (Spring-Summer 1981): 253–268.

49. Alvar, Manuel. "Los cuatro elementos en la obra de García Lorca." *CHA* 433–434 (July–August 1986):69–88.

50. Anderson, Andrew A. "García Lorca en Montevideo: Una cronología provisional.: *BH* 1,2 (January-June 1985):167–179.

51. Anderson, Andrew A. "Una amistad inglesa de Federico García Lorca." *Insula* 40,462 (May 1985):3–4.

52. Fernández Cifuentes, Luis. "García Lorca: Historia de una evaluación, evaluación de una historia." In: Luoreiro, Angel, G. (ed.). *Estelas, laberintos, nuevas sendas*. Barcelona: Anthropos, 1988. pp. 233–261.

53. Armas, Isabel de. "García Lorca y el segundo sexo." *CHA* 433–434 (July-August 1986):129–138C.

54. Babín, María Teresa. "The Voice of Nature in the Life of the Water: García Lorca's Vision From 1923 to 1936." In: Zdenek, Joseph W. (ed.). *The World of Nature in the Works of Federico García Lorca*. Rock Hill, S.C.: Winthrop College, pp.139–150.

55. Belarmi, Rabah. "Federico García Lorca, Jean Senac: Influences et convergences." In: Dejeux, Jean (ed.). *Espagne et Algérie au XXe siècle: Contacts culturels et création littéraire*. Paris: L'Harmattan, 1985. 189–206.

56. Benstock, Bernard. "The Assassin and the Censor: Political and Literary Tensions." *Cliol*. 11,3 (Spring 1982):219–238.

57. Bouet, Jacques. "F. García Lorca intériorisé par un poète roumain: M.R. Paraschivescu." In: Hommage à Jean-Louis Flecniakoska par ses collègues, amis et élèves des Universités de Montpellier, Avignon et Perpignan. Montpellier: Université Paul Valéry, 461 pp. 59-71.

58. Byrd, Suzanne. "La 'Fiesta del Cante Jondo' de Granada: ¿una españolada?" In: Loureiro, Angel G. (ed.). *Estelas, laberintos, nuevas sendas*. Barcelona: Anthropos, 1988. pp. 345–352.

59. Canales, Luis, "O Mundo Pansexual de García Lorca." *MGSL* 18,862 (April 9, 1983).

60. Cao, Antonio F. "Huellas lorquianas en el teatro de la guerra civil española." In: Gordon, Alan M. and Evelyn Rugg, (eds). *Actas del Sexto Congreso Internacional de Hispanistas celebrado en Toronto del 22 al 26 agosto de 1977*. pp. 149–153.

61. Caromna, Elena Reina. "Lo órfico y elegíaco en el poema de Emilio Prados 'Estancia en la muerte con Federico García Lorca.'" *ALEC* 9,1–3 (1984):29–48.

62. Casalduero, Joaquín. "Conversación con Paco García Lorca (14 marzo 1956)." *Hispania* 69,4 (December 1986):760.

63. Castagnino, Raúl H. "García Lorca: Arte y pueblo." *Boletín de la Acad. Argentina de Letras* 51, 201–202 (July-December 1986): 417–423.

64. Costa, René de. "La poesía y sus circunstancias: Un inédito de García Lorca." *Hispania* 69, 4 (December 1986):761–763.

65. Diaconu, Dana. "La suerte de Federico García Lorca en Rumania." *ASUI* 31(1985):75–82.

66. Díaz Sande, José Ramón. "Cincuentenario de García Lorca: Resumen de un año teatral.: *RYF* 215, 1061 (March 1987): 319–327.

67. Dobos, Erzsébet. "Nuevos datos sobre el viaje de Federico García Lorca por Cuba en el año 1930." *ALitASH*. 1980:22 (3–4):392–405.

68. Eisenberg, Daniel. "Nuevos documentos relativos a la edición de *Poeta en Nueva York* y otras obras de García Lorca." *ALE* 5, (1986–1987):106–107.

69. Flys, Michael J. "The Changing View of Nature in Federico García Lorca." In: Zdenek, Joseph W. (ed.). *The World of Nature in the Works of Federico García Lorca*. Rock Hill, S.C.: Winthrop College, pp. 19–28.

70. García-Posada, Miguel. "Air nocturne." *Europe* 616-617:51–56. (Tr. Charles Marcilly).

71. García-Posada, Miguel. "Lorca en 'La Pléiade'". *Insula* XXXVII, 430 (Sept. 1982):4–5.

72. Gazarian-Gautier, Marie-Lise. "Doors and Windows as a Luring Call of Nature in the Work of Federico García Lorca." In: Zdenek, Joseph W. (ed.). *The World of Nature in the Works of Federico García Lorca*. Rock Hill, S.C.: Winthrop College: pp. 73–80.

73. Georgescu, Paul Alexandru. "Un andaluz universal: Federico García Lorca. *Steaua* 32,9 [41 2] (Sept. 1981):56.

74. Gibson, Ian. "L' 'Apolitisme' de García Lorca." *Europe* 616–617:20–29. (Tr. Monique Martin).

75. González Montes, Yara. "Mecánica socio-económica en la obra de García Lorca." *GLR* 8,1 (Spring 1980):47–59.

76. Grande, Félix. "García Lorca y el flamenco." In: Loureiro, Angel G. (ed.) *Estelas, laberintos, nuevas sendas*. Barcelona: Anthropos, 1988. pp. 321–343.

77. Greenfield, Sumner M. and Jeanne P. Brownlow. "Federico García Lorca." *ALEC* 11,1–2(1986)

78. Gullón, Germán. "García Lorca y la Segunda República Española." *GLR*, 10,1 (Spring 1982):10–23.

79. Hempel, Wido. "El viejo y el amor: Apuntes sobre un motivo en la literatura española de Cervantes a García Lorca." In: Kossof, A. David, et. al. (eds.). *Actas del VIII Congreso de la Asociación de Hispanistas, I*. Madrid: Istmo, 1986. pp. 693–702.

80. Holmberg, Arthur. "Five Years After Franco, Lorca Is Alive Again in Spain." *NYT* (October 19, 1980):3. [Sec. 2].

81. Kobo, Khuan. "Kto zhe otdal prikaz ob ublistve Lorki?" *LG*. 12, 4922 (March 23, 1983):13, 14923 (March 30, 1983):110.

82. Johnson, Anita L. "García Lorca en la España democrática: La temporada teatral 1984–1985: *ALEC* 11,1–2 (1986); 161–175.

83. Laffranque, Marie. "A propos d'un livre récent sur Lorca: Le Poète vu par son frère." *BH* LXXXV, 1–2 (Jan. – June 1983):175–181.

84. Laffranque, Marie. "Poète et public." *Europe* 616, 617:115–127.

85. Marcilly, Charles. "Chronologie de Federico García Lorca." *Europe* 616–617:7–20.

86. Marcilly, Charles. "Il faut passer les ponts." *Europe* 616–617:29–50.

87. Marcilly, Charles. "Présence de Federico." *Europe* 616–617:29–50.

88. Martín, Eutimio. "En torno a un texto autobiográfico (inédito) de Federico G. Lorca." 227–259 In: *L'Autobiographie en Espagne*. Aix-en-Provence: Univ. de Provence;1982. 374 pp.

89. Martín, Eutimio. "Federico García Lorca: dos entrevistas desconocidas." *Insula* 35,402 (May 1980):1,4,15.

90. Martín, Eutimio. "Los puntos sobre las 'ies': Edición de la obra de Federico García Lorca." *Quimera* 17 (March 1982):15–18.

91. Martín, Eutimio. "Una leyenda de Victor Hugo en la obra de García Lorca." *Insula* XXXVII, 427 (June 1982):1,10.

92. Maurer, Christopher. "Sobre 'joven literatura' y política: Cartas de Pedro Salinas y de Federico García Lorca (1930–1935)." In: Loureiro, Angel G. (ed.). *Estelas, laberintos, nuevas sendas*. Barcelona: Anthropos, 1988. pp. 297–319.

93. Morelli, Gabriele. "Fortuna literaria de García Lorca en Italia." *Insula* 41, 478 (September 1986):4.

94. Morla Lynch, Carlos. "En Espagne avec Federico García Lorca: Pages d'un journal intime (1928–1936)." *Europe* 616–617:128–143 (Trs. Silvie Sesé and Bernard Sesé)

95. Newton, Candelas. "El jardín y su significado en la producción lorquiana." *Cruz Ansata* (Bayamón, Puerto Rico) 6 (1983):261–268.

96. O'Nan, Martha. "French Public and Scholarly Interest on García Lorca: 1980–81." *GLR*. 10,2 (Spring 1982):114–129.

97. Poeta, Salvatore J. "Elegía de Miguel Hernández en memoria de Federico García Lorca analizada." *HisJ* 8,2 (Spring 1985): 173–183.

98. Poeta, Salvatore J. "La 'Oda a Federico García Lorca' re-examinada." *GLR* 11,2 (1983):111–123.

99. Rodrigo, Antonina. "Federico García Lorca – Rafael Barradas: El 'ateneillo de Hospitalet'." *Insula* 41, 476-477 (July–August 1986):7–8.

100. Rogers, Paul Patrick. "García Lorca and His Friends: Some Anecdotes Recalled by Pictures." *LCUT* 13:12–26.

101. Rosenthal, David. "Lorca and the Catalans." *GLR* 8,2 (Fall 1980):137–150.

102. Salvador, Salvador, Francisco. "La significación de la muerte de García Lorca entre los intelectuales republicanos." In: Paolini, Gilbert (ed.). *La Chispa '87: Selected Proceedings.* New Orleans: Tulane University Press, 1987. pp. 271–279.

103. Sirimarco, María C. "Ricardo Molinari: Una rosa para Federico García Lorca." *CHA* 433–434 (July–August 1986):183–193.

104. Söderberg, Lasse. "Federico García Lorca." *Lyrikvännen* 4 (1983):158–161.

105. Tinnell, Roger D. "A Listing of Recordings of García Lorca's *Canciones populares antiguas* and of Recordings of Music Based on García Lorca Texts." *GLR* 11,1 (1983):1–23.

106. Ucelay, Margarita. "Federico García Lorca parla per als obrers catalans': Estudio preliminar a una entrevista de Federico García Lorca.'" *Boletín de la Fundación Federico García Lorca* I,1 (June 1987):38–57.

107. Villegas, Marcelino. "Una imagen taurina compartida por José Eustasio Rivera y Federico García Lorca." *CHA* 433–434 (July–August 1986):230–234.

108. Wahnon, Sultana. "García Lorca y la estética de posguerra." *Insula* 41, 476–477 (July–August 1986):12–13.

109. Walsh, John K. and B. Bussell Thompson. "García Lorca en Buenos Aires: Entrevista con D. Edmundo Guibourg." *GLR* 11,2 (1983):211–230.

110. Woensel, Maurice J.F. van. "Amelinha Canta García Lorca." *CdAr.* 200 (July 10, 1983):10–11.

111. Yarmus, Marcia D. "Federico García Lorca's Naming Practices: A Study in the Generic." In: Seits, Laurence E. (ed.). *In Honor of Allen Walker Read.* DeKalb, Il: N. Central Name Society, 1988. pp. 74–82.

112. Yuden, Florence L. "The Yes and No of Lorca's Ocean." In: Zdenek, Joseph W. (ed.). *The World of Nature in the Works of Federico García Lorca.* Rock Hill, S.C.: Winthrop College, pp. 117–127.

Poetry

General

113. Anderson, Andrew A. "García Lorca como poeta petrarquista." *CHA* 435–436 (September–October 1986):495–518.

114. Ayéndez Alder, Ruth. "Otro aspecto del viento en la obra de Federico García Lorca." *HisJ* 4,1 (Fall 1982):41–52.

115. Babín, María T. "El viejo y el nuevo mundo de Juan Ramón Jiménez y García Lorca." *SinN* 12,3 (April-June 1982):131–146.

116. Bardi, Ubaldo. "García Lorca e la poesia italiana del dopoguerra." *GLR* 11,1 (1983):25–60.

117. Bly, Robert. "García Lorca and Desire." *NewL* 40, 3–4 (Spring-Summer 1983):85–88.
118. Boland, Roy C. "Un poema de Salarrue inspirado por García Lorca." *Cultura* 68–69 (January–June 1980):188–191.
119. Chamberlain, Lori. "How Dead Men Write to Each Other." 51–56 In:Wellman, Don, Cola Franzen, and Irene Turner, (eds.). *Translations: Experiments in Reading.* Fasc. A. Cambridge, MA:O.ARS; 1983. pp.51–56.
120. Ciplijauskaité, Biruté. "El verso ajeno en el poema." *Hispania* 69,4 (December 1986):784–787.
121. Cirre, José Francisco. "Vanguardia y clasicismo en la 'Oda a Salvador Dalí'." In: Gallego Morell, A., Andrés Soria, and Nicolás Marín, (eds.). *Estudios sobre literatura y arte dedicados al profesor Emilio Orozco Díaz,* I. Granada:Univ. de Granada, 1979. pp. 297–302.
122. Cobb, Carl W. "Federico García Lorca and a Rejected Gypsy Ballad." *Hispania* 69,4 (December 1986):788–790.
123. Correa, Gustavo, "The Mythification of Nature in the Poetry of Federico García Lorca." In:Zdenek, Joseph W. (ed.). *The World of Nature in the Works of Federico García Lorca.* Rock Hill, S.C.:Winthrop College. pp. 1–17.
124. DiAntonio, Robert. "The Confluence of Childhood Fantasy and Mythic Primitivism: Two Early Poems by García Lorca." *RomN* 25,1 (Fall 1984): 11–15.
125. Durán, Manuel. "Lorca y las vanguardias." *Hispania* 69,4 (December 1986):764–770.
126. Durán, Manuel. "Notas sobre García Lorca, la vanguardia, Ramón Gómez de la Serna y las greguerías." *CHA* 433–434 (July-August 1986):221–229.
127. Dust, Patrick H. "Cosmic Love in Lorca and Guillén." 53–68 In: Jiménez Fajardo, Salvador, and John C. Wilcox (eds.). *At Home and Beyond: New Essays on Spanish Poets of the Twenties.* Lincoln, NE: Society of Spanish and Spanish-American Studies, 1983. pp. 53–68.
128. Ekstrom, Margareth V. "Thematic Comparisons of the Spanish Poetry of García Lorca and the Japanese Poetry of Basho." *GLR* 9,1 (Spring 1981):56–63.
129. García Lorca, Francisco. "Federico García Lorca ou le réalisme poétique." *Europe* 616–617:96–100.
130. Genoud de Fourcade, Mariana. "La poesía de Federico García Lorca a la luz de su poética." *Letras* (Univ. Católica Argentina)15–16 (April–August 1986):76–83.
131. Gleaves, Robert M. "Neruda and Lorca: A Meeting of Poetic Minds." *RS* 48:142–151.

132. Higginbotham, Virginia. "García Lorca and Hart Crane: Two Views from the Bridge." *Neophil.* 66,2 (Apr. 1982):219–226.
133. Madrid-Malo, Néstor. "García Lorca, sonetista." *BCB* 16,5 (May 1979):48–56.
134. Martín, Eutimio. "Descenso al Monte Carmelo: San Juan de la Cruz en García Lorca." *Quimera* 34 (December 1983):54–59.
135. Martín, Eutimio. "'Sobre un libro de versos'": El primer manifiesto poético de Federico García Lorca." *ALE* 4(1986):246–256.
136. Martín, Eutimio. "'Sombras': Una obra inédita de García Lorca." *Quimera* 36 (March 1984):51–55.
137. Martín, Eutimio and Gerard Dufour. "Presencia de Victor Hugo en Federico García Lorca. In: *Hommage à Monsieur le professeur Claude-Henri Fraches à l'occasion de son départ à la retraite.* Provence: Pubs. Univ. de Provence, 1984. pp. 135–157.
138. Martínez Cuitino, Luis. "Federico García Lorca y Argentina." *Insula* 39, 448 (March 1984):14.
139. Maurer, Christopher. "De la correspondencia de García Lorca: Datos inéditos sobre la transmisión de su obra. *"Boletín de la Fundación García Lorca* I, 1(June 1987):58–85.
140. McInnis, Judy B. "José Ortega y Gasset and Federico García Lorca." In: Marval-McNair, Nora de (ed.). *José Ortega y Gasset.* Westport, CT.: Greenwood, 1987. pp. 143–149.
141. McInnis, Judy B. "The Psychological Map of García Lorca's Aesthetics: Granada as Universal Image." *Comparatist* (May 8, 1984):33–42.
142. McSorley, Bonnie Shannon. "Nature's Sensual and Sexual Aspects in Three Gypsy Ballads of García Lorca." In:Zdenek, Joseph W., (ed.). *The World of Nature in the Works of Federico García Lorca.* Rock Hill, S.C.: Winthrop College, pp. 81–89.
143. Millán, María C. "Un inédito de Federico García Lorca." *CHA* 433–434 (July-August 1986):31–32.
144. Min, Yong-tae. "Lorca, poeta oriental." *CHA* 358:129–144.
145. Monsivais, Carlos. "García Lorca y México." *CHA* 433–434 (July-August 1986):249–255.
146. Newton, Candelas. "Emilio Carrere en la formación poética de García Lorca." *CH* 5,1 (1983):59–70.
147. Newton, Candelas. "Proyecciones de 'El jardín de las toronjas de luna' de García Lorca." *HisJ* 5,2 (Spring 1984):101–112.
148. Ortega, José. "Apunte sobre la visión infantil en la poesía de García Lorca." *NE* 47 (1982):37–40.
149. Ortega, José. "El gitano y el negro en la poesía de García Lorca." *CHA* 433–434 (July-August 1986): 146–168.
150. Ortega, José. "Juan Ramón Jiménez y Federico García Lorca: Dos poetas andaluces en Estados Unidos." *CHA* 376–378 (1981):875–885.

151. Ortega, José. "La visión infantil en la poesía de García Lorca." *Monographic Review/Revista Monográfica* 1 (1986):38–41.

152. Palley, Julian. "Lorca's Floating Images." *ALEC* 6 (1981):161–171.

153. Patout, Paulette. "La Poésie d'Alfonso Reyes et de García Lorca: Ressemblances, reminiscenes, influences?" In: Bonneville, Barcelona: LAIA, 1979. pp. 649–660.

154. Ramond, Michèle. "Federico García Lorca: El Otro (o la letra viva)." *CHA* 435–436 (September-October 1986):431–437.

155. Ríos-Font, Wadda C. "La poética de Salvador Dalí y la poesía de Federico García Lorca." *Plaza* 11 (Autumn 1986):48–56.

156. Ronay, Laszlo. "A pasztor es a profeta: Motivumok Radnoti Miklos kolteszeteben Alfol: Irodaimi Muvelodesi es Kritikai." *Folyoirst* 35,5 (1984):35–43.

157. Rosselli, Ferdinando. "Possibile lettura di un sonetto di Federico García Lorca." *Studi dell'Istituto Linguistico* 1 (1978):223–228.

158. Sahuquillo, Angel. "Presencia de Verlaine en la vida y en la obra de Federico García Lorca." In: Suomela-Harma, Elina and Olli Valikangas (eds.). *Actes du 5e Congrès des Romanistes Scandinaves* (Helsinski, August 13–17, 1986) Helsinksi: Soc. Neophilol, 1986. pp. 303–312.

159. Socrate, Mario. "L" Adán' di Lorca e la simultaneità del punto di vista." *SCr.* 15,1 [44] (Feb. 1981):46–67.

160. Ucatescu, Jorge. "Lenguaje poético y musical en García Lorca." *CHA* 435–436 (September–October 1986):455–467.

161. Uscatescu, Jorge and Tania Enache. "Lenguaje poético y musical en García Lorca, II. *RITL* 34, 2–3 (1986):87–91.

162. Velasco, Joseph. "La poesía erótica del primer Lorca." In: *Hommage à Jean-Louis Flecniakoska par ses collègues, amis et élèves des Universités de Montpellier, Avignon et Perpignan.* Montpellier: Université Paul Valéry. pp. 445–461.

163. Weldon, Alicia G. "Algunos escorzos comparativos de la poética de Góngora y García Lorca a trescientos años de distancia." *CHA* 384 (June 1982):625–639.

164. Xirau, Ramón. "Federico García Lorca: Poesía y poética." *CHA* 435–436. (September–October 1986):425–429.

Romancero gitano

165. Arango, Manuel A. "Lo mítico en el *Romancero gitano* de Federico García Lorca." *GLR* 11,2 (1983):125–138.

166. Crosbie, John. "Structure and Counter-Structure in Lorca's *Romancero gitano.*" *MLR* 77,1 (Jan. 1982):74–88.

167. Debicki, Andrew P. "Códigos expresivos en el *Romancero gitano.*" *TCrit* 14 (1979):143-154.

168. Harris, Derek. "The Theme of the Crucifixion in Lorca's *Romancero gitano.*" *BHS* LXIII, 4 (Oct. 1981):329-338.
169. Larkins, James E. "Myth upon Myth: Five Animals of the *Romancero gitano. Hispania* 64,1 (March 1981):14–22.
170. Larkins, James E. "The Mythical Aspect of Death in the Natural World of the *Romancero gitano.*" In: Zdenek, Joseph W., (ed.). *The World of Nature in the Works of Federico García Lorca:* Rock Hills, S.C.: Winthrop College. pp. 211–233.
171. Maio, Eugene A. "An Imaginary Companion in García Lorca's 'La casada infiel'." *GLR* 8,2 (Fall 1980):102–110.
172. Marín, Diego. "Algunos problemas interpretativos del *Romancero gitano.*" In: Paolini, Gilbert, (ed.). *La Chispa '81: Selected Proceedings, February, 26–28, 1981.* New Orleans: Tulane University, 1981. pp. 199-207.
173. Martín, Eutimio. "La Dimension socio-religieuse du *Romancero gitano:* 'Romance de la pena negra'." *Europe* 616–617:57–70.
174. McInnis, Judy B. and Elizabeth E. Bohning. "The Child, the Daemon and Death in Goethe's 'Erlkönig' and García Lorca's 'Romance de la luna, luna.'" *GLR* 9,2 (Fall 1981):109–127.
175. Selig, Karl Ludwig. "Lorca's 'Antoñito el Camborio' Poems and the Potential Subversion of the Ideal." *TLTL* 23,1 (Dec. 1983):32–37.
176. Turner, Harriet, S. "Lorquian Reflections: 'Romance del emplazado.'" *Hispania* 70,3 (September 1987):447–456.
177. Velasco, Joseph. "L'Aspect narratif dans le *Romancero gitano:* Essai d'interprétation du romance 'Muerto de amor'." In: *Mélanges à la mémoire d'André Joucla-Ruau.* Aix-en-Provence: Université de Provence, 1978. pp. 1205-1217.

Poeta en Nueva York

178. Anderson, Andrew A. "García Lorca en Montevideo: un testimonio desconocido y más evidencia sobre la evolución de *Poeta en Nueva York.*" *BH* LXXXIII, 1–2 (Jan.-June 1981):145–161.
179. Anderson, Andrew A. "Lorca's 'New York Poems': A contribution to the debate." *FMLS* 17,3 (July 1981):256-270.
180. Anderson, Andrew A. "The Evolution of García Lorca's Poetic Projects 1929–36 and the Textual Status of *Poeta en Nueva York.*" *BHS* LX,3 (July 1983):221–246.
181. Brumm, Anne-Marie. "Lorca's 'Santa Lucía y San Lázaro': Precursor to *Poet in New York,*" *NConL* 12,5 (Nov. 1982):10–12.
182. Dennis, Nigel. "On the First Edition of Lorca's *Poeta en Nueva York.*" *OHis* 1 (1979);47–83.
183. Glass, Elliot S. "'El cementerio judío': García Lorca's Historical Vision of the Jews." *Hispano* 25,75 (May 1982):33–49.

184. Halliburton, Lloyd. "The Son-Christ Image in *Poeta en Nueva York.*" *GLR* 8,2 (Fall 1980):111-126.
185. Higginbotham, Virginia. "Sounds of Fury: Listening to *Poeta en Nueva York.*" *Hispania* 69,4 (December 1986):778–784.
186. Ilie, Paul. "The Vanguard Infrastructure of "Poema doble del lago Eden." *Hispania* 69,4 (December 1986):770–778.
187. Millán, María C(lementa). "Hacia un esclarecimiento de los poemas americanos de Federico García Lorca: *Poeta en Nueva York* y otros poemas." *Insula* 37,431 (October 1982):1,14,15,16.
188. Ortega, José. "Apuntes para una teoría de la poética de García Lorca: *Poeta en Nueva York.*" *SinN* 14,1 (October-December 1983):7–18.
189. Ortega, José. "*Poeta en Nueva York:* Alienación social y libertad política." *CHA* 356:350–367.
190. Ortega, José. "*Poeta en Nueva York:* Alienación social y surrealismo." *NE* 18:45–54.
191. Ortega, José. "Retorno y denuncia de la ciudad: *Poeta en Nueva York.*" *SinN* 11,3 (Oct.–Dec. 1980)" 41–50.
192. Sabourín, Jesús. "Un gran libro sobre una gran crisis: *Poeta en Nueva York.*" *CasaA* 21,122 (Sept.–Oct. 1980):57–66.
193. Solotorevsky, Myrna. "'Vuelta de paseo' de Federico García Lorca." *RLet* 27 (1978):71–91.
194. Zdenek, Joseph W. "*Poeta en Nueva York:* Product of García Lorca's Subconsciousness or Superconsciousness?" *GLR* 10,2 (Spring 1982):62–74.

Other

195. Atencia, María Victoria. "Los seis poemas gallegos de Federico García Lorca." *Insula* XXXVII, 427 (June 1982):1,12.
196. Dumitrescu-Sîrbu, Domnita. "Estructura del vocabulario poético en *Diván del Tamarit* de Federico García Lorca." *RRL* 28 [20],1 (Jan.–June 1983):21–34.
197. Gómez S. Iglesias, Rafael. "El manuscrito autógrafo de *Llanto por Ignacio Sánchez Mejías,* de Federico García Lorca." *BBMP* 55 (1979):207–230.
198. Marcilly, Charles. "Las Suites de García Lorca: El jardín de las simientes no florecidas." *RO* 65 (October 1986):33–50.
199. Newton, Candelas, S. "Nostalgia del paraíso infantil en *Libro de poemas: el poeta sobre su Pegaso.*" *GLR* 8,1 (Spring 1980):73–81.
200. Newton, Candelas, S. "Two Aspects of Nature in *Libro de poemas:* Nature as the Lost Paradise and Nature as Teacher." In: Zdenek, Joseph W., (ed.). *The World of Nature in the Works of Federico García Lorca.* Rock Hill, S.C.: Winthrop College. pp. 29–42.

201. Nunes, María Luisa. "Absence and Presence in the Six Galician Poems of García Lorca." *GLR* 9,2 (Fall 1981):97–108.
202. Ramond, Michèle. "Les Rapports de l'écriture et de l'inconscient dans le poème liminaire du *Diván del Tamarit*." Europe 616–617:71–82.

Theater

General

203. Aguilar Pinal, Francisco. "La honra en el teatro de García Lorca." *Revista de Literatura* 48,86 (July-December 1986):447–454.
204. Alvarez-Altman, Grace. "The Empty Nest Syndrome in García Lorca's Major Dramas." *GLR* 11,2 (1983):149–159.
205. Anderson, Andrew A. "Some Shakespearean Reminiscences in García Lorca's Drama." *CLS* 22,2 (Summer 1985):187–210.
206. Anderson, Andrew A. "The Strategy of García Lorca's Dramatic Composition 1930–1936." *Romance Quarterly* 33,2 (May 1986):211–229.
207. Aszyk, Urszula. "Federico García Lorca y su teatro en Polonia." *CHA* 433–434 (July–August 1986):270–280.
208. Barbeito, Clara L. "Paralelos y convergencias en el teatro de Valle-Inclán y García Lorca." *GLR* 11,1 (1983):87–97.
209. Burton, Julianne. "The Greatest Punishment: Female and Male in Lorca's Tragedies." In: Miller, Beth, (ed. and introd.) *Women in Hispanic Literature: Icons and Fallen Idols*. Berkeley: U of California P, 1983. pp. 259–279.
210. Busette, Cedric. "Libido and Repression in García Lorca's Theater." In: Redmond, James (ed.). *Drama, Sex and Politics*. Cambridge: Cambridge University Press, 1985. pp. 173–182.
211. Cao, Antonio F. "Presencia de Lorca en el repertorio teatral internacional." *Insula* XXXVI, 418 (Sept. 1981):4.
212. Colecchia, Francesca. "The 'Prólogo' in the Theater of Federico García Lorca: Towards the Articulation of a Philosophy of Theater." *Hispania* 69,4 (December 1986): 791–796.
213. Colecchia, Francesca. "The Religious Ambience in the Trilogy: A Definition." *GLR* 10,1 (Spring 1982):24–42.
214. Dougherty, Dru. "El lenguaje del silencio en el teatro de García Lorca." *ALEC* 11,1–2 (1986):91–110.
215. Dowling, John. "La 'bestia fiera' de Federico García Lorca: El autor dramatico y su público." *Estreno* 12,2 (Fall 1986):16–20.
216. Feal, Carlos. "La idea del honor en las tragedias de Lorca." In: Morris, C. Brian (ed.). *Essays in Memory of Federico García Lorca*. Lanham, M.D.: University Press of America, 1988. p. 277–293.

217. Fernández-Cifuentes, Luis. "García Lorca y el teatro convencional." *Ibero* 17 (1983):66–99.

218. Finke, Wayne H. "Naming Practices in Federico García Lorca's Newly Discovered Plays." *LOS* 14(1987):139–160.

219. Frazier-Clemons, Brenda. "A Teaching Elite in the Theater: Federico García Lorca." *GLR* 11,2 (1983):171–179.

220. García de la Torre, José Manuel. "En torno a una influencia literaria: Valle-Inclán y García Lorca." In: Gordon, Alan M. and Evelyn Rugg. (eds.) *Actas del Sexto Congreso Internacional de Hispanistas*. Toronto: University of Toronto Press, 1980. pp. 297–300.

221. González del Valle, Luis T. "El teatro de Federico García Lorca." In: Gonzale del Valle, Luis T. *El teatro de Federico García Lorca y otros ensayos sobre literatura española e hispanoamericana*. Lincoln, NE: Society of Spanish and Spanish-American Studies, 1980. pp. 3–94.

222. Jiménez, María. "Crítica social en el teatro de García Lorca." *GLR* 11,2 (1983):139–148.

223. Klein, Dennis A. "Las sociedades creadas en el teatro de Federico García Lorca." *CHA* 433–434 (July–August 1986):283–292.

224. Klein, Dennis A. "The Possible Influence of Falla's *La vida breve* on Lorca's Later Plays." *GLR* 9,2 (Fall 1981):91–96.

225. Loughran, David K. "Imagery of Nature and its Function in Lorca's Poetic Drama: 'Reyerta' and *Bodas de sangre*." In: Zdenek, Joseph W., (ed.). *The World of Nature in the Works of Federico García Lorca*. Rock Hill, S.C.: Winthrop College, pp. 55–61.

226. Loughran, David K. "Lorca, Lope and the Idea of a National Theater: *Bodas de sangre* and *El caballero de Olmedo*." *GLR* 8 (Fall 1980):127–136.

227. Materna, Linda. "Los códigos genéricos sexuales y la presentación de la mujer en el teatro de García Lorca." In: Loureiro, Angel, G. (ed.). *Estelas, laberintos, nuevas sendas*. Barcelona: Anthropos, 1988. pp. 263–277.

228. Ortega, José. "Conciencia social en los tres dramas rurales de García Lorca." *GLR* 9,1 (Spring 1981):64–90.

229. Smoot, Jeanne J. "The Living Text in the Drama of John Millington Synge and Federico García Lorca I." In: Balakian, Anna, et. al. *Proceedings of the Xth Congress of the International Comparative Literature Association* (New York, 1982). New York: Garland Publishing, Inc. pp. 338–342.

230. Turner, Harriet. "Circularity and Closure in Lorca's Trilogy." In: Zdenek, Joseph W., (ed.). *The World of Nature in the Works of Federico García Lorca*. Rock Hill, S.C.: Winthrop College. pp. 101–115.

231. Velázquez Cueto, Gerardo. "Adiós al jardín: García Lorca y Chejov: *Insula* 41,476–477 (July–August 1986):13.

232. Velázquez-Cueto, Gerardo. "De Lorca a Martín Recuerda: Crónica de una violencia siempre anunciada." *Insula* 38,440–441 (July–August 1983):23.

233. Walsh, John. "Las mujeres en el teatro de Lorca." In: Loureiro, Angel G. (ed.). *Estelas, laberintos, nuevas sendas.* Barcelona: Anthropos, 1988. pp. 279–295.

234. Welles, Marcia L. "Lorca, Alberti, and *Los tontos del cine mudo.*" In: Jiménez Fajardo, Salvador, and John C. Wilcox, (eds.). *At Home and Beyond: New Essays on Spanish Poets of the Twenties.* Lincoln, NE: Society of Spanish and Spanish-American Studies, 1983. pp. 113–125.

Early Plays and The Love of Don Perlimplín

235. Ambrosi, Paola. "Il 'teatro de títeres' di F. García Lorca: *Retablillo de don Cristóbal* e *Los títeres de Cachiporra: Tragicomedia de don Cristóbal y la señá Rosita.*" *QLL* 3–4 (1978–1979):249–265.

236. Ayéndez-Alder, Ruth. "Imagery and Theme in *El maleficio de la mariposa.*" In: Zdenek, Joseph W., (ed.). *The World of Nature in the Works of Federico García Lorca.* Rock Hill, S.C.: Winthrop College. pp. 63–72.

237. Ayéndez -Alder, Ruth. "Revisión crítica de *El maleficio de la mariposa* de Federico García Lorca: *HisJ* 8,2 (Spring 1985):149–163.

238. Echevarría, M.B. "The Inner Space in *The Love of Don Perlimplín and Belisa in His Garden.*" *RR* 73,1 (Jan. 1982):98–109.

239. Giunti, Dario. "El paseo de Buster Keaton di F. García Lorca." *QLL* 3–4 (1978–1979):233–248.

240. González-del-Valle, Luis T. *"La niña que riega la albahaca y el príncipe preguntón* y las constantes dramáticas de Federico García Lorca." *ALEC* 7,2 (1982):253–264.

241. Martín, E.(utimio). *F.G.L. heterodoxo y mártir. Análisis y proyección de la obra juvenil inédita.* Madrid: Siglo XXI, 1986.

242. Martín, Eutimio. "Federico García Lorca, un precursor de la 'teología de la liberación'? Su primera obra dramática inédita." *Hispania* 69,4 (December 1986):803–807.

243. Menarini, Piero. "Les Deux Versions de *l'Idylle sauvage de don Cristóbal et de la señá Rosita.*" *Europe* 616–617:83–95. (Tr. by Monique Martin and Charles Marcilly.

244. Turel, Sarah. "La 'quimera' de García Lorca: Expresión surrealista de un mito." *CHA* 433–434 (July–August 1986:351–358.

245. Ucelay, Margarita. *"Amor de don Perlimplín con Belisa en su jardín* de Federico García Lorca: Notas para la historia de la obra: Textos, ediciones, fragmentos inéditos."￼ In: Molloy, Sylvia and Luis Fernández Cifuentes (eds.). *Essays on Hispanic Literature in Honor of Edmund L. King.* London: Tamesis, 1983. pp. 233–243.

La Zapatera Prodigiosa and Doña Rosita la Soltera

246. Aguirre, Elvira. "Una farsa violenta: *La zapatera prodigiosa* de F. García Lorca." *ExTL* 13,1 (1984–1985):53–57.

247. Aguirre, J.M. "El llanto y la risa de la zapatera prodigiosa." *BHS* LVIII, 3 (July 1981):241–250.

248. Anderson, Farris. *"La zapatera prodigiosa:* an Early Example of García Lorca's Metatheater." *KBQ* 28,3 (1981):279–294.

249. Canavaggio, Jean. "García Lorca ante el entremés cervantino: El telar de *La zapatera prodigiosa."* In: *El teatro menor en España a partir del Siglo XVI: Actas del Coloquio celebrado en Madrid 20–22 de mayo de 1982.* Madrid: Consejo Superior de Investigaciones Científicas, 1983. pp. 141–153.

250. Morris, C. Brian. "Divertissement as Distraction in Lorca's *La zapatera prodigiosa." Hispania* 69,4 (December 1986):797–03.

251. Nichols, Geraldine Cleary. "Maturity as Accomodation: Lorca's *La zapatera prodigiosa." MLN* 95:335–356.

252. Nichols, Geraldine Cleary. "Echoes of Calderón in Lorca: *La zapatera prodigiosa."* In: De Armas, Edward A., David M. Gitlitz, and José A. Madrigal, (eds.). *Critical Perspectives on Calderón de la Barca.* Lincoln, NE: Society of Spanish and Spanish American Studies, 1981. pp. 103–108.

253. Nickel, Catherine, "The Function of Language in García Lorca's *Doña Rosita la soltera." Hispania* 66,4 (Dec. 1983):522–531.

254. Rodrigo, Antonina. *"Doña Rosita la soltera:* teatro y realidad." In: Soria Olmedo, Andrés (ed.) *Lecciones sobre F.G.L.* Granada: Comisión Nacional del Cincuentenario, 1986.

255. Velázquez Cueta, Gerardo. "Actualidad y entendimiento de *Doña Rosita la soltera o el lenguaje de las flores. Insula* XXXVI, 410 (Jan. 1981):1,12.

The Trilogy

Bodas de sangre

256. Alvarez Altman, Grace. *"Blood Wedding:* A Literary Onomastic Interpretation." *GLR* 8,1 (Spring 1980):60–72.

257. Anderson, Andrew A. "García Lorca's *Bodas de sangre:* The Logic and Necessity of Act Three." *Hispano* 303,90 (May 1987):21–37.

258. Bejel, Emilio. *"Bodas de sangre* y la estructura dramática." *Thesaurus* 33 (1978);309–316.

259. Bejel, Emilio. "Las secuencias estructurales de *Bodas de sangre."* *Dispositio* 3 (1978):381–390.

260. Feal, Carlos. "El Lorca póstumo: *El público* y *Comedia sin título."* *ALEC* 6 (1981):43–62.

261. Feal, Carlos. "El sacrificio de la hombría en *Bodas de sangre."* *MLN* 99 (1986):270–287.

262. Feal, Carlos. "Eurípides y Lorca: Observaciones sobre el cuadro final de *Yerma."* In: Kossoff, A. David, et. al. *Actas del VIII Congreso de la Asociación Internacional de Hispanistas.* Madrid: Istmo, 1986. pp. 511–518.

263. Feito, Francisco E. "Synge y Lorca: De *Riders to the Sea* a *Bodas de Sangre."* *GLR* 9,2 (Fall 1981):144–152.

264. López, Daniel. *"Bodas de sangre* and *La dama del alba:* Compared and Contrasted." *REH* 15,3 (Oct. 1981):407–423.

265. Miller, Norman C. "Lullaby, Wedding Song, and Funeral Chant in García Lorca's *Bodas de sangre."* *Gestos* 3,5 (April 1988):41–51.

266. Molho, Maurice. *"Noces de sang:* Nécessité, liberté, conjoncture: Contribution à l'histoire d'Espagne." *Europe* 616–617:110–112.

267. Romero, Héctor. "Hacia un concepto dualista sobre el personaje trágico en *Bodas de sangre."* *GLR* 10,2 (Spring 1982):50–62.

268. Vermeylen, A. "Du fait divers à la tragédie: A propos de *Noces de sang* de García Lorca." *LR* 39,1–2 (February–May 1985):125–138.

Yerma

269. Alvarez-Altman, Grace. "Poly-Anthroponomycal Onomastic Technique in *Yerma* by Federico García Lorca." *Names* 30,2 (June 1982):93–103.

270. Alvarez Harvey, Maria Luisa. "Lorca's Yerma: Frigid ... or Mismatched?" *CLAJ* 23:460–469.

271. Anderson, Reed. "The Idea of Tragedy in García Lorca's *Yerma."* *Hispano* 25,74 (Jan. 1982):41–60.

272. Cate, Francie. "Los motivos de la espera y la esperanza en *Yerma* y *Doña Rosita la soltera."* *GLR* 10,2 (Spring 1982):94–113.

273. Greenfield, Sumner M. "Yerma, the Woman and the Work: Some Reconsiderations." *Estreno* 7,1 (Spring 1981):18–21.

274. Hernández, Mario. "Cronología y estreno de *Yerma,* poema trágico de García Lorca." *RABM* 82 (1979):289–315.

275. Ter Horst, Robert. "Nature Against Nature in *Yerma."* In: Zdenek, Joseph W., (ed.). *The World of Nature in the Works of Federico García Lorca.* Rock Hill, S.C.: Winthrop College, pp. 43–54.

276. Yarmus, Marcia D. "Federico García Lorca's *Yerma* and John Steinbeck's *Burning Bright:* A Comparative Study, "*GLR* 11,1 (1983):75–86.

La casa de Bernarda Alba

277. Alvarez-Altman, Grace. "Sexual Nihilism in *The House of Bernarda Alba:* A Literary Onomastic Vignette." *LOS* 11 (1984):178–195.
278. Anderson, Reed. "Christian Symbolism in Lorca's *La casa de Bernarda Alba.*" In: Brancaforte, Benito, Edward R. Mulvihill, and Roberto G. Sánchez, (eds.). *Homenaje a Antonio Sánchez Barbudo: Ensayos de literatura española moderna*. Madison, Wisconsin: University of Wisconsin, 1981. 394 pp. 219–230.
279. Arango L., Manuel Antonio. "Símbolos sociales en *La casa de Bernarda Alba* de Federico García Lorca." *CA* 5,256 (September-October 1984):111–121.
280. Barrick, Mac E. "'Los antiguos sabían muchas cosas': Superstition in *La casa de Bernarda Alba*. *HR* 48:469–477.
281. Duarte, Patricia Gladys. "Realismo y estilización en *La casa de Bernarda Alba* de Federico García Lorca." *Letras* (Univ. Catolica Argentina) 15–16 (April–August 1986):175–182.
282. Fiddian, Robin W. "Adelaida's Story and the Cyclical Design of *La casa de Bernarda Alba.*" *RomN* 21: 150–154.
283. Knapp, Bettina L. "Federico García Lorca's *The House of Bernarda Alba:* A Hermaphroditic Matriarchate." *MD* XXVII, 3 (Sept. 1984):382–394.
284. Richards, Katherine C. "Hypocrisy in *La casa de Bernarda Alba.*" *RomN* 22,1 (Fall 1981):10–13.
285. Rodríguez, Alfred. "Bernarda Alba, Creation as Defiance." *RomN* 21,3 (Spring 1981):279–282.
286. Rubio, Isaac. "Notas sobre el realismo de *La casa de Bernarda Alba* de García Lorca." *RCEH* 4(1980):160–182.
287. Rude, Roberta N., Harriet S. Turner. "The Circles and Mirrors of Women's Lives in *The House of Bernarda Alba.*" *LPER* 3,1 (Nov. 1982):75–82.
288. Seybolt, Richard A. "Characterization in *La casa de Bernarda Alba:* The Case of Martirio." *GLR* 8,2 (Fall 1980):82–90.
289. Seybolt, Richard A. "*La casa de Bernarda Alba:* A Jungian Analysis." *KRQ* 29,2 (1982):125–133.
290. Urbina, Eduardo. "De Calderón a Lorca: El tema del honor en *La casa de Bernarda Alba.*" 259–270. In: McGaha, Michael D., (ed. & pref.). *Approaches to the Theater of Calderón*. Washington, D.C.: UP of America; 1982. XII, 287 pp.

291. Weingarten, Barry E. "Bernarda Alba: Nature as Unnatural." In: Zdenek, Joseph W. (ed.). *The World of Nature in the Works of Federico García Lorca*. Rock Hill, S.C. Winthrop College. pp. 129–138.

The Surreal and the Later Plays

292. Anderson, Farris. "The Theatrical Design of Lorca's: *Así que pasen cinco años*." *JSSTC* 7 (1979):249–278.

293. Anderson Reed. "'Comedia sin título': Some Observations on the New García Lorca Manuscript." *GLR* 8,2 (Fall 1980): 91–101.

294. Bogumil, Sieghild. "Poesie des Theaters; Eine Analyse des Schauspiels *Así que pasen cinco años. Leyenda del tiempo en tres actos y cinco cuadros* von Federico García Lorca." *Sprachkunst* 15,1 (1984):95–117.

295. De Long-Tonelli, Beverly J. "The Trials and Tribulations of Lorca's *El público*. *GLR* 9,2 (Fall 1981):153–168.

296. Dolan, Kathleen. "Time, Irony and Negation in Lorca's Last Three Plays." *Hispania* 63:514–522.

297. Edwards, Gwynne, "Lorca and Buñuel: *Así que pasen cinco años* and *Un chien andalou.*" *GLR* 9,2 (Fall 1981):153–168.

298. Feal, Carlos. "El Lorca póstumo: *El público* y *Comedia sin título.*" *ALEC* 6 (Summer 1981):43–62.

299. Figure, Paul. "The Mystification of Love and Lorca's Female Image in *El público.*" *Cincinnati Romance Rev.* 2(1983):26–32.

300. García Lorca, Francisco. "Légende du temps: A propos de *Lorsque cinq ans seront passés.*" *Europe* 616–617:112–115 (Tr. by Marie Laffranque. Excerpt of an unpublished article.)

301. Jérez-Ferrán, Carlos. "La estética expresionista en *El público* de García Lorca." *ALEC* 11,1–2 (1986):111–127.

302. Londré, Felicia Hardison. "Lorca in Metamorphosis: His Posthumous Plays." *TJ* 35,1 (Mar. 1983):102–108.

303. Martín, Eutimio. "El teatro imposible de Federico García Lorca en escena en Polonia." *Quimera* 44 (n.d.):58–59.

304. Millán, María C. *"El público,* de García Lorca: Obra de hoy." *CHA* 433–434 (July–August 1986):399–407.

305. Ortega, José. "Surrealismo y erotismo: *Así que pasen cinco años* de García Lorca." *GLR* 10,2 (Spring 1982):75–93.

306. Zdenek, Joseph W. "Alter Ego and Personality Projection in García Lorca's *Así que pasen cinco años.*" *REH* 16,2 (May 1982):303–313.

Other

307. Anderson, Andrew. "García Lorca at Vassar College: Two Unpublished Letters." *GLR* 11,2 (1983):99–109.

308. Bardi, Ubaldo. "Federico García Lorca, Musician: Equipment for a Bibliography." *GLR* 9,1 (Spring 1981):30–42.
309. Mac Curdy, Grant G. "Bibliografía cronológica comentada de Federico García Lorca." *Hispania* 69,4 (December 1986): 757–760.
310. Mahieu, José A. "García Lorca y su relación con el cine." *CHA* 433–434 (July–August 1986):119–128.
311. Martín, Eutimio. "La pujante vitalidad del lorquismo: Bibliografía de y sobre Federico García Lorca." *CER* 11 (1986):175–190.
312. Maurer, Christopher. "Sobre la prosa temprana de García Lorca (1916–1918)." *CHA* 433–434 (July–August 1986):13–22.
313. Muñoz González, Luis. Simbolización y cubismo en García Lorca: Un ejemplo: *Acta Literaria* 12 (1987):45–54.
314. Ortega, José. "Bibliografía anotada de *Poeta en Nueva York* de García Lorca." *GLR* 8,1 (Spring 1980):36–46.
315. Ramond, Michèle, "Canéphore de cauchemar: Analyse d'un texte *d'Impressions et paysages* de F. García Lorca." In: *Mélanges à la memoire d'André Joucla Ruau.* (2 vols.). Aix-en-Provence: Université de Provence, 1978. pp. 1043–1055.
316. Ramond, Michèle. "Le Moi au convent: L'Episode des chiens dans *Impresiones y paisajes de Federico García Lorca.* In: *L'Autobiographie dans le monde hispanique: Actes du Colloque international de la Baume-les-Aix. 11-12-13 Mai 1979.* Aix-en-Provence: Université de Provence, pp. 47–61.
317. Sucharzewska, Jadwiga, Barbara Czopek, and Francesca Colecchia. "A Partially Annotated Bibliography of Homages to Federico García Lorca in Polish." *GLR* 10,1 (Spring 1982):1–8.
318. Sucharzewska, Jadwiga, Barbara Czopek, and Francesca Colecchia. "Performances of Lorca's Plays in Poland: On Stages, on Radio and on Television." *GLR* 9,1 (Spring 1981):1–29.
319. Sucharzewska, Jadwiga, Barbara Czopek and Francesca Colecchia. "Translations of Lorca's Works into Polish." *GLR* 8,1 (Spring 1980):1–35.
320. Wood, Elizabeth. "Richard Meale, 1932- ." In: Callaway, Frank and David [Evatt] Tunley, (eds.). *Australian Composition in the Twentieth Century.* Melbourne: Oxford University Press, 1978. pp. 159–172.

Translations, Newly Discovered Work, and Media Adaptations.

321. Arbeteta, B. (dir.). *Federico García Lorca* (selections) Madrid: Fidias, 1983. Selections read by Carmen Bernardos et al. Guitar: S. Pastor. Selections: B. Arbeteta. Cassette Programme and Notes.
322. Casteros, Marta Teresa, (ed.). *Inéditos de Federico García Lorca: Sonetos del amor oscuro, 1935–1936.*

323. Crumb, George. *Music of George Crumb.* (New York: Composers Recordings, 1985. Cassette, 58 min. (Spanish/English). 1963–1966, 1970.

324. Diggory, Edith Anne. Student Recital. Indiana University School of Music, March 13, 1981. Edith Diggory, soprano. Alejandro Cáceres, piano. Two tape decks. 52 min. Selected songs by Lorca. In Spanish.

325. Friedmann, John (tr). *The Gypsy Balladeer* (with Three Historical Romances). [s.l.: b.s.n.], 1984. 39 pp. Tr. of *Primer romancero gitano.*

326. García Lorca, Federico. *Cinq jardins cinq sens.* (Suite de cinq eaux-fortes de François Houtin avec texte et poèmes de Federico García Lorca). Paris: Boulogne-sur-Seine: Robert Blanchet, 1982. 31 pp. 5 leaves of plates. Texts and translations from André Belamich's tr. Editions Gallimard, 1954–1981.

327. García Lorca, Federico. *Lola la comedianta.* Madrid: Alianza, 1981. 215 pp. Piero Menarini, ed. Gerardo Diego, prolog. Piero Menarini, preliminary study. bibliog. Facsims. Critical edition.

328. Martínez Nadal, Rafael. *"Temat Publiczonósci."* Dialog W 25, ix:95–98. (Tr. of *El público* by Pioty Niklewicz.)

329. Maurer, Christopher, (ed. and tr.). *Deep Song and Other Prose.* London; Boston: Marion Boyars, 1980. xiii, 143 pp. bibliog. Also: New Directions Publishing Corporation, 1980.

330. Maurer, Christopher. (tr. and ed.). *How a City sings from November to November.* San Francisco: Cadmus Editions, 1984. 64 pp. music. portrait. Tr. of "Cómo canta una ciudad de noviembre a noviembre."

331. Piedro, Emiliano, (dir.). *Bodas de sangre.* TVE 1, 1981 videorecording 130 min. "an adaptation … set in the Southwest."

332. Rodríguez, Stella (tr.). *Theory and Play of the Duende; and, Imagination, Inspiration, and Evasion.* Dallas, Tex. (?): Kanathos, 1981. XII, 84 pp. preface. Randolph Severson. introd. Rafael Pedraza. Bilingual edition.

333. Vieru, Anatol. *Scène nocturne.* Electrecord ST-ECE 0416. n.p.:n.d. M. Ritual Marb'e. Marin Constantin, Conductor. One side, 33 1/3 rpm. Roumanian production based on poems by Lorca.

334. Zamora, Romulus, (dir.). *Bodas de sangre.* videorecording Sacramento, CA: California State University at Sacremento: Center for Instructional Media, 1979. 3 cassettes. 105 min. Romulus Zamora (director). (A bilingual adaptation set in the Southwest.)

Glossary of Abbreviations

Acta Lit	*Acta Literaria*
ALE	*Anales de Literatura Española*
ALEC	*Anales de Literatura Española Contemporánea*
ALitASH	*Acta Literaria Academiae Scientiarum Hungaricae*
ASUI	*Analele Stiintifici ale Universitatii "Al. I, Cuza" din Iasi (Serie Noma) e Lingvistica.*
BBMP	*Boletín Cultural y Bibliográfico*
BH	*Bulletin Hispanique*
BHS	*Bulletin of Hispanic Studies*

Boletín de la Academia Argentina de Letras

Boletín de la Fundación Federico García Lorca

CA	*Cuadernos Americanos*
CasaA	*Casa de la Américas*
CdAr	*Correio das Artes*
CER	*Cahiers d'Etudes Romanes*
CH	*Crítica Hispánica*
CHA	*Cuadernos Hispanoamericanos*
CLAJ	*College Language Association Journal*
ClioI	*ClioI: An Interdisciplinary Journal of Literature, History, and the Philosophy of History*
CLS	*Comparative Literature Studies*
Comparatist	*The Comparatist: Journal of the Southern Comparative Literature Association*

Cultura	*Cultura: Revista del Ministerio de Educación de El Salvador*
DAI	*Dissertation Abstracts International*
DialogW	*Dialog (Warsaw)*
Estreno	
ExTL	*Explicación de Textos Literarios*
FLMS	*Forum for Modern Language Studies* (Scotland)
Gestos	*Gestos: Teoría y Práctica del Teatro Hispánico*
GLR	*García Lorca Review*
HisJ	*Hispanic Journal* (Indiana, Pa.)
Hispano	*Hispanófila*
HR	*Hispanic Review*
Insula	*Insula: Revista de Letras y Ciencias Humanas*
Ibero	*Iberoromania*
JSSTC	*Journal of Spanish Studies: Twentieth Century*
KRQ	*Romance Quarterly* (Formerly: *Kentucky* Romance Quarterly)
LCUT	*Library Chronicle of the University of Texas*
Letras	*Letras* (Universidad Católica, Argentina)
LG	*Literatur in der Gesellschaft*
LOS	*Literary Onomastic Studies*
LPer	*Literature in Performance: A Journal of Literary and Performing Art*
LR	*Les Lettres Romanes*

MD   *Modern Drama*

MGSL   *Minas Gerais, Suplemento Literário*

MLN   *Modern Language Notes*

MLR   *Modern Language Review*

NB   *Namm och Bygd: Tidskrift för Nordisk ortnamnsforsk-ning /Journal for Nordic Place Name Research*

NE   *Nueva Estafeta*

NewL   *New Letters*

Neophil   *Neophilologus*

NYT   *New York Times*

OHis   *Ottawa Hispánica*

Parnassus   *Parnassus: Poetry in Review*

Plaza   *Plaza: Revista de Literatura*

QLL   *Quaderni di Lingue e Letterature*

Quimera   *Quimera: Revista de Literatura*

RABM   *Revista de Archivos, Bibliotecas y Museos*

RCEH   *Revista Canadiense de Estudios Hispánicos*

REH   *Revista de Estudios Hispánicos*

RHM   *Revista Hispánica Moderna*

RITL   *Revista de Istorie si Teorie Literara*

RL   *Revista de Literatura*

RLET   *Revista Letras* (Brazil)

RomN   *Romance Notes*

RRL   *Revue Roumaine de Linguistique* (Bucharest)

RR   *Romanic Review*

RS   *Research Studies*

RyF   *Razón y Fé*

SCr   *Strumenti Critici* (Turin)

SinN   *Sin Nombre*

Sprachkunst *Sprachkunst: Beiträge zur Literaturwissenschaft*

TCrit   *Texto Crítico*

Thesaurus   *Thesaurus: Boletín del Instituto Caro y Cuervo*

TJ   *Theater Journal*

TLTL   *Teaching Language Through Literature*